THE
NUMBERS
DON'T LIE

COMPARATIVE CAREER ANALYSES OF
JACK NICKLAUS & TIGER WOODS

WADE P. WHITE

authorHOUSE®

AuthorHouse™
1663 Liberty Drive
Bloomington, IN 47403
www.authorhouse.com
Phone: 833-262-8899

Published by AuthorHouse 10/31/2022

ISBN: 978-1-6655-6959-0 (sc)
ISBN: 978-1-6655-6958-3 (hc)
ISBN: 978-1-6655-6957-6 (e)

Library of Congress Control Number: 2022916101

Print information available on the last page.

Any people depicted in stock imagery provided by Getty Images are models,
and such images are being used for illustrative purposes only.
Certain stock imagery © Getty Images.

This book is printed on acid-free paper.

Because of the dynamic nature of the Internet, any web addresses or links contained in
this book may have changed since publication and may no longer be valid. The views
expressed in this work are solely those of the author and do not necessarily reflect the
views of the publisher, and the publisher hereby disclaims any responsibility for them.

CONTENTS

INTRODUCTION

"Years ago, somebody told me that when Tiger was a kid, he taped a list of my golf accomplishments on his closet. Well, if he's making a checkmark every time he matches me in something, he must have his pencil out pretty darn often." – Jack Nicklaus

Upon conclusion of the 2006 PGA Championship where Tiger Woods won by five shots, I retired to the Internet to read various articles and discussion boards regarding his triumph. As I already knew, the win marked Woods' 12th professional major championship victory with only six remaining to tie the record total of 18 set by Jack Nicklaus.

What I didn't know was while there were many comments written by both professional writers and amateur commentators about Woods being "on pace" to do this or "ahead of Nicklaus" to do that, which of these more obscure or detailed aspects were fact, which were fiction, and which required additional background or context.

I first played golf in 1981 and took an early interest in its history of players and championship records. Over time, my awareness drifted from following it as intently. Yet, Woods' major championship record chase renewed my interest enough that I began tracking his performance against that of Nicklaus.

Since Jack Nicklaus and Tiger Woods have stated repeatedly the standard for greatness in golf is defined by performance in the major championships, most of the comparative data in this book will revolve around those four championships and the players' records. For readers unfamiliar with the respective championships, they are:

- **Masters Tournament**
- **U.S. Open Championship**
- **Open Championship (aka "British Open")**
- **PGA Championship**

While the game of golf continues to evolve and the professional circuit adds significant events, the consensus among competitors, media, and fans alike is the four majors are the gold standard for the game's top players. These are the championships by which players are most remembered and careers best defined.

Such a standard is neither recent nor limited to the game of golf. Upon winning the "Impregnable Quadrilateral" or calendar-year Grand Slam in 1930, the great amateur Bobby Jones was rewarded with a ticker tape parade in New York City. The four championships at the time were the U. S. and British Open Championships along with the U.S. and British Amateur Championships, but the theory was the same. The year 1930 still resonates with many as the greatest year in golf as this feat has never been duplicated since with either the new or old version of the Grand Slam.

Ben Hogan won the "Triple Crown" in 1953, consisting of the first three Grand Slam events under the modern terminology. Unfortunately, he was unable to compete in the PGA Championship that year due to its schedule conflicting with the Open Championship. As with Jones, Hogan was celebrated in New York City with a ticker tape parade.

Outside of the game of golf, Roger Federer's performance in the Grand Slam events in professional tennis has elevated him to being widely regarded as the greatest professional men's player to date. However, many might make a case for Rod Laver. While Laver's championship total is fewer, he won the calendar-year Grand Slam twice. Nevertheless, the commonality is performance in the four Grand Slam championships. As Jimmy Connors wrote in his autobiography, <u>The Outsider</u>, *"Grand Slam events, which are also called the majors, are the ones where you make your reputation, then as now. They have the most ranking points, the most prize money, and they attract the most attention."* Consequently, a correlation exists between the greater the event, its inherent pressure, and the player who masters that pressure the best over time. This theory is no different, regardless of sport.

For Nicklaus and Woods, the composition of the major championships has remained static. That makes a comparative analysis fairly straightforward. However, the more I began to study their major championship performances, the further I delved into their total records. Thus, while this book will focus largely on the major championships, it will not focus *exclusively* on them.

There is more to the careers of Jack Nicklaus and Tiger Woods than just the major championships. Therefore, time will also be spent delineating how they fared in other aspects (i.e. money titles, Player of the Year, scoring, etc.). It is with these ancillary areas that a proper context should be placed as the criteria for achievement has changed over the years.

For the discerning reader, please note the following caveats pertaining to both players' records:

- When running calculations/spreadsheets on placements for Jack Nicklaus, Tiger Woods, and applicable competitors, any ties were treated as discrete so the results would compute properly. While any ties do not change the records favorably or unfavorably, they will be referenced when possible.
- The focus of this book should be on the most competitive range of professional years for both players. For Jack Nicklaus, 1962 through 1986 made sense as it encompassed his first and last victories. Therefore, a similar range was set for Tiger Woods. Due to injuries in his later years, I included September of 1996 through the 2022 Open Championship. And although Woods missed a few years, the ages of he and Nicklaus were similar throughout.

Also, the acronyms below will be sprinkled throughout various charts. The references are:

- DNP   Did Not Play
- MC   Missed Cut
- N/A   Not Available
- T-   Tied for (placement)
- WD   Withdrew

Growing up, I repeatedly heard my father utter the words, *"Let's put this in perspective."* The overriding goal of this book is simply that – to better place in perspective prominent points of the careers of Jack Nicklaus and Tiger Woods while breaking down myths surrounding each player relative to the other and their respective eras.

It would be naïve to believe through these pages, I will singlehandedly sway the legions of Tiger Woods' fans to second-guess their position or move many Jack Nicklaus fans into aligning themselves otherwise. Therefore, my goal is not to develop a case for one or the other as the greatest player, but to provide copious data, both old and new – and in new formats – to add to the debate.

Regardless of player preference, I hope the reader will acknowledge the effort that went into compiling the data in the following pages. In addition, I will attempt to present the information with a lack of subjectivity. Whether agreeing or disagreeing with the conclusions or formats, the reader should discover representations of statistics, contexts, and *perspectives* perhaps not previously considered.

AMATEUR SUMMARY

*"When I won the Amateur at Pebble (in 1961), I played 3-iron or 4-iron into that green half the time for my second shot." – Jack Nicklaus on the 14ᵗʰ hole at Pebble Beach (565-yard par five) **Golf Digest** – "Weighing in for the U.S. Open" June 1983*

*"He's lean, he's strong, his swing is marvelous. I couldn't see the ball come off the club for the first 27 holes. It came off the club that fast." – Buddy Marucci on Tiger Woods after the 1995 U.S. Amateur final **Sports Illustrated** – "Encore! Encore!" September 1995*

While the majority of this book will cover the records of Jack Nicklaus and Tiger Woods during their professional careers – notably in the major championships – the following provides a summary of their records as amateurs.

Along with Bobby Jones, who won five U.S. Amateur Championships, four U.S. Open Championships, three Open Championships, and one British Amateur Championship, both Nicklaus and Woods are considered the greatest amateurs to play the game – each having been the top-ranked amateurs their final three years prior to turning professional. While there are similarities, their records do not mirror each other as closely as one might expect.

Jack Nicklaus Amateur Summary – Top-ranked Amateur (1959 – 1961)			
Age	Event	Result	Commentary
12	Columbus District Junior Golf League Championship	1	
13	Ohio State Junior Championship (13 – 15 yrs)	1	

13	Columbus Junior Match-Play Championship (13 – 15 yrs)	1	
13	Columbus Junior Stroke-Play Championship (13 – 15 yrs)	1	
13	Broke 70 for 18 holes		Shot 69 at Scioto Country Club.
14	Tri-State High School Championship (OH, KY, IN)	1	Shot 68 to win the individual title.
14	Columbus Junior Match-Play Championship (13 – 15 yrs)	1	Won the final 6 & 5.
14	Columbus Junior Stroke-Play Championship (13 – 15 yrs)	1	Shot 70-69 – 139.
14	Ohio State Junior Championship (13 – 15 yrs)	1	
15	Ohio Jaycees Championship	1	Shot 67-68 – 135.
15	Columbus Junior Match-Play Championship (13 – 15 yrs)	1	Won the final 6 & 5.
15	Columbus Junior Stroke-Play Championship (13 – 15 yrs)	1	Shot 71-72-73 – 216.
15	Ohio State Junior Championship (13 – 15 yrs)	1	
16	Ohio High School State Championship	1	
16	Columbus Amateur Match-Play Championship	1	Won the final 5 & 4.
16	Columbus Junior Match-Play Championship	1	
16	Ohio State Open	1	Shot 76-70-64-72 – 282 at this former PGA-sanctioned event.
16	Ohio Jaycees Championship	1	
17	Tri-State High School Championship (OH, KY, IN)	1	
17	Ohio High School State Championship	1	
17	Ohio Jaycees Championship	1	
17	U.S. National Jaycees Championship	1	
17	U.S. Open	MC	First of 44 consecutive U.S. Opens
18	Trans-Mississippi Amateur	1	Won the final 9 & 8.
18	Queen City Open Championship	1	
18	U.S. Open	T-41	
18	Rubber City Open	12	First PGA-sanctioned tournament
19	U.S. Amateur Championship	1	Youngest winner since 1909 defeating two-time champion Charles Coe.1-up.
19	Trans-Mississippi Amateur	1	Won the final 3 & 2.

19	North and South Amateur Championship	1	
19	Royal St. George's Challenge Cup	1	
19	Walker Cup	2-0-0	
19	Masters	MC	
19	U.S. Open	MC	
19	Gleneagles – Chicago Open	T-26	PGA-sanctioned tournament
19	Motor City Open	T-45	PGA-sanctioned tournament
19	Buick Open	T-12	PGA-sanctioned tournament
20	U.S. Amateur Championship	T-16	Eliminated in the fourth round.
20	World Amateur Team Championship	1	Shot a record 11-under par 269 to win by 13 shots.
20	Colonial Invitational	1	
20	Masters	T-13	Low Amateur
20	U.S. Open	2	Low Amateur shooting a then-record two-under par 282 (broken in 2019); the only player to shoot all four rounds at par or better.
21	U.S. Amateur Championship	1	20-under par for 138 holes; defeated future professional Dudley Wysong 8 & 6 in the final.
21	NCAA Championship	1	First player to win along with the U.S. Amateur in the same year.
21	NCAA Big Ten Conference Championship	1	Won the individual competition by 22 shots.
21	Western Amateur Championship	1	
21	Walker Cup	2-0-0	
21	Masters	T-7	Charles Coe tied for second as Low Amateur.
21	U.S. Open	T-4	Low Amateur; one-under par for the final 54 holes.
21	Colonial National Invitation	T-38	PGA-sanctioned tournament
21	Buick Open	T-24	PGA-sanctioned tournament
21	American Golf Classic	T-55	PGA-sanctioned tournament

Tiger Woods Amateur Summary – Top-ranked Amateur (1994 – 1996)			
Age	**Event**	**Result**	**Commentary**
8	Optimist International Junior World	1	
9	Optimist International Junior World	1	
11	Broke 70 for 18 holes		Location undetermined

3

12	Optimist International Junior World	1	
13	Optimist International Junior World	1	
14	Optimist International Junior World	1	
14	Insurance Youth Golf Classic	1	Youngest champion
15	U.S. Junior Amateur Championship	1	Youngest champion
15	Optimist International Junior World	1	
15	Southern California Junior Championship	1	
15	PING / Phoenix Junior (AJGA)	1	
15	Edgewood Tahoe Junior Classic (AJGA)	1	
15	CIF – SCGA High School Invitational Championship	1	
15	Los Angeles City Junior Championship	1	
15	Orange Bowl Junior International	1	
16	U.S. Junior Amateur Championship	1	First two-time champion
16	PING / Phoenix Junior (AJGA)	1	
16	Insurance Youth Golf Classic	1	
16	Nabisco Mission Hills Desert Junior (AJGA)	1	
16	Pro Gear San Antonio Shootout (AJGA)	1	
16	Nissan Open	MC	First PGA Tour event
17	U.S. Junior Amateur Championship	1	Only three-time champion and in succession.
17	Nissan Open	MC	PGA Tour event
17	Honda Classic	MC	PGA Tour event
17	GTE Byron Nelson Classic	MC	PGA Tour event
18	U.S. Amateur Championship	1	Defeated Trip Kuehne 2-up becoming the youngest champion at the time.
18	Western Amateur Championship	1	
18	Southern California Golf Association Amateur Championship	1	
18	Pacific Northwest Amateur Championship	1	
18	William Tucker Invitational	1	
18	Jerry Pate Invitational	1	
18	World Amateur Team Championship	6	Shot 70-75-67-72 – 284.
18	Nestle Invitational	MC	PGA Tour event
18	Buick Classic	MC	PGA Tour event
18	Motorola Western Open	MC	PGA Tour event

18	Johnnie Walker Classic	T-34	First European Tour event
19	U.S. Amateur Championship	1	Defeated Buddy Marucci 2-up winning his second title in succession.
19	Stanford Invitational	1	
19	Walker Cup	2-2-0	
19	Masters	T-41	Low Amateur and only amateur to make the cut.
19	U.S. Open	WD	Withdrew due to second round wrist injury.
19	Open Championship	T-68	
19	Western Open	T-57	PGA Tour event
19	Scottish Open	T-48	European Tour event
20	U.S. Amateur Championship	1	Defeated Steve Scott 1-up on the 38th hole to become the only player to win three in succession.
20	NCAA Championship	1	Third player to win with the U.S. Amateur in the same year.
20	Pac-10 Championship	1	
20	NCAA West Regional	1	
20	John A. Burns Invitational	1	
20	Cleveland Golf Championship	1	
20	Tri-Match (Stanford, AZ, AZ State)	1	
20	Cougar Classic	1	
20	Masters	MC	
20	U.S. Open	T-82	
20	Open Championship	T-22	Low Amateur with a record-tying score of three-under par 281.
20	Scottish Open	MC	European Tour event

Both performances are of the highest caliber with a few embellishments below.

Nicklaus:

- At age 16, won the Ohio State Open, previously a PGA-sanctioned tournament against a field largely consisting of professionals.
- At age 17, qualified for the U.S. Open Championship.
- At age 18, placed 12th in his first PGA-sanctioned tournament (non-major).
- At age 19, won the U.S. Amateur Championship being the second-youngest at the time (Robert Gardner, 1909).

- At age 20, finished second in the U.S. Open to Arnold Palmer while playing the final 36 holes with Ben Hogan. Nicklaus was the only player to shoot par or better over four rounds and his score of two-under par 282 remained the lowest by an amateur for 59 years (Viktor Hovland, 2019).
- At age 20, won the individual title at the World Amateur Team Championship by 13 shots having four straight rounds in the 60s for a total of 11-under par 269.
- At age 21, won the U.S. Amateur and the NCAA Championship becoming the first player to win both in the same year.
- At age 21, tied for fourth in the U.S. Open having played the final 54 holes in one-under par.

Woods:
- From ages 15 through 17, won three consecutive USGA Junior Championships, becoming the first two-time and thus far only three-time winner.
- At age 16, competed in his first PGA Tour event shooting 72-75 (missed cut).
- At age 18, won the U.S. Amateur Championship being the youngest at the time.
- At age 20, won the U.S. Amateur for the third and final time becoming the first (and to date only) player to win three in succession.
- At age 20, won the U.S. Amateur and the NCAA Championship becoming the third player at the time to win both in the same year (Nicklaus, Phil Mickelson).
- At age 20, finished tied for 22nd in the Open Championship with a record-tying aggregate score of 281 (Iain Pyman, 1993).

While Woods won an unprecedented three consecutive U.S. Amateur titles from 1994 through 1996, Nicklaus won it twice in 1959 and 1961. Much has rightfully been made regarding Woods' consecutive wins – especially on the heels of three straight USGA Junior titles – yet the accomplishments of Nicklaus during 1960 when he did not win the U.S. Amateur were also significant as noted below.

- Shot a record 11-under par 269 to win the World Amateur Team Championship individual title by 13 shots. This score and margin of victory remained the record until 2014 and was a tournament Woods placed sixth in with a score of even-par 284 at age 18.

- Finished as Low Amateur in the U.S. Open by shooting a record two-under par 282 to place second. This remained the record score by an amateur until 2019.
- Finished tied with William J. Patton for Low Amateur in the Masters by shooting a five-over par 293 to tie for 13th place.

Let's review Nicklaus' and Woods' performances specifically in official events against touring professionals of the day.

Jack Nicklaus & Tiger Woods Placements Against Professionals as Amateurs (PGA-sanctioned Events)										
	Wins	2 - 5	6 - 10	11 - 20	21 - 30	31 - 40	41 - 50	51 - 100	MC	WD
Nicklaus	0	2	1	3	2	1	2	1	3	0
Woods	0	0	0	0	1	0	1	3	8	1
Variance	0	2	1	3	1	1	1	(2)	(5)	(1)

Nicklaus' first event above was the 1957 U.S. Open at age 17, while Woods' first was the 1992 Nissan Los Angeles Open at age 16 – both missed the cut. With Nicklaus competing in 15 events and Woods in 14, the distribution is nearly even. Ironically, Nicklaus' three top placements were also his three missed cuts – two top-five U.S. Open finishes and one tie for seventh in the Masters. Woods' top finish was a tie for 22nd in the 1996 Open Championship.

The following provides a summary of Nicklaus and Woods as amateurs vs. professionals during PGA-sanctioned events and major championships.

Jack Nicklaus PGA-sanctioned Events – Amateur Summary		
Total Events Played	15	
Major Championships Played	8	
Total Rounds Completed	54	
Total Stroke Average	73.04	
Major Championship Stroke Average	73.62	
Low 18-hole Score	66	
High 18-hole Score	80	
Median 18-hole Score	73	
Rounds in the 60s & Percentage	7	12.96%
Rounds in the 70s & Percentage	45	83.33%
Rounds in the 80s & Percentage	2	3.70%
Victories & Percentage	0	0.00%
Top-10 Placements & Percentage	3	20.00%
Missed Cuts & Percentage	3	20.00%
Withdrawals & Percentage	0	0.00%

Tiger Woods PGA-sanctioned Events – Amateur Summary		
Total Events Played	14	
Major Championships Played	6	
Total Rounds Completed	37	
Total Stroke Average	73.70	
Major Championship Stroke Average	73.00	
Low 18-hole Score	66	
High 18-hole Score	80	
Median 18-hole Score	74	
Rounds in the 60s & Percentage	3	8.11%
Rounds in the 70s & Percentage	33	89.19%
Rounds in the 80s & Percentage	1	2.70%
Victories & Percentage	0	0.00%
Top-10 Placements & Percentage	0	0.00%
Missed Cuts & Percentage	8	57.14%
Withdrawals & Percentage	1	7.14%

Coincidentally, for both players as amateurs, their play against the professionals spanned five years. Nicklaus' performance exceeds that of Woods. The record immediately above for Woods does not include three European Tour events summarized below.

- **1994 Johnnie Walker Classic**
  - 74-71-74-72 = 291
    - T-34
- **1995 Scottish Open**
  - 69-71-75-78 = 293
    - T-48
- **1996 Scottish Open**
  - 81-75 = 156
    - MC

What conclusions can be drawn from a review of their amateur days? Woods having started golf at a younger age amassed a staggering amateur record. He was totally dominant among the other amateurs at the junior and post-junior levels. Many of Woods' wins were unprecedented.

Nicklaus' record is also quite commanding. Although having started the game at age 10, he did not compete in the expanse of tournaments early on and was not as much of a national presence as a junior golfer.

Once Nicklaus turned 18, he began to dominate the amateur ranks completely. During his last three years as an amateur, the one exception to Woods is the lack of three successive U.S. Amateur titles. Yet, as illustrated, his "off" year of 1960 was nevertheless record-setting with achievements Woods did not equal.

What also stands out is while Nicklaus did not overpower the amateur level nationally during his junior years in the manner Woods did, he was better against the professionals in the events he played – especially the major championships.

CUP MATCHES

"It is really a great thing to know that although a man can be paid for playing a game he loves, he can at the same time play for the honor of his team and his country." – *Samuel Ryder*

Although not weighed heavily when discussing the records of Jack Nicklaus and Tiger Woods, the following is a summary of their Walker Cup, World Cup, Ryder Cup, and Presidents Cup performances along with commentary.

Walker Cup

As an amateur, Nicklaus competed on two Walker Cup teams (1959 and 1961) representing the United States vs. Great Britain & Ireland. With the format prior to 1963 being 36 holes per match, there were only two per year – one foursomes match and one singles match. In each year, Nicklaus was undefeated bringing his record to 4-0-0. Below summarize his results:

Jack Nicklaus Walker Cup Record							
	Win	Loss	Halve	Points Won	Points Lost	Net Points	Percentage Won
Foursomes	2	0	0	2.00	0.00	2.00	100.00%
Singles	2	0	0	2.00	0.00	2.00	100.00%
Total	4	0	0	4.00	0.00	4.00	100.00%

In 1995, Woods competed in his first and only Walker Cup. At that time, there were two 18-hole matches per day – one foursomes followed by one singles. Woods was victorious in the opening foursomes match, then lost his subsequent singles match. The following day, the match results were reversed with Woods on the losing end of the opening foursomes match and winning his singles match. This left Woods with a relatively flat record of 2-2-0. Below summarize his results:

Tiger Woods Walker Cup Record							
	Win	Loss	Halve	Points Won	Points Lost	Net Points	Percentage Won
Foursomes	1	1	0	1.00	1.00	0.00	50.00%
Singles	1	1	0	1.00	1.00	0.00	50.00%
Total	2	2	0	2.00	2.00	0.00	50.00%

World Cup of Golf

Upon turning professional, Nicklaus and Woods were able to compete in the World Cup of Golf (Canada Cup from 1953 through 1966). This was a two-man team event with participants from all over the world and very prestigious through the 1970s. After the inaugural year's 36-hole stroke-play competition, from 1954 through 1999, the format was 72-hole stroke-play, which yielded an individual and team champion. Beginning in 2000, the format was changed to alternating rounds of team stroke-play only, based on four-ball and foursomes.

Nicklaus competed in seven World Cup events from 1963 through 1973. He was a part of winning teams on six occasions and the individual champion three times. The following graphic illustrates his record in the event.

Jack Nicklaus World Cup Record – Yearly Placements							
	1963	1964	1965	1966	1967	1971	1973
Team	1	1	3	1	1	1	1
Individual	1	1	2	3	2	1	3

Woods competed three times in the World Cup during 1999, 2000, and 2001. He was a part of the winning team in 1999 and 2000, while finishing second via playoff in 2001. With the format change in 2000, Woods only won the individual title in 1999. The following graphic summarizes his record.

Tiger Woods World Cup Record – Yearly Placements			
	1999	2000	2001
Team	1	1	2
Individual	1	N/A	N/A

Ryder Cup

During his career, Nicklaus played his way onto six Ryder Cup teams from 1969 through 1981. However, due to the PGA of America guidelines, he was not eligible to begin accumulating points until January of 1967 – five full years after he began his playing career in 1962. Furthermore, captain selections of multiple players were not implemented until 1989. What does each of these caveats mean?

Unlike today where a player can begin qualifying for a Ryder Cup (and Presidents Cup) team immediately, Nicklaus was ineligible for the teams of 1963, 1965, and a full two-years' worth of qualifying points for the 1967 team. And while Nicklaus had a substandard year in 1979, it is likely Captain Billy Casper would have selected him for that team, if able.

Thus, Nicklaus missed three Ryder Cup teams he would have easily qualified for due to his playing performances in 1962/1963, 1964/1965, and 1966/1967 had the five-year restriction not been in place.

Below provides a reference of Nicklaus and Woods and their competitive years relative to their Ryder Cup team participation:

Jack Nicklaus		Tiger Woods	
Year	**Ryder Cup Team Status**	**Year**	**Ryder Cup Team Status**
1963	Ineligible	1997	Member
1965	Ineligible	1999	Member
1967	Denied Full Eligibility	2002	Member
1969	Member	2004	Member
1971	Member	2006	Member
1973	Member	2008	Member (injured)
1975	Member	2010	Member (captain selection)
1977	Member	2012	Member
1979	Did Not Qualify (no captain selection option)	2014	Did Not Qualify (injured)
1981	Member	2016	Did Not Qualify (injured)
1983	Non-playing Captain	2018	Member (captain selection)

| 1985 | Did Not Qualify (no captain selection option) | 2021 | Did Not Qualify (injured) |

With the above taken into consideration, here are both players' records in the Ryder Cup.

Jack Nicklaus Ryder Cup Record							
	Win	Loss	Halve	Points Won	Points Lost	Net Points	Percentage Won
Four-balls	5	3	1	5.50	3.50	2.00	61.11%
Foursomes	8	1	0	8.00	1.00	7.00	88.89%
Singles	4	4	2	5.00	5.00	0.00	50.00%
Total	17	8	3	18.50	9.50	9.00	66.07%

Tiger Woods Ryder Cup Record							
	Win	Loss	Halve	Points Won	Points Lost	Net Points	Percentage Won
Four-balls	5	10	0	5.00	10.00	(5.00)	33.33%
Foursomes	4	9	1	4.50	9.50	(5.00)	32.14%
Singles	4	2	2	5.00	3.00	2.00	62.50%
Total	13	21	3	14.50	22.50	(8.00)	39.19%

Nicklaus leads Woods overall at 66.07% vs. 39.19%. Nicklaus' record in four-ball and foursomes team performances are both significantly superior at 61.11% and 88.89% compared to Woods at 33.33% and 32.14%, respectively. Woods leads the singles record comparison at 62.50% vs. a relatively flat 50.00% for Nicklaus.

In summary, while Woods qualified for seven teams and was a captain selection twice thus far in his career with Nicklaus qualifying for six, the criteria have not been consistent over time. Under the current selection qualifications, the probability of Nicklaus being a member of 10 Ryder Cup teams is high. For the years 1963, 1965, and 1967, he would have qualified without question, as his play was exceptional in each, along with the preceding years to assist in point accumulations. And for each of these years under the format in place, Nicklaus would have been eligible for six additional singles matches, along with other team competition. It would be interesting to see how his record would have changed had he been a member of the four teams inclusive of a captain selection in 1979.

With respect to competition, it is widely known that in 1977, Nicklaus spearheaded the addition of the remaining European countries for eligibility to compete against the United States. In 1979, the Ryder Cup officially began as a match between the United States and Europe as opposed to Great Britain & Ireland. In 1981, Nicklaus had his best annual Ryder Cup performance at 4-0-0 as the United States defeated the unified European team.

Presidents Cup

In 1994, another cup match began that pitted the United States against an international squad of players exclusive of Europe. These Presidents Cup matches occur during the years the Ryder Cup does not. Due to the recent year of inception, Nicklaus did not compete. However, Woods has been a member of eight teams since 1998. The following displays his record in the event.

Tiger Woods Presidents Cup Record							
	Win	Loss	Halve	Points Won	Points Lost	Net Points	Percentage Won
Four-balls	7	9	0	7.00	9.00	(2.00)	43.75%
Foursomes	11	4	1	11.50	4.50	7.00	71.88%
Singles	6	2	0	6.00	2.00	4.00	75.00%
Total	24	15	1	24.50	15.50	9.00	61.25%

While the above shows Woods with a flat record in the four-ball competitions as in the Ryder Cup, his record in foursomes play improved considerably. The commonality in both the Ryder Cup and Presidents Cup is Woods' exceptional performance in singles play; the latter a 75.00% success rate. For singles matches in the combined Cups, he registered a 10-4-2 record, or 11 points out of a possible 16 – a win percentage of 68.75%.

SCORING

"If you are going to tell me that the golfers of today should be shooting the same scores on the same courses that golfers did 20 years ago, you are crazy. The golfers of today may not be that much better individually, but because of the competition we have and the scores you are forced to shoot, our ability to score today versus 20 years ago is night and day." – Jack Nicklaus **Golf Digest** *– "Weighing in for the U.S. Open" June 1983*

"With the length he (Tiger) had, the way he controlled the golf ball and never missed a putt, and the great chipping, it was time for me to hang up my hat." – Jack Nicklaus on playing with Tiger Woods in the 2000 PGA Championship **Golf Digest** *– December 2002*

When analyzing careers across different eras, the element with the highest variability would likely be scoring. Many factors come into play to influence scores including course conditioning, equipment, knowledge of technique, training advancements, weather, etc. Regardless, the following provides a good description of how Jack Nicklaus and Tiger Woods scored during their eras. One commonality between them is both played somewhat limited schedules with a focus on venues lending themselves to more difficult conditions.

Vardon Trophy

The most logical place to begin when reviewing the scoring records of Nicklaus and Woods is to examine the Vardon Trophy and its winners. Beginning in 1988, qualifying for the Vardon Trophy simply entailed having the lowest *adjusted* stroke average for a minimum of 60 PGA-sanctioned/affiliated rounds during the year while not withdrawing from a tournament once a round was underway. By this measure, Woods won the Vardon Trophy a record nine times in the following years with the corresponding adjusted stroke averages.

- **1999:**   68.43
- **2000:**   67.79
- **2001:**   68.81
- **2002:**   68.56
- **2003:**   68.41
- **2005:**   68.66
- **2007:**   67.79
- **2009:**   68.05
- **2013:**   68.98

From a straight average, Woods' aggregate is a remarkable 68.39. Woods led scoring in 2006, as well, with an average of 68.12, but only completed 55 rounds. Thus, Jim Furyk (68.87) emerged as the Vardon Trophy winner. Also, Woods' *actual* scoring average in 2008 was 69.00, slightly better than Vardon Trophy winner Sergio Garcia's adjusted average of 69.12. However, Woods only competed in five stroke-play events prior to knee surgery, so the number of rounds was too small to assess as a Vardon Trophy win. Conversely, Woods won the 2013 Vardon Trophy, but Steve Stricker had a lower stroke average (68.95) with 51 rounds completed.

Perhaps the most glaring omission from Nicklaus' professional record is the lack of a Vardon Trophy. With the number of regular tournament and major championship victories, money titles, etc. Nicklaus amassed, it seems an afterthought he would have won several. Although he never won the award, he led scoring eight years. The following should clear up any confusion.

Prior to the PGA Tour (or Tournament Players Division) being established in late 1968 and its subsequent development, players were subject to PGA of America guidelines. For Vardon Trophy eligibility, a player needed to first compete for five years. Once that timeframe expired, the minimum number of rounds to be played in a season for the Vardon Trophy was 80 – scoring was actual strokes and Open Championship rounds did not count as they do today.

Below shows the years Nicklaus led in scoring compared to the Vardon Trophy winner:

Year	Jack Nicklaus	Vardon Trophy Winner	Variance
1964	69.96	70.01	(0.05)
1965	70.09	70.59	(0.50)
1971	70.08	70.41	(0.33)
1972	70.23	70.91	(0.68)
1973	69.81	70.69	(0.88)
1974	70.06	70.53	(0.47)
1975	69.87	70.50	(0.63)
1976	70.17	70.56	(0.39)

Per the above data, Nicklaus' straight average score was 70.03 and he was an average of .49 strokes lower than the respective Vardon Trophy winners. Nicklaus was ineligible for the award during 1964 and 1965, which were his third and fourth seasons as a touring professional. During the years 1971 through 1976, Nicklaus never played 80 rounds within the United States in a single season. Even if Open Championship rounds were included for the latter six years, he was still below the minimum.

A further analysis of the Vardon Trophy in Nicklaus' peak playing years is illustrated below. Again, the data excludes Open Championship scores for all players.

Year	Vardon Trophy Winner	Vardon Trophy Scoring Average	Nicklaus Scoring Average (Rank)	Scoring Average Leader	Scoring Average Leader (Stroke Average)
1962	Arnold Palmer	70.27	70.80 (4)	Arnold Palmer	70.27
1963	Billy Casper	70.58	70.42 (2)	Gary Player	70.40
1964	Arnold Palmer	70.01	69.96 (1)	Jack Nicklaus	69.96
1965	Billy Casper	70.59	70.09 (1)	Jack Nicklaus	70.09
1966	Billy Casper	70.16	70.58 (2)	Billy Casper	70.16
1967	Arnold Palmer	70.18	70.23 (2)	Arnold Palmer	70.18

1968	Billy Casper	69.82	69.97 (2)	Billy Casper	69.82
1969	Dave Hill	70.34	71.06 (13)	Dave Hill	70.34
1970	Lee Trevino	70.64	70.75 (3)	Tom Weiskopf	70.63
1971	Lee Trevino	70.41	70.08 (1)	Jack Nicklaus	70.08
1972	Lee Trevino	70.91	70.23 (1)	Jack Nicklaus	70.23
1973	Bruce Crampton	70.69	69.81 (1)	Jack Nicklaus	69.81
1974	Lee Trevino	70.53	70.06 (1)	Jack Nicklaus	70.06
1975	Bruce Crampton	70.50	69.87 (1)	Jack Nicklaus	69.87
1976	Don January	70.56	70.17 (1)	Jack Nicklaus	70.17
1977	Tom Watson	70.32	70.37 (2)	Tom Watson	70.32
1978	Tom Watson	70.16	71.07 (8)	Tom Watson	70.16
1979	Tom Watson	70.27	72.49 (89)	Tom Watson	70.27
1980	Lee Trevino	69.73	70.85 (7)	Lee Trevino	69.73
1981	Tom Kite	69.80	70.69 (6)	Tom Kite	69.80
1982	Tom Kite	70.21	70.90 (12)	Tom Kite	70.21
1983	Raymond Floyd	70.61	70.87 (5)	Raymond Floyd	70.61
1984	Calvin Peete	70.56	70.75 (2)	Calvin Peete	70.56
1985	Don Pooley	70.36	71.81 (75)	Don Pooley	70.36
1986	Scott Hoch	70.08	71.51 (52)	Scott Hoch	70.08

With the above data, a summary of the top-10 scoring performances of Nicklaus and Woods during the prescribed timeframe can be shown along with their weighted averages.

Jack Nicklaus (1962 – 1986) & Tiger Woods (1997 – 2022) Top-10 Placements in Scoring											
	1	2	3	4	5	6	7	8	9	10	Average
Nicklaus	8	6	1	1	1	1	1	1	0	0	2.65
Woods	9	4	1	0	0	0	1	0	0	0	1.80
Variance	(1)	2	0	1	1	1	0	1	0	0	0.85

Here the consistency of Nicklaus is on full display. For 20 years, he was able to finish no worse than eighth place in scoring and led the category eight times. For his 25-year period under review, Nicklaus was eighth or better 80 percent of the time and within these 20 top-10 finishes, he was first eight times, or 40 percent.

As for Woods, his dominance resonates. While he was in the top 10 on five fewer occasions than Nicklaus at 15, he led the category nine times, or 60 percent. This exceeds Nicklaus by one in leading the scoring average and represents a higher percentage of category wins (60 percent vs. 40 percent) relative to overall placements wherein Woods was no worse than seventh. Again, this does not include Woods' year of 2008 as the sample size was too small. The likelihood of Woods leading that year had he been able to complete the season is high and placing no worse than seventh, a certainty.

The preceding described why Nicklaus is not mentioned as a Vardon Trophy recipient, while being the leading player of his era. With this category and several others, the above points out the criteria to achieve various awards have not remained constant over time.

18-hole Tournament Scores as Professionals (60s)

How do the players compare at going low? The following illustrates how Nicklaus and Woods measure up against one another with their rounds shot below 70 in tournament play.

Below provides a summary of Nicklaus and Woods with their total rounds in the 60s as professionals from 1962 through 1986 for Nicklaus and 1996 through 2022 for Woods:

	Jack Nicklaus (1962 – 1986)	Tiger Woods (1996 – 2022)	Variance
Total Rounds	697	762	(65)
Lowest Round	62 (3)	61 (4)	1
Average	67.64	66.99	(0.65)

Both performances represent superb numbers with an advantage across the board to Woods. What this does not include is Nicklaus' 59 shot in an exhibition in 1973, nor his rounds in the four-person World Series of Golf matches. This also does not include Woods' rounds in the four-person PGA Grand Slam of Golf, where he shot a low of 61 in 2002.

In addition, Nicklaus' full number of rounds in the 60s when competing in professional events through 1986 is as follows (excludes the 64 shot in the 1956 Ohio Open).

	Amateur	As Professional (1962 – 1986)	Total
Total Rounds	7	697	704
Lowest Round	66	62 (3)	62 (3)
Average	67.86	67.64	67.64

For Woods, his distribution of rounds in the 60s when competing against professionals through 2022 results in the following distribution.

	Amateur	As Professional (1996 – 2022)	Total
Total Rounds	3	762	765
Lowest Round	66	61 (4)	61 (4)
Average	68.00	66.99	66.99

While Nicklaus had more rounds in the 60s as an amateur than Woods, their stroke averages are nearly even for that period. Woods' lowest competitive round of 61 on four occasions as a professional is a shot less than Nicklaus' three rounds of 62 and his total number of sub-70 rounds is greater by 61.

Major Championships – Rounds Below 70

The following is a summary of Nicklaus and Woods with their rounds in the 60s in major championships as professionals for the timeframes referenced.

	Jack Nicklaus (1962 – 1986)	Tiger Woods (1997 – 2022)	Variance
Total Rounds	120	101	19
Lowest Round	63	63	0
Average	67.85	67.46	0.39

For the aggregate performance of rounds shot below 70 in major championships above, Nicklaus and Woods do not disappoint. While Nicklaus leads Woods in total rounds by 19, Woods leads on average by .39 shots per round. Both players are part of a contingent discussed later in this chapter having shot a then-record 63 (Nicklaus in the 1980 U.S. Open and Woods in the 2007 PGA Championship); each going on to win.

In addition, Nicklaus' number of rounds in the 60s in major championships from his amateur days through 1986 is as follows.

	Amateur	As Professional (1962 – 1986)	Total
Total Rounds	2	120	122
Lowest Round	69 (2)	63	63
Average	69.00	67.85	67.87

For Woods, his complete distribution of rounds in the 60s shot in major championships from 1995 through 2022 results in the following.

	Amateur	As Professional (1997 – 2022)	Total
Total Rounds	2	101	103
Lowest Round	66	63	63
Average	67.50	67.46	67.46

Both performances are the best the game has yet produced. The following chart and four tables will subdivide this summary among the four majors.

Jack Nicklaus (1962 – 1986) & Tiger Woods (1997 – 2022) Major Championship Distribution of Scores (60s)						
	Masters	U.S. Open	Open	PGA	Total	Average
Nicklaus	32	22	28	38	120	30.00
Woods	26	20	25	30	101	25.25
Variance	6	2	3	8	19	4.75
Nicklaus % Of Total	26.67%	18.33%	23.33%	31.67%	100.00%	
Woods % Of Total	25.74%	19.80%	24.75%	29.70%	100.00%	
Variance	0.93%	(1.47%)	(1.42%)	1.97%		

The above is a good composite of Nicklaus and Woods with respect to the distribution of their 18-hole rounds below 70 in major championship play for the years specified. While both show a reasonably even comparative proportion among the four championships with the U.S. Open having the least and the

PGA Championship the most, Nicklaus had more sub-70 rounds, but also completed more rounds. Here is the proportion for both players.

Jack Nicklaus (1962 – 1986) & Tiger Woods (1997 – 2022) Major Championship Proportion of Scores (60s)						
	Masters	U.S. Open	Open	PGA	Total	Average
Nicklaus (Actual)	32	22	28	38	120	30.00
Nicklaus (Attempts)	96	98	99	96	389	97.25
Percentage	33.33%	22.45%	28.28%	39.58%	30.85%	
Woods (Actual)	26	20	25	30	101	25.25
Woods (Attempts)	88	73	72	79	312	78.00
Percentage	29.55%	27.39%	34.72%	37.97%	32.37%	
Variance (Number)	6	2	3	8	19	4.75
Variance (Percentage)	3.78%	(4.94%)	(6.44%)	1.61%	(1.52%)	

The above data show while Nicklaus had 19 more rounds below 70 in the major championships, Woods has a better ratio of rounds under 70 to the total number he played.

Does having more rounds below 70 translate to a lower average in score? The data are shown below.

Masters	Jack Nicklaus (1962 – 1986)	Tiger Woods (1997 – 2022)	Variance
Total Rounds	32	26	6
Lowest Round	64	65 (2)	(1)
Average	67.75	67.50	0.25

U.S. Open	Jack Nicklaus (1962 – 1986)	Tiger Woods (1997 – 2022)	Variance
Total Rounds	22	20	2
Lowest Round	63	65	(2)
Average	67.82	68.00	(0.18)

Open Championship	Jack Nicklaus (1962 – 1986)	Tiger Woods (1997 – 2022)	Variance
Total Rounds	28	25	3

Lowest Round	65 (2)	64	1
Average	67.86	67.08	0.78

PGA Championship	Jack Nicklaus (1962 – 1986)	Tiger Woods (1997 – 2022)	Variance
Total Rounds	38	30	8
Lowest Round	64	63	1
Average	67.95	67.37	0.58

This exploded view is impressive. Although Nicklaus shot 19 more rounds in the 60s, Woods' scoring average for rounds under 70 is slightly lower in three of the four championships.

Lowest 72-hole Aggregate Scores as Professionals

Woods' lowest 72-hole aggregate as a professional is 257 (2007 Tour Championship). For the next review, this will be the lower end of the scoring range up to 272 to see where Nicklaus and Woods reside regarding their scoring ability over the years. Below are the results:

	Jack Nicklaus (1962 – 1986)	Tiger Woods (1996 – 2022)	Variance
Total Scores (257 to 272)	29	96	(67)
Lowest Score	265	257	8
Average	270.45	268.35	2.10

Despite the relative closeness of the scoring average above, Woods' total number of aggregate scores within this range towers over Nicklaus at more than three to one. Woods' singular low of 257 compared to Nicklaus at 265 is substantial. These two elements are not meant to denigrate Nicklaus as both were effective during their respective eras. Woods' results coincide with his greater average margins of victory.

Lowest 72-hole Under Par Scores as Professionals

Like the preceding review, Woods' lowest 72-hole score relative to par was 25-under. This will be the lower end of the scoring range up to 10-under par. The following shows how Nicklaus and Woods fared within these parameters.

	Jack Nicklaus (1962 – 1986)	Tiger Woods (1996 – 2022)	Variance
Total Scores (-25 to -10)	103	159	(56)
Lowest Score	-21	-25 (2)	4
Average	-12.95	-14.94	1.99

The results in the "under par" comparison equate closely to the "aggregate" comparison. Woods leads Nicklaus in number (a three to two ratio), but the overall margins are less. Woods' four-shot variance is also significant, especially since he achieved the score twice. With these two analyses in mind, the same type of criteria will be applied to major championship play.

Lowest 72-hole Aggregate Scores in Major Championships

Prior to 2018, both Nicklaus and Woods scored personal record low aggregates of 269 in major championships for 72 holes. For Nicklaus, it came during the 1977 Open Championship where he finished second to Tom Watson (and 10 shots ahead of Hubert Green in third place). In Woods' case, he shot the number during the 2000 Open Championship where he won by eight.

Woods broke this figure by three shots in chasing Brooks Koepka during the 2018 PGA Championship. While Koepka won, Woods finished in second place. Coincidentally, both players' lowest aggregates in major championships resulted in second-place finishes. For this review, 266 will represent the lower end of the scoring range and 284 the upper. Below are the results:

	Jack Nicklaus (1962 – 1986)	Tiger Woods (1997 – 2022)	Variance
Total Scores (266 to 284)	51	45	6
Lowest Score	269	266	3
Average	279.78	278.31	1.47

In this scenario, Nicklaus and Woods are close. Nicklaus has more rounds within the range having completed more major championships, but Woods is better by 1.47 strokes for the average. For each player, the average is much different than the low total 72-hole aggregates. The following four tables will subdivide this summary among the four major championships.

Low 72-hole Aggregate – Masters	Jack Nicklaus (1962 – 1986)	Tiger Woods (1997 – 2022)	Variance
Total Scores (266 to 284)	13	13	0
Lowest Score	271	270	1
Average	279.92	278.54	1.38

Low 72-hole Aggregate – U.S. Open	Jack Nicklaus (1962 – 1986)	Tiger Woods (1997 – 2022)	Variance
Total Scores (266 to 284)	9	9	0
Lowest Score	272	272	0
Average	279.89	280.33	(0.44)

Low 72-hole Aggregate – Open Championship	Jack Nicklaus (1962 – 1986)	Tiger Woods (1997 – 2022)	Variance
Total Scores (266 to 284)	12	11	1
Lowest Score	269	269	0
Average	279.92	278.55	1.37

Low 72-hole Aggregate – PGA Championship	Jack Nicklaus (1962 – 1986)	Tiger Woods (1997 – 2022)	Variance
Total Scores (266 to 284)	17	12	5
Lowest Score	274 (2)	266	8
Average	279.53	276.33	3.20

This exploded view is notable. While Nicklaus has more rounds in the range, the gap is narrower. The greatest disparity is in the PGA Championship numbers where Nicklaus has nearly 50 percent more scores, yet Woods' average is over three shots lower.

Lowest 72-hole Under Par Scores in Major Championships

Woods' lowest 72-hole score relative to par in major championship play was 19-under, while Nicklaus achieved a mark of 17-under. Therefore, the former will be the lower end of the scoring range up to four-under par. The following shows how Nicklaus and Woods fared during their careers within these parameters.

	Jack Nicklaus (1962 – 1986)	Tiger Woods (1997 – 2022)	Variance
Total Scores (-19 to -4)	35	25	10
Lowest Score	-17	-19	2
Average	-6.97	-10.96	3.99

Woods leads in the ability to go exceptionally low, while Nicklaus again has more championships within the range. Woods' average of four shots better is significant. Nicklaus shows his overall consistency with 10 more championships, having also played more. The following four tables will subdivide this summary among the four majors.

Low 72-hole Under Par – Masters	Jack Nicklaus (1962 – 1986)	Tiger Woods (1997 – 2022)	Variance
Total Scores (-19 to -4)	13	13	0
Lowest Score	-17	-18	1
Average	-8.08	-9.46	1.38

Low 72-hole Under Par – U.S. Open	Jack Nicklaus (1962 – 1986)	Tiger Woods (1997 – 2022)	Variance
Total Scores (-19 to -4)	3	1	2
Lowest Score	-8	-12	4
Average	-5.67	-12.00	6.33

Low 72-hole Under Par – Open Championship	Jack Nicklaus (1962 – 1986)	Tiger Woods (1997 – 2022)	Variance
Total Scores (-19 to -4)	10	4	6
Lowest Score	-11	-19	8

Average	-6.44	-14.00	7.56

Low 72-hole Under Par – PGA Championship	Jack Nicklaus (1962 – 1986)	Tiger Woods (1997 – 2022)	Variance
Total Scores (-19 to -4)	9	7	2
Lowest Score	-9	-18 (2)	9
Average	-6.33	-11.86	5.53

The above view provides several insights. As expected, the results are most alike for the Masters. Due to the same course being similar year after year and the parallels in Nicklaus' and Woods' games, it makes sense.

However, with the U.S. Open being the most difficult setup, Woods' single tournament within the range at -12 skews matters. This was his 15-shot winning margin in 2000. When compared as an average to Nicklaus at -5.67, the difference is substantial. Nicklaus again had two more championships than Woods where his lowest at -8 and second lowest at -5 were winning scores and his third at -4 references his second-place finish in 1982.

For the Open Championship, Nicklaus showed great consistency with 10 results compared to Woods' four. But again, Woods went exceptionally low for his three victories at -19, -18, and -14. All three represented multiple-shot wins at margins of eight, two, and five, respectively. What is also interesting is while Nicklaus won the Open three times as did Woods, only two of his winning scores are included in the range; 1970 at -5 and 1978 at -7. As mentioned, Nicklaus' lowest championship in relation to par was his second-place finish to Tom Watson in 1977 at -11, which was also his lowest aggregate (269) in all majors he played.

Woods' results in the PGA Championship are superior. Nicklaus again has more rounds within the range at nine vs. seven, but the gap is narrower. Woods completed two winning championships at -18 and a second-place finish at -14 which contributed to his average of -11.86 compared to Nicklaus at -6.33. And like the 1977 Open Championship, Nicklaus' low score in relation to par came in 1983 where he finished at -9, one shot behind Hal Sutton.

Major Championship Scoring – Extended Review

The following details the scoring performances of Nicklaus and Woods in each major championship as professionals for the prescribed date ranges. The first section covers the actual scores by round and 18-hole playoff (as applicable). Second, the data are provided on a per round/playoff basis in relation to par. Lastly, the data are presented for each player as professionals in age ranges during their 20s and 30s.

Major Championship Scoring – Raw Scores & Scores in Relation to Par

Since the Masters is played each year at the same site, the charting of scores as both raw data and in relation to par is very uniform.

Jack Nicklaus & Tiger Woods Masters – Raw Scores as Professionals					
	Round 1	Round 2	Round 3	Round 4	Playoff
Nicklaus – All	70.48	72.17	71.26	70.09	70.00
Woods – All	71.64	70.64	69.95	71.23	N/A
Variance	(1.16)	1.53	1.31	(1.14)	N/A
Nicklaus – 60s	11	4	5	12	0
Woods – 60s	2	8	9	7	N/A
Variance	9	(4)	(4)	5	N/A
Nicklaus – 60s %	44.00%	16.67%	21.74%	52.17%	0.00%
Woods – 60s %	9.09%	36.36%	40.91%	31.82%	N/A
Variance	34.91%	(19.69%)	(19.17%)	20.36%	N/A

Jack Nicklaus & Tiger Woods Masters – Relation to Par as Professionals					
	Round 1	Round 2	Round 3	Round 4	Playoff
Nicklaus – All	(1.52)	0.17	(0.74)	(1.91)	(2.00)
Woods – All	(0.36)	(1.36)	(2.05)	(0.77)	N/A
Variance	(1.16)	1.53	1.31	(1.14)	N/A
Nicklaus – Under Par	16	13	10	13	1

Woods – Under Par	11	12	14	14	N/A
Variance	5	1	(4)	(1)	N/A
Nicklaus – Under Par %	64.00%	54.17%	43.48%	56.52%	100.00%
Woods – Under Par %	50.00%	54.55%	63.64%	63.64%	N/A
Variance	14.00%	(0.38%)	(20.16%)	(7.12%)	N/A

Nicklaus was able to start faster and close stronger when reviewing the numbers of rounds in the 60s and under par. Woods made up ground during the second round and especially the third round, having the only scoring average under 70.

For additional context on the Masters records of Nicklaus and Woods, I have incorporated the following tables with point values for the number of occasions each player shot multiple rounds in the 60s and under par, per event. Each time a player shot four consecutive rounds in the 60s or under par, one point will be awarded, while .75 points for three rounds, and .50 points for two rounds. The details are below.

Jack Nicklaus & Tiger Woods **Masters – Point Values (Multiple Sub-70 Rounds Per Event)**						
	4	**3**	**2**	**Total**	**Total Events Played**	**Percentage**
Nicklaus	0	2	8	10	25	40.00%
Woods	0	2	7	9	22	40.91%
Variance	0	0	1	1	3	(0.91%)
Points (N)	0.00	1.50	4.00	5.50		
Points (W)	0.00	1.50	3.50	5.00		
Variance	0.00	0.00	0.50	0.50		

Jack Nicklaus & Tiger Woods Masters – Point Values (Multiple Sub-par Rounds Per Event)						
	4	**3**	**2**	**Total**	**Total Events Played**	**Percentage**
Nicklaus	1	8	8	17	25	68.00%
Woods	5	5	6	16	22	72.73%
Variance	(4)	3	3	2	3	(4.73%)
Points (N)	1.00	6.00	4.00	11.00		
Points (W)	5.00	3.75	3.00	11.75		
Variance	(4.00)	2.25	1.00	(0.75)		

Both charts show a near evenness in overall point values earned. However, Woods' most glaring achievement is the 5:1 ratio over Nicklaus of championships he completed all rounds under par. Nicklaus shows great consistency and volume, but also played more championships.

For the following data on the U.S. Open, since the sites varied along with par, there will be less uniformity with respect to scoring.

Jack Nicklaus & Tiger Woods U.S. Open – Raw Scores as Professionals					
	Round 1	**Round 2**	**Round 3**	**Round 4**	**Playoff**
Nicklaus – All	72.92	71.20	72.43	71.22	71.00
Woods – All	72.20	71.00	71.31	71.56	71.00
Variance	0.72	0.20	1.12	(0.34)	0.00
Nicklaus – 60s	3	6	3	10	0
Woods – 60s	4	7	4	5	0
Variance	(1)	(1)	(1)	5	0
Nicklaus – 60s %	12.00%	24.00%	13.04%	43.48%	0.00%
Woods – 60s %	20.00%	35.00%	25.00%	31.25%	0.00%
Variance	(8.00%)	(11.00%)	(11.96%)	12.23%	0.00%

Jack Nicklaus & Tiger Woods U.S. Open – Relation to Par as Professionals					
	Round 1	Round 2	Round 3	Round 4	Playoff
Nicklaus – All	2.40	0.68	1.91	0.70	0.50
Woods – All	2.00	0.80	1.06	1.31	0.00
Variance	0.40	(0.12)	0.85	(0.61)	0.50
Nicklaus – Under Par	4	9	4	10	0
Woods – Under Par	5	7	5	5	0
Variance	(1)	2	(1)	5	0
Nicklaus – Under Par %	16.00%	36.00%	17.39%	43.48%	0.00%
Woods – Under Par %	25.00%	35.00%	31.25%	31.25%	0.00%
Variance	(9.00%)	1.00%	(13.86%)	12.23%	0.00%

Both players started their U.S. Opens similarly with Nicklaus having nine scores in the 60s for the first two rounds compared to Woods at 11; each improving during the second relative to the first. Nicklaus then shot 13 rounds under 70 over the weekend vs. Woods' total of nine. Woods performed better during "moving day" for both rounds in the 60s and under par, while Nicklaus was stronger in both categories during the final round, yet competed in more events and made a greater number of cuts.

Jack Nicklaus & Tiger Woods U.S. Open – Point Values (Multiple Sub-70 Rounds Per Event)					
	4	3	2	Total	Total Events Played	Percentage
Nicklaus	0	0	6	6	25	24.00%
Woods	0	2	2	4	20	20.00%
Variance	0	0	4	2	5	5.00%
Points (N)	0.00	0.00	3.00	3.00		
Points (W)	0.00	1.50	1.00	2.50		
Variance	0.00	(1.50)	2.00	0.50		

Jack Nicklaus & Tiger Woods U.S. Open – Point Values (Multiple Sub-par Rounds Per Event)						
	4	3	2	Total	Total Events Played	Percentage
Nicklaus	0	1	7	8	25	32.00%
Woods	0	2	3	5	20	25.00%
Variance	0	(1)	4	3	5	7.00%
Points (N)	0.00	0.75	3.50	4.25		
Points (W)	0.00	1.50	1.50	3.00		
Variance	0.00	(0.75)	2.00	1.25		

The data above are almost a watered-down version of the preceding Masters view. Surprisingly, Nicklaus never had three rounds in the 60s during a single U.S. Open, while Woods accomplished this feat twice. Nicklaus is more consistent and leads in overall points, but Woods ultimately went lower on occasion.

For the Open Championship, there are fewer courses in the rotation, but as with the U.S. Open, the sites will vary along with the respective par.

Jack Nicklaus & Tiger Woods Open Championship – Raw Scores as Professionals					
	Round 1	Round 2	Round 3	Round 4	Playoff
Nicklaus – All	73.32	70.40	71.38	70.29	72.00
Woods – All	70.50	71.15	71.13	70.88	N/A
Variance	2.82	(0.75)	0.25	(0.59)	N/A
Nicklaus – 60s	4	8	6	10	0
Woods – 60s	9	6	6	4	N/A
Variance	(5)	2	0	6	N/A
Nicklaus – 60s %	16.00%	32.00%	25.00%	41.67%	0.00%
Woods – 60s %	45.00%	30.00%	37.50%	25.00%	N/A
Variance	(29.00%)	2.00%	(12.50%)	16.67%	N/A

Jack Nicklaus & Tiger Woods Open Championship – Relation to Par as Professionals					
	Round 1	**Round 2**	**Round 3**	**Round 4**	**Playoff**
Nicklaus – All	1.92	(1.00)	(0.04)	(1.13)	0.00
Woods – All	(0.70)	(0.05)	(0.06)	(0.31)	N/A
Variance	2.62	(0.95)	0.02	(0.81)	N/A
Nicklaus – Under Par	8	15	9	13	0
Woods – Under Par	11	7	8	6	N/A
Variance	(3)	8	1	7	N/A
Nicklaus – Under Par %	32.00%	60.00%	37.50%	54.17%	0.00%
Woods – Under Par %	55.00%	35.00%	50.00%	37.50%	N/A
Variance	(23.00%)	25.00%	(12.50%)	16.67%	N/A

Woods' performance on average in the first round is far superior to Nicklaus in raw scores and in relation to par; almost three shots for both over the first 18 holes. Nicklaus' inauspicious start to his professional career in the Open with an 80 did not help, however, he is flat, regardless. Yet, for as mundane as Nicklaus was, Woods is conversely every bit as impressive. While Nicklaus leads Woods for the second and fourth rounds in both sections, Woods' numbers for the opening round variances across both are substantial.

Jack Nicklaus & Tiger Woods Open Championship – Point Values (Multiple Sub-70 Rounds Per Event)						
	4	**3**	**2**	**Total**	**Total Events Played**	**Percentage**
Nicklaus	0	1	7	8	25	32.00%
Woods	1	1	5	7	20	35.00%
Variance	(1)	0	2	1	5	(3.00%)
Points (N)	0.00	0.75	3.50	4.25		
Points (W)	1.00	0.75	2.50	4.25		
Variance	(1.00)	0.00	1.00	0.00		

Jack Nicklaus & Tiger Woods Open Championship – Point Values (Multiple Sub-par Rounds Per Event)						
	4	3	2	Total	Total Events Played	Percentage
Nicklaus	1	6	8	15	25	60.00%
Woods	3	2	3	8	20	40.00%
Variance	(2)	4	5	7	5	20.00%
Points (N)	1.00	4.50	4.00	9.50		
Points (W)	3.00	1.50	1.50	6.00		
Variance	(2.00)	3.00	2.50	3.50		

The Open Championship provides another great look at Nicklaus' consistency and Woods' taking the performance to a brief, higher level. Woods was able to shoot four rounds in the 60s during his great run in 2000, which Nicklaus did not accomplish. He also led by a three to one margin in championships with all four rounds below par. However, Nicklaus wins out in total volume of rounds below 70 and under par, therefore, even with more championships played and cuts made, his ratios are greater.

Lastly, the PGA Championship is in line with the U.S. Open with respect to the number of sites used on a yearly basis. Let's see how the results compare.

Jack Nicklaus & Tiger Woods PGA Championship – Raw Scores as Professionals					
	Round 1	Round 2	Round 3	Round 4	Playoff
Nicklaus – All	70.88	71.16	70.78	70.00	N/A
Woods – All	71.27	69.73	70.50	70.24	N/A
Variance	(0.39)	1.43	0.28	(0.24)	N/A
Nicklaus – 60s	9	10	8	11	N/A
Woods – 60s	6	10	7	7	N/A
Variance	3	0	1	4	N/A
Nicklaus – 60s %	36.00%	40.00%	34.78%	47.83%	N/A
Woods – 60s %	27.27%	45.45%	38.89%	41.18%	N/A
Variance	8.73%	(5.45%)	(4.11%)	6.65%	N/A

Jack Nicklaus & Tiger Woods PGA Championship – Relation to Par as Professionals					
	Round 1	Round 2	Round 3	Round 4	Playoff
Nicklaus – All	0.20	0.48	0.09	(0.70)	N/A
Woods – All	0.41	(1.14)	(0.39)	(0.71)	N/A
Variance	(0.21)	1.62	0.48	0.01	N/A
Nicklaus – Under Par	11	13	11	12	N/A
Woods – Under Par	9	13	9	7	N/A
Variance	2	0	2	5	N/A
Nicklaus – Under Par %	44.00%	52.00%	47.83%	52.17%	N/A
Woods – Under Par %	40.91%	59.09%	50.00%	41.18%	N/A
Variance	3.09%	(7.09%)	(2.17%)	10.99%	N/A

Woods shows strength in the middle two rounds, which helped position himself many times as the front-runner toward victory. Nicklaus shows greater strength in first and final round performances. Nicklaus leads in the total number of rounds in the 60s and under par by eight and nine rounds, respectively, but competed in three more events and missed fewer cuts.

Jack Nicklaus & Tiger Woods PGA Championship – Point Values (Multiple Sub-70 Rounds Per Event)						
	4	3	2	Total	Total Events Played	Percentage
Nicklaus	0	4	9	13	25	52.00%
Woods	1	4	5	10	22	45.45%
Variance	(1)	0	3	2	3	(6.55%)
Points (N)	0.00	3.00	4.50	7.50		
Points (W)	1.00	3.00	2.50	6.50		
Variance	(1.00)	0.00	2.00	1.00		

Jack Nicklaus & Tiger Woods PGA Championship – Point Values (Multiple Sub-par Rounds Per Event)						
	4	3	2	Total	Total Events Played	Percentage
Nicklaus	0	8	10	18	25	72.00%
Woods	2	6	5	13	22	59.09%
Variance	(2)	2	5	5	3	12.91%
Points (N)	0.00	6.00	5.00	11.00		
Points (W)	2.00	4.50	2.50	9.00		
Variance	(2.00)	1.50	2.50	2.00		

Judging by these two schematics, the PGA Championship afforded Nicklaus and Woods the best opportunities to score. Woods has the honor of shooting all four rounds in the 60s during a single event, as well as all four rounds under par for the same championship plus one other. While Nicklaus accomplished neither, he succeeds over Woods in consistency and longevity spanning a greater number of championships played. Therefore, his overall point values are higher along with corresponding percentages.

With the performances of Nicklaus and Woods identified above in each major championship per the point system described, let's combine the four calculations into an aggregate representation.

Jack Nicklaus & Tiger Woods Major Championships – Point Values (Multiple Sub-70 Rounds Per Event)						
	4	3	2	Total	Total Events Played	Percentage
Nicklaus	0	7	30	37	100	37.00%
Woods	2	9	19	30	84	35.71%
Variance	(2)	(2)	11	7	16	1.29%
Points (N)	0.00	5.25	15.00	20.25		
Points (W)	2.00	6.75	9.50	18.25		
Variance	(2.00)	(1.50)	5.50	2.00		

For sub-70 rounds per major championship, Nicklaus has the lead. However, he has competed 16 times more than Woods and made more cuts. Yet, from a percentage basis, the numbers are close. Woods converted two championships with all four rounds under 70 – two greater than Nicklaus. Woods also leads Nicklaus in championships with three rounds per event below 70. Nicklaus shines with three out of every 10 having two rounds of the four under 70, which he was able to accomplish 11 times more than Woods.

					Total Events Played	
Jack Nicklaus & Tiger Woods **Major Championships – Point Values (Multiple Sub-par Rounds Per Event)**						
	4	**3**	**2**	**Total**		**Percentage**
Nicklaus	2	23	33	58	100	58.00%
Woods	10	15	17	42	84	50.00%
Variance	(8)	8	16	16	16	8.00%
Points (N)	2.00	17.25	16.50	35.75		
Points (W)	10.00	11.25	8.50	29.75		
Variance	(8.00)	6.00	8.00	6.00		

Above displays another great composite of Nicklaus and Woods with respect to completing major championships with at least two of the four rounds below par. Woods convincingly leads with 10 championships having all four rounds under par to Nicklaus' total of two. And despite competing in 16 additional majors, Nicklaus is well ahead of Woods for events with three of the four rounds below par as well as two rounds. On 56 occasions out of 100 (56.00%) – or out of 93 (60.22%), when deducting the six missed cuts and one withdrawal – Nicklaus shot either half or three-quarters of the rounds per major championship under par.

Major Championship Aggregate Scoring Summary

The following shows an overall scoring comparison in the major championships via the numbers listed above in a composite table.

Jack Nicklaus & Tiger Woods Major Championship Aggregate – Raw Scores as Professionals					
	Round 1	Round 2	Round 3	Round 4	Playoff
Nicklaus – All	71.90	71.22	71.46	70.40	71.00
Woods – All	71.40	70.61	70.65	70.99	71.00
Variance	0.50	0.61	0.81	(0.59)	0.00
Nicklaus – 60s	27	28	22	43	0
Woods – 60s	21	31	26	23	0
Variance	6	(3)	(4)	20	0
Nicklaus – 60s %	27.00%	28.28%	23.66%	46.24%	0.00%
Woods – 60s %	25.00%	36.90%	36.11%	32.39%	0.00%
Variance	2.00%	(8.62%)	(12.45%)	13.85%	0.00%

Jack Nicklaus & Tiger Woods Major Championship Aggregate – Relation to Par as Professionals					
	Round 1	Round 2	Round 3	Round 4	Playoff
Nicklaus – All	0.75	0.08	0.30	(0.76)	(0.25)
Woods – All	0.32	(0.48)	(0.50)	(0.18)	0.00
Variance	0.43	0.56	0.80	(0.58)	(0.25)
Nicklaus – Under Par	39	50	34	48	1
Woods – Under Par	36	39	36	32	0
Variance	3	11	(2)	16	1
Nicklaus – Under Par %	39.00%	50.51%	36.56%	51.61%	25.00%
Woods – Under Par %	42.86%	46.43%	50.00%	45.07%	0.00%
Variance	(3.86%)	4.08%	(13.44%)	6.54%	25.00%

The next outline provides a summary of the aggregate scoring data for Nicklaus and Woods with an emphasis on their strengths and weaknesses.

- **Strengths**
  - Nicklaus
    - Final Round Average
      - 70.40

- - - Final Round Performance
      - 46.24% of the time Nicklaus shot in the 60s
      - 51.61% of the time Nicklaus shot under par to close
    - Total Rounds (60s)
      - 120/389 = 30.85%
    - Total Rounds Under Par
      - 172/389 = 44.22%
  - Woods
    - Second Round Average
      - 70.61
    - Third Round Performance
      - 36.11% of the time Woods shot in the 60s
      - 50.00% of the time Woods shot under par
    - Total Rounds (60s)
      - 101/312 = 32.37%
    - Total Rounds Under Par
      - 143/312 = 45.83%
- **Weaknesses**
  - Nicklaus
    - First Round Average
      - 71.90
  - Woods
    - First Round Average
      - 71.40
- **Average 18-hole Scores (Raw Scores)**
  - Nicklaus
    - 71.25
  - Woods
    - 70.92
- **Average 18-hole Scores (Relation to Par)**
  - Nicklaus
    - .101
  - Woods
    - (.199)

For Nicklaus from 1962 through 1986 and Woods from 1997 through 2022, Woods beat Nicklaus by an average of .33 shots via raw score and .30 shots in relation to par over 18 holes. In addition, Nicklaus shot 19 more rounds in the 60s and 29 more rounds under par than did Woods. With Nicklaus competing in more championships and missing fewer cuts, their corresponding percentages to the total rounds played were 30.85% and 44.22%, respectively for Nicklaus compared to 32.37% and 45.83%, respectively for Woods.

Collective of Sub-70 & Sub-par Major Championship Rounds

As a further review of major championship performances by Nicklaus and Woods, the below data provide how each fared with multiple rounds under 70. Similarly, the subsequent graphic shows the number of times both players shot all rounds at par or better.

Jack Nicklaus & Tiger Woods Multiple Rounds in the 60s Per Major Championship as Professionals						
	4	3	2	Total	Events Played	Percent
Nicklaus (1962 – 1986)	0	7	29	36	100	36.00%
Woods (1997 – 2022)	2	8	19	29	84	34.52%
Variance	(2)	(1)	10	7	16	1.48%
Nicklaus – 60s %	0.00%	7.00%	29.00%			
Woods – 60s %	2.47%	9.88%	23.46%			
Variance	(2.47%)	(2.88%)	5.54%			

The above displays Woods' dominance and Nicklaus' consistency/longevity. On two occasions, Woods shot four straight rounds within a major championship under 70. They were:

- **2000 Open Championship**
  - 67-66-67-69
- **2006 PGA Championship**
  - 69-68-65-68

Woods won both events by eight shots and five shots, respectively.

Nicklaus did not shoot four straight rounds below 70 in a major championship. His three closest efforts were:

- **1974 PGA Championship**
    - ○ 69-69-70-69
- **1977 Open Championship**
    - ○ 68-70-65-66
- **1980 PGA Championship**
    - ○ 70-69-66-69

In the first two events, Nicklaus finished second by a shot to Lee Trevino and Tom Watson, respectively. In the third event, he won by seven shots.

Jack Nicklaus & Tiger Woods All Rounds at Par or Better Per Major Championship as Professionals							
	Masters	U.S. Open	Open	PGA	Total	Events Played	Percent
Nicklaus (1962 – 1986)	5	0*	5	2	12	100	12.00%
Woods (1997 – 2022)	9	1	4	5	19	84	22.62%
Variance	(4)	(1)	1	(3)	(7)	16	(10.62%)
Nicklaus – Sub-par %	5.00%	0.00%	5.00%	2.00%			
Woods – Sub-par %	10.71%	1.19%	4.76%	5.95%			
Variance	(5.71%)	(1.19%)	0.24%	(3.95%)			

The preceding graphic shows Woods ahead of the pace Nicklaus set for major championship play in which all rounds were shot at par or better during a single event. *It should be noted that Nicklaus did accomplish this feat in the 1960 U.S. Open as an amateur, but since the focus is on the professional records, there is only an asterisk. Regardless, Woods achieved this milestone 19 times compared to 12 for Nicklaus. So, not only is Woods' total greater, his proportion is considerably greater.

Major Championship Scoring Per Age Decade

To review the scoring prowess of Nicklaus and Woods at a granular level and during their prime playing years, the following shows how each fared in certain age ranges. The same format will be used as above per major championship and scoring silos of raw data and in relation to par. The only difference will be the data are segregated in the players' ages from 21 through 29 followed by 30 through 39.

Jack Nicklaus & Tiger Woods Masters – Raw Scores as Professionals (20s)					
	Round 1	Round 2	Round 3	Round 4	Playoff
Nicklaus – All	70.38	73.25	71.00	70.71	70.00
Woods – All	72.56	69.44	68.33	71.00	N/A
Variance	(2.18)	3.81	2.67	(0.29)	N/A
Nicklaus – 60s	4	1	1	3	0
Woods – 60s	0	5	6	3	N/A
Variance	4	(4)	(5)	0	N/A
Nicklaus – 60s %	50.00%	12.50%	14.29%	42.86%	0.00%
Woods – 60s %	0.00%	55.56%	66.67%	33.33%	N/A
Variance	50.00%	(43.06%)	(52.38%)	9.53%	N/A

Jack Nicklaus & Tiger Woods Masters – Relation to Par as Professionals (20s)					
	Round 1	Round 2	Round 3	Round 4	Playoff
Nicklaus – All	(1.63)	1.25	(1.00)	(1.29)	(2.00)
Woods – All	0.56	(2.56)	(3.67)	(1.00)	N/A
Variance	(2.19)	3.81	2.67	(0.29)	N/A
Nicklaus – Under Par	5	3	3	3	1
Woods – Under Par	4	5	7	7	N/A
Variance	1	(2)	(4)	(4)	N/A
Nicklaus – Under Par %	62.50%	37.50%	42.86%	42.86%	100.00%
Woods – Under Par %	44.44%	55.56%	77.78%	77.78%	N/A
Variance	18.06%	(18.06%)	(34.92%)	(34.92%)	N/A

Woods experienced difficulty getting off to a good start in the first round of the Masters, yet made up for it with exceptional performances in the second and third rounds. Woods' efforts in the third round positioned himself well for his four victories from ages 21 through 29. Nicklaus opened well and closed well, but his second-round performances were flat. Still, he captured three green jackets during his eligible eight years.

Jack Nicklaus & Tiger Woods U.S. Open – Raw Scores as Professionals (20s)					
	Round 1	**Round 2**	**Round 3**	**Round 4**	**Playoff**
Nicklaus – All	73.25	70.88	72.57	71.00	71.00
Woods – All	70.44	69.33	71.78	71.11	N/A
Variance	2.81	1.55	0.79	(0.11)	N/A
Nicklaus – 60s	0	2	1	3	0
Woods – 60s	3	5	1	3	N/A
Variance	(3)	(3)	0	0	N/A
Nicklaus – 60s %	0.00%	25.00%	14.29%	42.86%	0.00%
Woods – 60s %	33.33%	55.56%	11.11%	33.33%	N/A
Variance	(33.33%)	(30.56%)	3.18%	9.53%	N/A

Jack Nicklaus & Tiger Woods U.S. Open – Relation to Par as Professionals (20s)					
	Round 1	**Round 2**	**Round 3**	**Round 4**	**Playoff**
Nicklaus – All	3.00	0.63	2.43	0.86	0.00
Woods – All	0.33	(0.78)	1.67	1.00	N/A
Variance	2.67	1.41	0.76	(0.14)	N/A
Nicklaus – Under Par	0	3	1	3	0
Woods – Under Par	3	5	1	3	N/A
Variance	(3)	(2)	0	0	N/A
Nicklaus – Under Par %	0.00%	37.50%	14.29%	42.86%	0.00%
Woods – Under Par %	33.33%	55.56%	11.11%	33.33%	N/A
Variance	(33.33%)	(18.06%)	3.18%	9.53%	N/A

Woods handily beats Nicklaus in overall performance in the U.S. Open when both players were in their 20s. Even though Woods had an additional year, the margins are large enough to make that a moot point. While as an amateur at ages 20 and 21, Nicklaus performed very well in the U.S. Open relative to Woods at age 20, the objective here is to stay within their professional appearances. Both players won two championships in this age bracket, but Woods leads in scoring, rounds in the 60s, and in relation to par.

Jack Nicklaus & Tiger Woods Open Championship – Raw Scores as Professionals (20s)					
	Round 1	**Round 2**	**Round 3**	**Round 4**	**Playoff**
Nicklaus – All	74.00	69.88	71.75	71.75	N/A
Woods – All	69.78	70.11	71.56	70.22	N/A
Variance	4.22	(0.23)	0.19	1.53	N/A
Nicklaus – 60s	0	4	2	2	N/A
Woods – 60s	3	4	4	3	N/A
Variance	(3)	0	(2)	(1)	N/A
Nicklaus – 60s %	0.00%	50.00%	25.00%	25.00%	N/A
Woods – 60s %	33.33%	44.44%	44.44%	33.33%	N/A
Variance	(33.33%)	5.56%	(19.44%)	(8.33%)	N/A

Jack Nicklaus & Tiger Woods Open Championship – Relation to Par as Professionals (20s)					
	Round 1	**Round 2**	**Round 3**	**Round 4**	**Playoff**
Nicklaus – All	2.50	(1.63)	0.25	0.25	N/A
Woods – All	(1.33)	(1.00)	0.44	(0.89)	N/A
Variance	3.83	(0.63)	(0.19)	1.14	N/A
Nicklaus – Under Par	1	6	3	4	N/A
Woods – Under Par	5	4	5	4	N/A
Variance	(4)	2	(2)	0	N/A
Nicklaus – Under Par %	12.50%	75.00%	37.50%	50.00%	N/A
Woods – Under Par %	55.56%	44.44%	55.56%	44.44%	N/A
Variance	(43.06%)	30.56%	(18.06%)	5.56%	N/A

This review exhibits greater balance between the players than the U.S. Open. Nicklaus was flat in the opening rounds, but he rebounded nicely in the second rounds on average being under par 75.00% of the time. Woods leads most categories, but by smaller margins except for his sizable opening round advantage. With Woods having won two titles during this timeframe compared to Nicklaus' one, the better total performance is expected.

Jack Nicklaus & Tiger Woods PGA Championship – Raw Scores as Professionals (20s)					
	Round 1	Round 2	Round 3	Round 4	Playoff
Nicklaus – All	69.88	72.88	71.14	69.00	N/A
Woods – All	71.11	69.11	69.78	70.67	N/A
Variance	(1.23)	3.77	1.36	(1.67)	N/A
Nicklaus – 60s	4	1	3	3	N/A
Woods – 60s	2	6	4	3	N/A
Variance	2	(5)	(1)	0	N/A
Nicklaus – 60s %	50.00%	12.50%	42.86%	42.86%	N/A
Woods – 60s %	22.22%	66.67%	44.44%	33.33%	N/A
Variance	27.78%	(54.17%)	(1.58%)	9.53%	N/A

Jack Nicklaus & Tiger Woods PGA Championship – Relation to Par as Professionals (20s)					
	Round 1	Round 2	Round 3	Round 4	Playoff
Nicklaus – All	(0.75)	2.25	0.43	(1.71)	N/A
Woods – All	0.22	(1.78)	(1.11)	(0.22)	N/A
Variance	(0.97)	4.03	1.54	(1.49)	N/A
Nicklaus – Under Par	5	2	3	4	N/A
Woods – Under Par	4	6	5	3	N/A
Variance	1	(4)	(2)	1	N/A
Nicklaus – Under Par %	62.50%	25.00%	42.86%	57.14%	N/A
Woods – Under Par %	44.44%	66.67%	55.56%	33.33%	N/A
Variance	18.06%	(41.67%)	(12.70%)	23.81%	N/A

Nicklaus only won a single PGA Championship prior to turning 30, while Woods won back-to-back titles at ages 23 and 24. The chart above delineates a more even distribution of performance, with a slight advantage to Woods. Each player is flat when the other performed well. Woods shows strength in second rounds with two out of every three times shooting below 70 and leads Nicklaus in rounds below 70 and in relation to par each by four. And again, Nicklaus closes well in the final rounds.

Jack Nicklaus & Tiger Woods Aggregate – Raw Scores as Professionals (20s)					
	Round 1	Round 2	Round 3	Round 4	Playoff
Nicklaus – All	71.88	71.72	71.62	70.66	70.50
Woods – All	70.97	69.50	70.36	70.75	N/A
Variance	0.91	2.22	1.26	(0.09)	N/A
Nicklaus – 60s	8	8	7	11	0
Woods – 60s	8	20	15	12	N/A
Variance	0	(12)	(8)	(1)	N/A
Nicklaus – 60s %	25.00%	25.00%	24.14%	37.93%	0.00%
Woods – 60s %	22.22%	55.56%	41.67%	33.33%	N/A
Variance	2.78%	(30.56%)	(17.53%)	4.60%	N/A

Jack Nicklaus & Tiger Woods Aggregate – Relation to Par as Professionals (20s)					
	Round 1	Round 2	Round 3	Round 4	Playoff
Nicklaus – All	0.78	0.63	0.52	(0.45)	(1.00)
Woods – All	(0.06)	(1.53)	(0.67)	(0.28)	N/A
Variance	0.84	2.16	1.19	(0.17)	N/A
Nicklaus – Under Par	11	14	10	14	1
Woods – Under Par	16	20	18	17	N/A
Variance	(5)	(6)	(8)	(3)	N/A
Nicklaus – Under Par %	34.38%	43.75%	34.48%	48.28%	50.00%
Woods – Under Par %	44.44%	55.56%	50.00%	47.22%	N/A
Variance	(10.06%)	(11.81%)	(15.52%)	1.06%	N/A

With the aggregate results gathered, the below items provide another high-level view for Nicklaus and Woods as professionals in their 20s with an emphasis on strengths and weaknesses.

- **Strengths**
  - Nicklaus
    - Final Round Scoring Average
      - 70.66
    - Final Round Performance
      - 37.93% shot in the 60s
      - 48.28% shot under par to close
    - Total Rounds (60s)
      - 34/124 = 27.42%
    - Total Rounds Under Par
      - 50/124 = 40.32%
  - Woods
    - Second Round Scoring Average
      - 69.50
    - Second Round Performance
      - 55.56% shot in the 60s
      - 55.56% shot under par
    - Third Round Performance
      - 50.00% shot under par
    - Total Rounds (60s)
      - 55/144 = 38.19%
    - Total Rounds Under Par
      - 71/144 = 49.31%
- **Weaknesses**
  - Nicklaus
    - First Round Scoring Average
      - 71.88
  - Woods
    - First Round Performance
      - 22.22% shot in the 60s
- **Scoring Average (18-hole Raw Scores)**
  - Nicklaus
    - 71.47

- o   Woods
  - ▪ 70.40
- **Scoring Average (18-hole Relation to Par)**
  - o   Nicklaus
    - ▪ .36
  - o   Woods
    - ▪ (.63)

As professionals from ages 20 through 29, Woods (nine years) beats Nicklaus (eight years) by an average of 1.07 shots via raw score and .99 shot in relation to par per all 18-hole rounds in major championships. Woods' percentage of rounds in the 60s and rounds under par are greater than Nicklaus' number relative to their total attempts. Incredibly, Woods did not miss a single 36-hole cut in the 36 major championships he played, while Nicklaus missed just three cuts in the 32 he competed.

Jack Nicklaus & Tiger Woods Masters – Raw Scores as Professionals (30s)					
	Round 1	**Round 2**	**Round 3**	**Round 4**	**Playoff**
Nicklaus – All	69.50	71.50	71.20	69.30	N/A
Woods – All	71.22	71.22	70.56	70.56	N/A
Variance	(1.72)	0.28	0.64	(1.26)	N/A
Nicklaus – 60s	6	2	3	7	N/A
Woods – 60s	1	2	2	3	N/A
Variance	5	0	1	4	N/A
Nicklaus – 60s %	60.00%	20.00%	30.00%	70.00%	N/A
Woods – 60s %	11.11%	22.22%	22.22%	33.33%	N/A
Variance	48.89%	(2.22%)	7.78%	36.67%	N/A

Jack Nicklaus & Tiger Woods Masters – Relation to Par as Professionals (30s)					
	Round 1	**Round 2**	**Round 3**	**Round 4**	**Playoff**
Nicklaus – All	(2.50)	(0.50)	(0.80)	(2.70)	N/A
Woods – All	(0.78)	(0.78)	(1.44)	(1.44)	N/A
Variance	(1.72)	0.28	0.64	(1.26)	N/A
Nicklaus – Under Par	8	7	4	7	N/A

Woods – Under Par	4	5	6	5	N/A
Variance	4	2	(2)	2	N/A
Nicklaus – Under Par %	80.00%	70.00%	40.00%	70.00%	N/A
Woods – Under Par %	44.44%	55.56%	66.67%	55.56%	N/A
Variance	35.56%	14.44%	(26.67%)	14.44%	N/A

Nicklaus competed in all 10 Masters events from age 30 through 39 and won two. Woods missed the 2014 edition but did not win a single green jacket in the other nine attempts. This lends probability Nicklaus would have performed better overall during that age bracket – and he did. Apart from third round performance, Nicklaus leads Woods convincingly. Nicklaus' record for this 10-year period at the Masters is beyond reproach with an uncanny ability to sustain rounds in the 60s and under par.

Jack Nicklaus & Tiger Woods U.S. Open – Raw Scores as Professionals (30s)					
	Round 1	Round 2	Round 3	Round 4	Playoff
Nicklaus – All	73.40	71.40	73.20	71.10	71.00
Woods – All	73.63	71.88	70.67	72.67	71.00
Variance	(0.23)	(0.48)	2.53	(1.57)	0.00
Nicklaus – 60s	1	3	1	4	0
Woods – 60s	1	2	3	1	0
Variance	0	1	(2)	3	0
Nicklaus – 60s %	10.00%	30.00%	10.00%	40.00%	0.00%
Woods – 60s %	12.50%	25.00%	50.00%	16.67%	0.00%
Variance	(2.50%)	5.00%	(40.00%)	23.33%	0.00%

Jack Nicklaus & Tiger Woods U.S. Open – Relation to Par as Professionals (30s)					
	Round 1	Round 2	Round 3	Round 4	Playoff
Nicklaus – All	2.60	0.60	2.40	0.30	1.00
Woods – All	3.38	1.63	0.33	2.33	0.00
Variance	(0.78)	(1.03)	2.07	(2.03)	1.00

Nicklaus – Under Par	2	4	1	4	0
Woods – Under Par	1	2	4	1	0
Variance	1	2	(3)	3	0
Nicklaus – Under Par %	20.00%	40.00%	10.00%	40.00%	0.00%
Woods – Under Par %	12.50%	25.00%	66.67%	16.67%	0.00%
Variance	7.50%	15.00%	(56.67%)	23.33%	0.00%

Both Nicklaus and Woods won the U.S. Open once in their 30s – and at age 32. Nicklaus in his 11th year as a professional and Woods in his 12th. Nicklaus was able to compete in all 10 and Woods in eight. However, Woods' third round performances stand out, while Nicklaus leads in first, second, and fourth round prowess.

Jack Nicklaus & Tiger Woods Open Championship – Raw Scores as Professionals (30s)					
	Round 1	Round 2	Round 3	Round 4	Playoff
Nicklaus – All	70.60	70.60	70.90	69.20	72.00
Woods – All	69.38	72.00	71.33	71.83	N/A
Variance	1.22	(1.40)	(0.43)	(2.63)	N/A
Nicklaus – 60s	4	2	3	6	0
Woods – 60s	6	2	1	1	N/A
Variance	(2)	0	2	5	N/A
Nicklaus – 60s %	40.00%	20.00%	30.00%	60.00%	0.00%
Woods – 60s %	75.00%	25.00%	16.67%	16.67%	N/A
Variance	(35.00%)	(5.00%)	13.33%	43.33%	N/A

Jack Nicklaus & Tiger Woods Open Championship – Relation to Par as Professionals (30s)					
	Round 1	Round 2	Round 3	Round 4	Playoff
Nicklaus – All	(1.00)	(1.00)	(0.70)	(2.40)	0.00
Woods – All	(1.88)	0.75	0.00	0.50	N/A
Variance	0.88	(1.75)	(0.70)	(2.90)	N/A

Nicklaus – **Under Par**	7	6	5	6	0
Woods – **Under Par**	6	2	2	2	N/A
Variance	1	4	3	4	N/A
Nicklaus – **Under Par %**	70.00%	60.00%	50.00%	60.00%	0.00%
Woods – **Under Par %**	75.00%	25.00%	33.33%	33.33%	N/A
Variance	(5.00%)	35.00%	16.67%	26.67%	N/A

Nicklaus won two Open Championships in his 30s while competing in 10 and had zero missed cuts. Woods won the championship once in eight attempts and missed two cuts. Even with Woods' exceptional first round performance with 75.00% under par and under 70, Nicklaus is ultimately superior. Nicklaus' combined lead over Woods in rounds under par and under 70 is 17, thus translating to more accomplished second, third, and final rounds. If Woods had played in 2008 and 2011, the variance would likely be less.

Jack Nicklaus & Tiger Woods **PGA Championship – Raw Scores as Professionals (30s)**					
	Round 1	**Round 2**	**Round 3**	**Round 4**	**Playoff**
Nicklaus – All	71.20	71.10	70.33	70.89	N/A
Woods – All	71.56	70.22	70.67	71.17	N/A
Variance	(0.36)	0.88	(0.34)	(0.28)	N/A
Nicklaus – 60s	4	5	4	3	N/A
Woods – 60s	3	2	2	2	N/A
Variance	1	3	2	1	N/A
Nicklaus – 60s %	40.00%	50.00%	44.44%	33.33%	N/A
Woods – 60s %	33.33%	22.22%	33.33%	33.33%	N/A
Variance	6.67%	27.78%	11.11%	0.00%	N/A

Jack Nicklaus & Tiger Woods **PGA Championship – Relation to Par as Professionals (30s)**					
	Round 1	**Round 2**	**Round 3**	**Round 4**	**Playoff**
Nicklaus – All	0.60	0.50	(0.22)	0.33	N/A
Woods – All	0.33	(1.00)	(0.67)	(0.17)	N/A

Variance	0.27	1.50	0.45	0.50	N/A
Nicklaus – Under Par	4	6	6	3	N/A
Woods – Under Par	4	5	3	2	N/A
Variance	0	1	3	1	N/A
Nicklaus – Under Par %	40.00%	60.00%	66.67%	33.33%	N/A
Woods – Under Par %	44.44%	55.56%	50.00%	33.33%	N/A
Variance	(4.44%)	4.44%	16.67%	0.00%	N/A

Woods won this title twice in the age range above and leads Nicklaus across the board in round-by-round scoring averages in relation to par. However, Nicklaus leads Woods in total rounds shot in the 60s by seven and rounds under par by five with Woods playing in two fewer championships. Nicklaus' consistency throughout this event during the decade is evident by winning three times and missing just one 36-hole cut vs. three missed cuts for Woods.

Jack Nicklaus & Tiger Woods Aggregate – Raw Scores as Professionals (30s)					
	Round 1	Round 2	Round 3	Round 4	Playoff
Nicklaus – All	71.18	71.15	71.44	70.10	71.50
Woods – All	71.44	71.29	70.78	71.44	71.00
Variance	(0.26)	(0.14)	0.66	(1.34)	0.50
Nicklaus – 60s	15	12	11	20	0
Woods – 60s	11	8	8	7	0
Variance	4	4	3	13	0
Nicklaus – 60s %	37.50%	30.00%	28.21%	51.28%	0.00%
Woods – 60s %	32.35%	23.53%	29.63%	25.93%	0.00%
Variance	5.15%	6.47%	(1.42%)	25.35%	0.00%

Jack Nicklaus & Tiger Woods Aggregate – Relation to Par as Professionals (30s)					
	Round 1	Round 2	Round 3	Round 4	Playoff
Nicklaus – All	(0.08)	(0.10)	0.18	(1.15)	0.50
Woods – All	0.15	0.06	(0.56)	0.11	0.00

Variance	(0.23)	(0.16)	0.74	(1.26)	0.50
Nicklaus – Under Par	21	23	16	20	0
Woods – Under Par	15	14	15	10	0
Variance	6	9	1	10	0
Nicklaus – Under Par %	52.50%	57.50%	41.03%	51.28%	0.00%
Woods – Under Par %	44.12%	41.18%	55.56%	37.04%	0.00%
Variance	8.38%	16.32%	(14.53%)	14.24%	0.00%

With the above aggregate results defined, the below items provide another high-level view for Nicklaus and Woods as professionals in their 30s with an emphasis on strengths and weaknesses.

- **Strengths**
  - Nicklaus
    - Final Round Scoring Average
      - 70.10
    - Final Round Performance
      - 51.28% shot in the 60s
      - 51.28% shot under par to close
    - Total Rounds (60s)
      - 58
    - Total Rounds Under Par
      - 80
    - First, Second, & Final Rounds
      - Shot under par more than half the time
        - 57.50% in the second round
  - Woods
    - Third Round Scoring Average
      - 70.78
    - Third Round Performance
      - 55.56% shot under par

- **Weaknesses**
  - Nicklaus
    - Third Round Scoring Average
      - 71.44
  - Woods
    - First Round & Final Round Scoring Averages
      - 71.44
- **Scoring Average (Raw Scores)**
  - Nicklaus
    - 70.98
  - Woods
    - 71.25
- **Scoring Average (Relation to Par)**
  - Nicklaus
    - (0.28)
  - Woods
    - (0.01)

As professionals from ages 30 through 39, Nicklaus beat Woods by an average of .27 shots via raw score and .27 shots in relation to par. Nicklaus shot 24 more rounds in the 60s and 26 more rounds under par than Woods, yet Woods missed six major championships due to injury. Lastly, Nicklaus only missed one 36-hole cut in 40 major championships, while Woods missed the weekend seven times in 34 attempts.

Record Major Championship Scores

Prior to the third round of the 2017 Open Championship wherein Branden Grace shot an eight-under par 62, the lowest 18-hole score in a men's major championship was 63. As expected, both Nicklaus (first round, 1980 U.S. Open) and Woods (second round, 2007 PGA Championship) are included among the 35 players who accomplished this feat 38 times; Greg Norman, Vijay Singh, and Brooks Koepka achieved it twice. Of these 35 players, nine went on to win; Koepka twice. And of these nine players, Nicklaus and Woods are again included. The following lists chronologically per major championship all players who shot 63.

Masters – Scores of 63 (2)				
Year	Player	Round	To Par	Win (Yes / No)
1986	Nick Price	3	-9	No
1996	Greg Norman	1	-9	No

U.S. Open – Scores of 63 (6)				
Year	Player	Round	To Par	Win (Yes / No)
1973	Johnny Miller	4	-8	Yes
1980	Jack Nicklaus	1	-7	Yes
1980	Tom Weiskopf	1	-7	No
2003	Vijay Singh	2	-7	No
2017	Justin Thomas	3	-9	No
2018	Tommy Fleetwood	4	-7	No

Open Championship – Scores of 63 (12)				
Year	Player	Round	To Par	Win (Yes / No)
1977	Mark Hayes	2	-7	No
1980	Isao Aoki	3	-8	No
1986	Greg Norman	2	-7	Yes
1990	Paul Broadhurst	3	-9	No
1991	Jodie Mudd	4	-7	No
1993	Nick Faldo	2	-7	No
1993	Payne Stewart	4	-7	No
2010	Rory McIlroy	1	-9	No
2016	Phil Mickelson	1	-8	No
2016	Henrik Stenson	4	-8	Yes
2017	Haotung Li	4	-7	No
2019	Shane Lowry	3	-8	Yes

PGA Championship – Scores of 63 (18)				
Year	Player	Round	To Par	Win (Yes / No)
1975	Bruce Crampton	2	-7	No
1982	Raymond Floyd	1	-7	Yes
1984	Gary Player	2	-9	No

1993	Vijay Singh	2	-8	No
1995	Michael Bradley	2	-8	No
1995	Brad Faxon	4	-8	No
2000	Jose Maria Olazabal	3	-9	No
2001	Mark O'Meara	2	-7	No
2005	Thomas Bjorn	3	-7	No
2007	Tiger Woods	2	-7	Yes
2011	Steve Stricker	1	-7	No
2013	Jason Dufner	2	-7	Yes
2015	Hiroshi Iwata	2	-9	No
2016	Robert Streb	2	-7	No
2018	Brooks Koepka	2	-7	Yes
2018	Charl Schwartzel	2	-7	No
2019	Brooks Koepka	1	-7	Yes
2022	Bubba Watson	2	-7	No

Let's review a summary of the above detail.

- **Total Scores & Corresponding Percentages**
  - Masters: 2 (5.26%)
  - U.S. Open: 6 (15.79%)
  - Open Championship: 12 (31.58%)
  - PGA Championship: 18 (47.37%)
- **Score Distribution Per Round & Corresponding Percentages**
  - First Round: 8 (21.05%)
  - Second Round: 16 (42.11%)
  - Third Round: 7 (18.42%)
  - Fourth Round: 7 (18.42%)
- **Scores Per Decade & Corresponding Percentages**
  - 1970s: 3 (7.89%)
  - 1980s: 7 (18.42%)
  - 1990s: 8 (21.05%)
  - 2000s: 5 (13.16%)
  - 2010s: 14 (36.84%)

- o 2020s: 1 (2.63%)
- **Scores Per Era**
  - o Nicklaus Era: 10
  - o Woods Era: 20
- **Champions**
  - o Nicklaus Era: 4 (40.00%)
    - Miller
    - Nicklaus
    - Floyd
    - Norman
  - o Woods Era: 6 (30.00%)
    - Woods
    - Dufner
    - Stenson
    - Lowry
    - Koepka
      - 2018 & 2019

The Masters may take heat for being the only major championship played on the same course and having the weakest field – or at least the smallest field. However, just two scores of 63 are included in the total of 38. And until 2020, the Masters was the only major where four consecutive rounds in the 60s had not been shot during a tournament. Cameron Smith accomplished the feat with his 15-under-par tie for second behind Dustin Johnson. These two elements add luster to the event. Conversely, the PGA Championship having arguably the strongest field occupies nearly half the total scores with 18.

Inclusive of Nicklaus and Woods, nearly two-thirds of the scores were shot in the first and second rounds of the championships. This is likely a product of the greater number of players in the field prior to the 36-hole cut and/or the inherent post-cut pressure.

With respect to the eras of Nicklaus and Woods, the number of champions having shot 63 is similarly distributed. For the eight scores of 63 shot post-Nicklaus era and pre-Woods era, there were no champions. While the Nicklaus era leads in the ratio of champions to number of rounds shot at 40.00%, the Woods era has twice as many 63s posted at 20.

However, not all 63s are created equal. Due to the number of scores and the fact they were completed across varying championships and timeframes, there should be a method to differentiate the performances. The 38 rounds are ranked below relative to the total field average when each 63 was shot.

	Major Championships – Scores of 63 Ranked				
Year	Championship	Player (Round)	Field Average	Variance	Rank
1984	PGA Championship	Gary Player (2)	74.50	11.50	1
1980	U.S. Open	Jack Nicklaus (1)	74.36	11.36	2
1980	U.S. Open	Tom Weiskopf (1)	74.36	11.36	2
1977	Open Championship	Mark Hayes (2)	74.25	11.25	4
1986	Open Championship	Greg Norman (2)	74.08	11.08	5
1973	U.S. Open	Johnny Miller (4)	73.77	10.77	6
1982	PGA Championship	Raymond Floyd (1)	73.65	10.65	7
1996	Masters	Greg Norman (1)	73.29	10.29	8
2011	PGA Championship	Steve Stricker (1)	73.11	10.11	9
2019	PGA Championship	Brooks Koepka (1)	73.06	10.06	10
2015	PGA Championship	Hiroshi Iwata (2)	72.94	9.94	11
1975	PGA Championship	Bruce Crampton (2)	72.92	9.92	12
2016	Open Championship	Henrik Stenson (4)	72.80	9.80	13
2007	PGA Championship	Tiger Woods (2)	72.79	9.79	14
2022	PGA Championship	Bubba Watson (2)	72.60	9.60	15
1993	Open Championship	Nick Faldo (2)	72.58	9.58	16
2013	PGA Championship	Jason Dufner (2)	72.29	9.29	17
2018	U.S. Open	Tommy Fleetwood (4)	72.20	9.20	18
2016	Open Championship	Phil Mickelson (1)	72.03	9.03	19
2017	U.S. Open	Justin Thomas (3)	72.01	9.01	20
2003	U.S. Open	Vijay Singh (2)	71.90	8.90	21
1993	PGA Championship	Vijay Singh (2)	71.88	8.88	22
2010	Open Championship	Rory McIlroy (1)	71.75	8.75	23
1995	PGA Championship	Michael Bradley (2)	71.59	8.59	24
2005	PGA Championship	Thomas Bjorn (3)	71.43	8.43	25
2001	PGA Championship	Mark O'Meara (2)	71.36	8.36	26
1990	Open Championship	Paul Broadhurst (3)	71.19	8.19	27
1980	Open Championship	Isao Aoki (3)	71.08	8.08	28

2000	PGA Championship	Jose Maria Olazabal (3)	71.00	8.00	29
1986	Masters	Nick Price (3)	70.98	7.98	30
1991	Open Championship	Jodie Mudd (4)	70.78	7.78	31
2016	PGA Championship	Robert Streb (2)	70.69	7.69	32
1993	Open Championship	Payne Stewart (4)	70.58	7.58	33
1995	PGA Championship	Brad Faxon (4)	70.19	7.19	34
2017	Open Championship	Haotung Li (4)	70.13	7.13	35
2019	Open Championship	Shane Lowry (3)	70.08	7.08	36
2018	PGA Championship	Brooks Koepka (2)	69.59	6.59	37
2018	PGA Championship	Charl Schwartzel (2)	69.59	6.59	37

With the scores ranked in this manner, the following can be ascertained.

- At age 48 and with a shot margin of 11.50, Gary Player is the oldest competitor and leads the listing with the largest variance between his score and the field average.
- Nine of the top 10 scores shot relative to the field averages were completed in the first or second rounds of the respective major championships. The 10th was Johnny Miller's final round in the 1973 U.S. Open. With the criteria in place, championship, venue, and round number, Miller's score may be the best of all listed.
- Jack Nicklaus, Raymond Floyd, and Brooks Koepka (2019 PGA Championship) were the only wire-to-wire winners.
- Coinciding with a shot variance of 1.57 (74.36 vs. 72.79) between field averages for Nicklaus and Woods, respectively, Nicklaus finished 12 places higher in the ranking.

In reference to Branden Grace, his third-round of 62 in the 2017 Open Championship was just 7.03 shots better than the field average that day of 69.03.

Largest 72-hole Victory Margins as Professionals

Woods' largest 72-hole victory margin as a professional was 15 shots during the 2000 U.S. Open. For the following review, this will represent the lower end of the scoring range up to four shots to see where Nicklaus and Woods reside during their respective careers.

	Jack Nicklaus (1962 – 1986)	Tiger Woods (1997 – 2022)	Variance
Range (15 to 4) – Total	15	25	(10)
Highest Margin	9 (2)	15	(6)
Average	6.07	6.72	(0.65)

One of the hallmarks of Woods has been his ability to dominate against the fields he has competed. As displayed above, Nicklaus' record in this regard is solid, but Woods' record is phenomenal. Now, let's review the same criteria under major championships only.

Largest 72-hole Major Championship Victory Margins

As stated, Woods' largest margin of victory occurred in the 2000 U.S. Open where he won by 15 shots. Thus, it will be the lower end of the scoring range up to four shots. The following shows how Nicklaus and Woods fared in major championships within this scale.

	Jack Nicklaus (1962 – 1986)	Tiger Woods (1997 – 2022)	Variance
Range (4 to 15) – Total	4	5	(1)
Highest Margin	9	15	(6)
Average	6.00	9.00	(3.00)

Woods leads Nicklaus throughout. With wins in the 2000 U.S. Open, 1997 Masters, and 2000 Open Championship by a combined 35 shots, it makes Nicklaus' three largest margins of nine, seven, and four – 20 shots – in the 1965 Masters, 1980 PGA Championship, and 1967 U.S. Open / 1973 PGA Championship, respectively, seem almost lackluster. The following applies the criteria to each major championship.

Largest 72-hole Victory Margins – Masters	Jack Nicklaus (1962 – 1986)	Tiger Woods (1997 – 2022)	Variance
Range (4 to 15) – Total	1	1	0
Highest Margin	9	12	(3)
Average	9.00	12.00	(3.00)

Largest 72-hole Victory Margins – U.S. Open	Jack Nicklaus (1962 – 1986)	Tiger Woods (1997 – 2022)	Variance
Range (4 to 15) – Total	1	1	0
Highest Margin	4	15	(11)
Average	4.00	15.00	(11.00)

Largest 72-hole Victory Margins – Open	Jack Nicklaus (1962 – 1986)	Tiger Woods (1997 – 2022)	Variance
Range (4 to 15) – Total	0	2	(2)
Highest Margin	0	8	(8)
Average	0.00	6.50	(6.50)

Largest 72-hole Victory Margins – PGA	Jack Nicklaus (1962 – 1986)	Tiger Woods (1997 – 2022)	Variance
Range (4 to 15) – Total	2	1	1
Highest Margin	7	5	2
Average	5.50	5.00	0.50

This granular view again shows Woods' dominance over his competition and superiority under the prescribed criteria when compared to Nicklaus. However, when each player's competition is analyzed later, the results in this chapter will take on a new dimension.

Scoring Wrap-up

After all the copious detail in this chapter, below provides a high-level scoring comparison between Jack Nicklaus and Tiger Woods for their respective 25-year periods as professionals.

Jack Nicklaus & Tiger Woods 18-hole Tournament Scores as Professionals (1st 25 Years)						
	60s	70s	80s	Total	Stroke Average	Low Round	High Round
Nicklaus	697	1,208	10	1,915	70.59	62 (3)	83
Woods	762	744	4	1,510	69.54	61 (4)	85
Variance	(65)	464	6	405	1.05	1 (1)	(2)
Nicklaus %	36.40%	63.08%	0.52%	100.00%			
Woods %	50.46%	49.27%	0.26%	100.00%			
Variance %	(14.06%)	13.81%	0.26%				
Nicklaus Avg	67.64	72.21	80.80				
Woods Avg	66.99	72.08	82.00				
Variance Avg	0.65	0.13	(1.20)				

Jack Nicklaus & Tiger Woods 18-hole Major Championship Scores as Professionals (1st 25 Years)						
	60s	70s	80s	Total	Stroke Average	Low Round	High Round
Nicklaus	120	266	3	389	71.25	63	83
Woods	101	209	2	312	70.92	63	81
Variance	19	57	1	77	0.33	0	2
Nicklaus %	30.85%	68.38%	0.77%	100.00%			
Woods %	32.37%	66.99%	0.64%	100.00%			
Variance %	(1.52%)	1.39%	0.13%				
Nicklaus Avg	67.85	72.39	81.33				
Woods Avg	67.46	72.50	80.50				
Variance Avg	0.39	(0.11)	0.83				

63

VENUE VERSATILITY

"(Jack's) major contributions to golf have been in the field of reconnaissance and preparation, course analysis, and tactical planning. To a fair degree, his phenomenal successes have represented a triumph of strength and talent over technique. Many of his famous victories were won when he was off his game." – Peter Dobereiner **Golf Digest Special Edition Lessons from Golf's Greatest Swings** *– Spring/Summer 1996*

"One thing that makes Tiger Tiger is that he's more willing to bring a shot from the practice tee onto the course than any golfer I know." – Butch Harmon

When reviewing the careers of Jack Nicklaus and Tiger Woods, it is necessary to examine how they performed on various tournament sites. Such a study should solidify similarities in their games and versatility as players. Since this is an examination of the two best players in professional golf encompassing two different eras, the impact technology has had on the game should also be realized.

Total PGA Victory Distribution

Woods leads Nicklaus in the total number of PGA victories at 82 wins compared to 73. What is not typically detailed is the distribution of their respective win totals. The below table provides a high-level summary.

Jack Nicklaus & Tiger Woods PGA Victory Distribution Summary			
	Nicklaus	Woods	Variance
Total Number of Victories	73	82	(9)
Total Major Championship Victories	18	15	3
Total Full-field Non-major Victories	46	41	5
Total Limited-field Victories	9	26	(17)
Total Major Championships & Full-field Victories	64	56	8
Total Different Victories	35	27	8
Total Different Victory Sites	48	39	9

While Nicklaus has nine fewer wins than Woods, his distribution shows greater versatility. Not only did Nicklaus win three more major championships, he won more full-field, non-major events (46 vs. 41). That combination of 64 wins comprises 87.67% of his 73 PGA victories. Nicklaus' 73 victories were achieved on 48 different courses where the number of different wins was 35.

For Woods' 82 wins, his combined major championship and full-field total of 56 is 68.29%. Woods' victories were achieved on 39 different courses where the number of different wins was 27. Each number is lower than Nicklaus' and as a percentage of the overall.

The full detail of the summary above would be too voluminous to effectively list. Thus, I have included only the top five events won by each player from most repeat victories to least.

Jack Nicklaus Top PGA Victory Distribution Detail				
Tournament Name	Tournament Type	Victories	Number of Venues	Percentage of Total Victories
Masters	Major Championship	6	1	8.22%
PGA Championship	Major Championship	5	5	6.85%
Tournament of Champions	Limited-field	5	2	6.85%
Sahara Invitational	Full-field	4	1	5.48%
U.S. Open	Major Championship	4	3	5.48%

Nicklaus' most dominant performance was during the Masters at the Augusta National Golf Club with six victories. Although he did win five PGA Championships and five Tournament of Champions titles, they were spread across seven sites. Of Nicklaus' 73 victories, 24 (32.88%) reside in the above chart. Nicklaus also won four times at the Paradise Valley Country Club and at Pebble Beach Golf Links, but these are considerably less than what Woods accomplished for this particular measurement.

Tiger Woods Top PGA Victory Distribution Detail				
Tournament Name	**Tournament Type**	**Victories**	**Number of Venues**	**Percentage of Total Victories**
Arnold Palmer Invitational	Full-field	8	1	9.76%
WGC Bridgestone Invitational	Limited-field	8	1	9.76%
Farmers Insurance Open	Full-field	7	1	8.54%
WGC Cadillac Championship	Limited-field	7	6	8.54%
Masters	Major Championship	5	1	6.09%
Memorial Tournament	Full-field	5	1	6.09%

With eight victories at the Arnold Palmer Invitational and the WGC Bridgestone Invitational, Woods has done something unprecedented in professional golf. Formerly, Sam Snead held the record alone for most wins in a single tournament with eight at the Greater Greensboro Open, yet Woods has equaled that for two events. Of Woods' 82 PGA victories, 40 (48.78%) occurred in the above six tournaments on 11 different courses. In addition, he won seven Farmers Insurance Open titles. When including the 2008 U.S. Open, Woods won eight times at the Torrey Pines Golf Course.

Another review of the two graphics confirms Nicklaus' ongoing presence in major championships with three of the top five events being the Masters, PGA, and U.S. Open. For Woods, he has proven a greater level of superiority with a total differential of 16 wins in six events vs. five for Nicklaus, yet they are comprised of less-prestigious titles.

Major Championship Victory Distribution

The following shows the listing of major championship victory sites for Nicklaus and Woods along with their distribution of wins.

Jack Nicklaus Major Championship Victory Site Distribution		
Site	**Number of Victories**	**Percentage of Total Victories**
Augusta National Golf Club	6	33.33%
Baltusrol Golf Club	2	11.11%
Old Course at St. Andrews	2	11.11%
Oakmont Country Club	1	5.56%
Pebble Beach Golf Links	1	5.56%
Muirfield	1	5.56%
Canterbury Golf Club	1	5.56%
Dallas Athletic Club	1	5.56%
Firestone Country Club	1	5.56%
Oak Hill Country Club	1	5.56%
PGA National Golf Club	1	5.56%

Tiger Woods Major Championship Victory Site Distribution		
Site	**Number of Victories**	**Percentage of Total Victories**
Augusta National Golf Club	5	33.33%
Medinah Country Club	2	13.33%
Old Course at St. Andrews	2	13.33%
Bethpage Black Course	1	6.67%
Pebble Beach Golf Links	1	6.67%
Torrey Pines Golf Course	1	6.67%
Royal Liverpool Golf Club	1	6.67%
Southern Hills Country Club	1	6.67%
Valhalla Golf Club	1	6.67%

With the exception of Nicklaus' 18 wins to Woods' 15, the distribution among tournament sites is similar. Nicklaus won his 18 titles on 11 courses with three titles being multiple-victory sites. For Woods, his 15 titles were won on nine courses with three titles being multiple-victory sites, as well. Two of the three multiple victories for each player were at Augusta National and St. Andrews, which adds even greater similarity between careers.

Major Championship Site Overlap Performance

A subsequent review of Nicklaus' and Woods' comparative performances in major championships delineates how each performed – their best placements – at the same venues that overlapped their careers. Realizing course conditions varied over the years, the graphic provides insight to how versatile each player was during their peak performances.

Jack Nicklaus & Tiger Woods Major Championship Site Overlap Comparison					
Nicklaus			Woods		
Masters					
Site	Victories	Best Finish	Site	Victories	Best Finish
Augusta National Golf Club	6	1	Augusta National Golf Club	5	1
Masters Total / Average	6	1.00	Masters Total / Average	5	1.00
U.S. Open					
Site	Victories	Best Finish	Site	Victories	Best Finish
Southern Hills Country Club	0	T-10	Southern Hills Country Club	0	T-12
Winged Foot Golf Club	0	T-10	Winged Foot Golf Club	0	MC (2)
Oakland Hills Country Club	0	T-4*	Oakland Hills Country Club	0	T-82*
Oakmont Country Club	1	1	Oakmont Country Club	0	T-2
Olympic Club	0	3	Olympic Club	0	T-18
Merion Golf Club	0	2	Merion Golf Club	0	T-32
Pebble Beach Golf Links	1	1	Pebble Beach Golf Links	1	1
Shinnecock Hills Golf Club	0	T-8	Shinnecock Hills Golf Club	0	T-17

U.S. Open Total / Average	2	4.88	U.S. Open Total / Average	1	23.43

Open Championship					
Site	Victories	Best Finish	Site	Victories	Best Finish
Royal Troon Golf Club	0	4	Royal Troon Golf Club	0	T-9
Royal Lytham & St. Annes	0	3	Royal Lytham & St. Annes	0	T-3
Old Course at St. Andrews	2	1	Old Course at St. Andrews	2	1
Royal Birkdale Golf Club	0	T-2	Royal Birkdale Golf Club	0	3
Muirfield	1	1	Muirfield	0	T-6
Royal Liverpool Golf Club	0	2	Royal Liverpool Golf Club	1	1
Carnoustie Golf Links	0	T-2	Carnoustie Golf Links	0	T-7
Turnberry	0	2	Turnberry	0	MC
Royal St. George's Golf Club	0	T-23	Royal St. George's Golf Club	0	T-4
Open Championship Total / Average	**3**	**4.10**	**Open Championship Total / Average**	**3**	**3.89**

PGA Championship					
Site	Victories	Best Finish	Site	Victories	Best Finish
Southern Hills Country Club	0	T-6	Southern Hills Country Club	1	1
Oak Hill Country Club	1	1	Oak Hill Country Club	0	T-39
Atlanta Athletic Club	0	T-4	Atlanta Athletic Club	0	T-29
PGA Championship Total / Average	**1**	**3.67**	**PGA Championship Total / Average**	**1**	**23.00**
Major Championship Total / Average	**12**	**3.59**	**Major Championship Total / Average**	**10**	**10.92**

Crossover					
Site	Victories	Best Finish	Site	Victories	Best Finish
Baltusrol Golf Club (U.S. Open)	2	1	Baltusrol Golf Club (PGA)	0	T-4
Hazeltine National Golf Club (U.S. Open)	0	T-46	Hazeltine National Golf Club (PGA)	0	2 (2)
Medinah Country Club (U.S. Open)	0	T-7	Medinah Country Club (PGA)	2	1

Crossover Total / Average				2	13.75	Crossover Total / Average				2	2.00

Overall Total / Average				14	4.90	Overall Total / Average				12	9.27

*As amateurs

Nicklaus leads Woods below as summarized.

- **Total Victories:** 14 vs. 12
- **Top-10 Placements:** 29 vs. 22
- **Average Placement:** 4.90 vs. 9.27 (excludes missed cuts)
- **Missed Cuts:** 0 vs. 3

Even with course and equipment changes along with different fields, the table shows Nicklaus was more efficient and able to successfully adapt his game to a greater number of venues under the pressure of major championship play. What is also interesting is the disparity of Nicklaus' tie for fourth place to Woods' tie for 82nd place at Oakland Hills and 10-shot differential when each were 21 and 20-year-old amateurs, respectively, playing the U.S. Open.

Let's review how many of those courses have augmented over time via total yardage. It is not difficult to find some of the same courses Nicklaus and Woods competed on to be lengthened anywhere from 300 to 500 yards. If the same courses are not available, new courses in tournament rotations exceeding 7,400 or 7,500 yards are included.

When television commentators point out a course's total yardage has been increased by numbers like 300 to 500 yards, it seems like a huge difference. And it would be if the equipment over time had not changed. The following provides a closer look.

Driving Distance

In 1980, the PGA Tour commenced quantifying official player statistics for a range of categories. One of the most popular measures has been driving distance.

While there are no official statistics prior to 1980, this will offer insight relative to the topic of total course yardages from the Nicklaus era to the Woods era.

Below lists the PGA Tour driving distance leader averages per decade with comparative data:

Year	Distance Leader Average	Variance (Yards)	Variance (%)
1980	274.3	N/A	N/A
1990	279.6	5.3	1.93%
2000	301.4	21.8	7.80%
2010	315.5	14.1	4.68%
2020	322.1	6.6	2.09%

Below provides the same data per the PGA Tour driving distance mean (average) over the same time periods:

Year	Distance Mean Average	Variance (Yards)	Variance (%)
1980	256.5	N/A	N/A
1990	262.3	5.8	2.26%
2000	272.7	10.4	3.96%
2010	287.3	14.6	5.35%
2020	296.4	9.1	3.17%

Below are the same data per the PGA Tour driving distance median (midpoint of all players) over the same time periods:

Year	Distance Median Average	Variance (Yards)	Variance (%)
1980	256.7	N/A	N/A
1990	263.1	6.4	2.49%
2000	273.2	10.1	3.84%
2010	287.9	14.7	5.38%
2020	297.3	9.4	3.27%

For this study, I originally selected the median vs. mean to compare thinking it would blunt any larger variances an average may not. However, I added the average (mean) later and discovered little variation between the two. Therefore, subsequent comparisons will revolve around the leaders and median only.

Regardless, all schematics show steady, if not significant increases between decades with an average yardage gain of 11.95 yards and corresponding percentage increase of 4.13% for the distance leader and 10.15 yards and 3.75%, respectively, for the median.

If this comparative data is expanded, the driving distance leader in 2020 was 47.8 yards longer at an average than the leader in 1980 or 17.43% greater. For the median, the corresponding numbers are 40.6 yards and 15.82% greater. Both are significant variations and do not cover Nicklaus' prime playing years.

Except perhaps for the freakishly-long 6'5", 240-lb. George Bayer from the 1950s and early 1960s, Nicklaus was considered the longest hitter of the 1960s and among the top two longest hitters of the 1970s (i.e. Tom Weiskopf). Note Tom Watson from "Golf Digest" in June of 1983, *"And 10 years ago, (Jack) was much longer than he is now. I mean, there was nobody who could hit it up with him. And certainly, no one could hit it up with him 20 years ago."*

Thus, a supposition of where the driving distance leader during the 1960s and 1970s would fall relative to the earlier chart is a moot point. It is common knowledge Nicklaus averaged 275 – 280 yards in driving distance during his peak years (greater in the early- to mid-1960s) as even his 10th-place ranking in 1980 at age 40 registered 269.0 yards.

It would be more applicable to project the median distance for the 1960s and 1970s. Due to the percentage increase from 1980 through 1990 being 2.49%, let's use that figure to determine a realistic number for 1970 and 1960.

- **1970:** 256.7 *(1980 actual median)* ÷ 1.0249 = 250.5 projected median yards
- **1960:** 250.5 *(1970 projected median)* ÷ 1.0249 = 244.4 projected median yards

With these two numbers calculated, the distance median table is augmented.

Year	Distance Median Average	Variance (Yards)	Variance (%)
1960	244.4	N/A	N/A
1970	250.5	6.1	2.49%
1980	256.7	6.2	2.49%
1990	263.1	6.4	2.49%
2000	273.2	10.1	3.84%
2010	287.9	14.7	5.38%
2020	297.3	9.4	3.27%

When this comparative data is expanded, the median in 2020 was 52.9 yards longer at an average than in 1960, or 21.64% greater. For 1970, the corresponding figures are 46.8 yards, or 18.68% greater.

Let's circle back to Nicklaus and Woods for added context. Both players' immense power was well-known during their amateur days. Upon arrival to the professional circuit, they were either the longest drivers or without question, the second-longest drivers.

As noted, George Bayer may have been the only player to exceed a young Nicklaus in power. For Woods, John Daly had a stranglehold on the driving distance category from 1991 through 2002 (excluding 1994, when he did not compete). From 1997 through 2001, Woods was runner-up three times and in third place twice for this measurement.

Officially for Nicklaus, the earliest data available is from 1980. At age 40, he finished 10th in driving distance with an average of 269.0 yards. Below displays how Nicklaus compared to the driving distance leader as well as the median performer.

- **Leader:**   274.3
- **Nicklaus:**   269.0
- **Variance (Yards):**   5.3
- **Variance (Percentage):**   1.97

- **Nicklaus:**   269.0
- **Median:**   256.7
- **Variance (Yards):**   12.3
- **Variance (Percentage):**   4.79

The first section shows how close Nicklaus in 10th place was to the leader Dan Pohl. Consequently, all players within the leading 10 spots were very bunched up. In the second tranche, Nicklaus is more than twice the number of yards and percentage ahead of the median than he was behind the leader.

Due to Woods having missed the 2016 season and effectively all of 2017, a comparison between him and Nicklaus at age 40 is not available. Therefore, the next closest age for both players is 42; Nicklaus in 1982 and Woods in 2018. A relative view is provided.

- **Leader:**   275.3
- **Nicklaus:**   264.6
- **Variance (Yards):**   10.7
- **Variance (Percentage):**   4.04

- **Nicklaus:**   264.6
- **Median:**   256.3
- **Variance (Yards):**   8.3
- **Variance (Percentage):**   3.24

Two years removed from 1980, Nicklaus ranked 22nd in driving distance vs. 10th and on average was 4.4 yards shorter per drive. As expected, he was further behind the leader and closer to the median for the year.

- **Leader:**   319.7
- **Woods:**   303.6
- **Variance (Yards):**   16.1
- **Variance (Percentage):**   5.30

- **Woods:**   303.6
- **Median:**   296.0
- **Variance (Yards):**   7.6
- **Variance (Percentage):**   2.57

With Tiger at age 42, the percentages reflect some consistency compared to Nicklaus. Tiger placed 32nd on the driving distance list for the year. Thus, he was slightly more adrift of the leader and a bit closer the median from percentage bases.

Lastly, let's implement a reasonable data extrapolation for a younger Nicklaus and compare to known data for Woods at the same age based on the previous formulary.

At ages 25, Nicklaus (1965) and Woods (2001) were already established as the best players of their eras. During these years, each won the Masters plus four additional tournaments, led in money earned, and in scoring. By estimating wisely, we can deduce how Nicklaus would compare in driving distance to a median in 1965. Once gathered, we can approximate to Woods' same data for 2001.

Having won the long-driving contest at the PGA Championship in 1963 with an effort of 341 yards and 17 inches, plus dismantling Augusta National in 1965 for the then-record score of 271, an estimate of Nicklaus' average drive at 280 yards is safe. Pertaining to his third round of the latter, Nicklaus described three drives at 320 yards and one at 330 yards, with several others implied at roughly 300 yards. For the median, an average yardage of the previous calculations for 1960 and 1970 above in the amount of 247.5 shall be used.

- **Nicklaus:**   280.0
- **Median:**   247.5
- **Variance (Yards):**   32.5
- **Variance (Percentage):**   13.13

The gaps from the bases of yardage and percentage are both significant. That is to be expected, since Nicklaus was at best the longest hitter that year and at worst, the second-longest. Yet, the figures are educated guesses. To make the numbers more convergent, below deducts two yards from Nicklaus and adds three to the median.

- **Nicklaus:**   278.0
- **Median:**   250.5
- **Variance (Yards):**   27.5
- **Variance (Percentage):**   10.98

Even with a composite adjustment of five yards to the disadvantage of Nicklaus, his power is still apparent. Recognizing the data are hypothetical, the actual results would likely not vary by much. Nicklaus at approximately 12 percent greater in average driving distance than the median professional of the day is very realistic. So, how does Woods measure up?

- **Woods:**   297.6
- **Median:**   279.5
- **Variance (Yards):**   18.1
- **Variance (Percentage):**   6.48

During 2001, Woods finished third in driving distance at nearly 300 yards per tee shot and the effect of technology is in full bloom. Although a placement of third for Woods is exceptional, he is closer to the median in yardage and percentage per average drive than the projected data for Nicklaus at the same age. Moreover, in the year 2001, Nicklaus would only approximate both the median (279.5) and mean (278.8) in driving distance with a direct transfer of the hypothetical data for 1965.

The preceding data should add perspective to the upcoming discussion of same-course yardages and yardage expansions for Nicklaus and Woods during major championship play.

Major Championship Course Yardage Progression

The following table shows 11 major championship sites from the year 1962 when Nicklaus won his first through the Woods era where the same venue held at least one other major championship. The schematic also conveys the applicable yardage changes over the years.

Major Championship Site Yardage Comparisons						
Year	Site	Event	Yardage	Variance	Par	Champion
1963	Augusta National Golf Club	Masters	6,850	N/A	72	Nicklaus
1965	Augusta National Golf Club	Masters	6,980	130	72	Nicklaus
1966	Augusta National Golf Club	Masters	6.980	0	72	Nicklaus
1972	Augusta National Golf Club	Masters	6,980	0	72	Nicklaus
1975	Augusta National Golf Club	Masters	7,020	40	72	Nicklaus
1986	Augusta National Golf Club	Masters	6,905	(115)	72	Nicklaus
1997	Augusta National Golf Club	Masters	6,925	20	72	Woods
2001	Augusta National Golf Club	Masters	6,985	60	72	Woods
2002	Augusta National Golf Club	Masters	7,270	285	72	Woods
2005	Augusta National Golf Club	Masters	7,290	20	72	Woods
2010	Augusta National Golf Club	Masters	7,435	145	72	Mickelson
2015	Augusta National Golf Club	Masters	7,435	0	72	Spieth
2019	Augusta National Golf Club	Masters	7,475	40	72	Woods
1967	Baltusrol Golf Club	U.S. Open	7,015	N/A	70	Nicklaus
1980	Baltusrol Golf Club	U.S. Open	7,076	61	70	Nicklaus
1993	Baltusrol Golf Club	U.S. Open	7,116	40	70	Janzen
2005	Baltusrol Golf Club	PGA Championship	7,392	276	70	Mickelson
2016	Baltusrol Golf Club	PGA Championship	7,428	36	70	Walker
1965	Bellerive Country Club	U.S. Open	7,191	N/A	70	Player
2018	Bellerive Country Club	PGA Championship	7,316	125	70	Koepka

1975	Firestone Country Club	PGA Championship	7,180	N/A	70	Nicklaus
2010	Firestone Country Club	WGC Bridgestone Invitational	7,400	220	70	Mahan
2018	Firestone Country Club	WGC Bridgestone Invitational	7,400	0	70	Thomas
1975	Medinah Country Club	U.S. Open	7,032	N/A	71	L. Graham
1999	Medinah Country Club	PGA Championship	7,401	369	72	Woods
2006	Medinah Country Club	PGA Championship	7,561	160	72	Woods
1967	Muirfield	Open Championship	6,887	N/A	71	Nicklaus
1972	Muirfield	Open Championship	6,892	5	71	Trevino
2002	Muirfield	Open Championship	7,034	142	71	Els
2013	Muirfield	Open Championship	7,245	211	71	Mickelson
1968	Oak Hill Country Club	U.S. Open	6,962	N/A	70	Trevino
1980	Oak Hill Country Club	PGA Championship	6,964	2	70	Nicklaus
2003	Oak Hill Country Club	PGA Championship	7,134	170	70	Micheel
2013	Oak Hill Country Club	PGA Championship	7,163	29	70	Dufner
1962	Oakmont Country Club	U.S. Open	6,894	N/A	71	Nicklaus
1973	Oakmont Country Club	U.S. Open	6,921	27	71	Miller
1978	Oakmont Country Club	PGA Championship	6,989	68	71	Mahaffey
1983	Oakmont Country Club	U.S. Open	6,972	(17)	71	L. Nelson
2007	Oakmont Country Club	U.S. Open	7,230	258	70	Cabrera
2016	Oakmont Country Club	U.S. Open	7,254	24	70	D. Johnson
1970	Old Course at St. Andrews	Open Championship	6,951	N/A	72	Nicklaus
1978	Old Course at St. Andrews	Open Championship	6,933	(18)	72	Nicklaus
1984	Old Course at St. Andrews	Open Championship	6,933	0	72	Ballesteros

2000	Old Course at St. Andrews	Open Championship	7,115	182	72	Woods
2005	Old Course at St. Andrews	Open Championship	7,279	164	72	Woods
2010	Old Course at St. Andrews	Open Championship	7,279	0	72	Oosthuizen
2015	Old Course at St. Andrews	Open Championship	7,297	18	72	Z. Johnson
2022	Old Course at St. Andrews	Open Championship	7,297	0	72	Smith
1972	Pebble Beach Golf Links	U.S. Open	6,812	N/A	72	Nicklaus
1977	Pebble Beach Golf Links	PGA Championship	6,804	(8)	72	Wadkins
1982	Pebble Beach Golf Links	U.S. Open	6,825	21	72	T. Watson
2000	Pebble Beach Golf Links	U.S. Open	6,846	21	71	Woods
2010	Pebble Beach Golf Links	U.S. Open	7,040	194	71	McDowell
2019	Pebble Beach Golf Links	U.S. Open	7,075	35	71	Woodland
1967	Royal Liverpool Golf Club	Open Championship	6,995	N/A	70	DeVicenzo
2006	Royal Liverpool Golf Club	Open Championship	7,258	263	72	Woods
2014	Royal Liverpool Golf Club	Open Championship	7,312	54	72	McIlroy

From the earliest applicable date to the latest, the highlights of this table are below.

- **Augusta National Golf Club**
  - Date Range: 57 years
  - Total Yardage Increase: 625 yards
  - Average Yardage Increase Per Hole: 34.72 yards
- **Baltusrol Golf Club**
  - Date Range: 50 years
  - Total Yardage Increase: 413 yards
  - Average Yardage Increase Per Hole: 22.94 yards

- **Bellerive Country Club**
  - Date Range: 54 years
  - Total Yardage Increase: 125 yards
  - Average Yardage Increase Per Hole: 6.94 yards
- **Firestone Country Club**
  - Date Range: 44 years
  - Total Yardage Increase: 220 yards
  - Average Yardage Increase Per Hole: 12.22 yards
- **Medinah Country Club**
  - Date Range: 32 years
  - Total Yardage Increase: 529 yards
  - Average Yardage Increase Per Hole: 29.39 yards
- **Muirfield**
  - Date Range: 47 years
  - Total Yardage Increase: 358 yards
  - Average Yardage Increase Per Hole: 19.89 yards
- **Oak Hill Country Club**
  - Date Range: 46 years
  - Total Yardage Increase: 201 yards
  - Average Yardage Increase Per Hole: 11.17 yards
- **Oakmont Country Club**
  - Date Range: 55 years
  - Total Yardage Increase: 360 yards
  - Average Yardage Increase Per Hole: 20.00 yards
- **Old Course at St. Andrews**
  - Date Range: 53 years
  - Total Yardage Increase: 346 yards
  - Average Yardage Increase Per Hole: 19.22 yards
- **Pebble Beach Golf Links**
  - Date Range: 48 years
  - Total Yardage Increase: 263 yards
  - Average Yardage Increase Per Hole: 14.61 yards
- **Royal Liverpool Golf Club**
  - Date Range: 48 years
  - Total Yardage Increase: 317 yards
  - Average Yardage Increase Per Hole: 17.61 yards

For the courses listed, the averages are:

- **Average Date Range:**   48.55 years
- **Average Total Yardage Increase:**   341.55 yards
- **Average Yardage Increase Per Hole:**   18.98 yards

Augusta National remained somewhat steady until 2002 when noticeable increases began and continued primarily through 2010. However, the scorecard reflecting Nicklaus' 64 during the third round of the 1965 Masters showed a total yardage of 6,990 yards, which exceeded the official 6,925 yardage Woods won on in 1997. Even in 1975 when Nicklaus won at 12-under par by one shot over Johnny Miller and Tom Weiskopf, the course was playing at 7,020 yards.

Whether the yardage in 1965 was 6,990 as noted above in the third round, officially 6,980, or 6,925 as in 1997, the variances are negligible. However, this adds a new perspective on Nicklaus' then-record of 17-under par 271 where he won by nine shots over Arnold Palmer and Gary Player compared to Woods' then-record of 18-under par 270 in 1997 where he won by 12 strokes over Tom Kite. Let's review the driving distance designations for the two years in the same manner as previously outlined.

- **Nicklaus 1965:**   278.0
- **Median 1965:**   250.5
- **Variance (Yards):**   27.5
- **Variance (Percentage):**   10.98

- **Woods 1997:**   294.8
- **Median 1997:**   267.2
- **Variance (Yards):**   27.6
- **Variance (Percentage):**   10.33

When using the more conservative data for Nicklaus in 1965 as developed earlier in this chapter, the relative similarities to Woods in 1997 are striking. Woods finished the year in driving distance with a second-place ranking and when compared to the year's median driving distance, he was nearly identical in average yardage ahead as Nicklaus was (27.5 yards vs. 27.6 yards, respectively) and only .65% less by percentage variance (10.98% vs. 10.33%, respectively). Now, let's view the two silos of data in a combined, chronological comparison and the similarities are once again pronounced.

- **Nicklaus 1965:** 278.0
- **Woods 1997:** 294.8
- **Variance (Yards):** 16.8
- **Variance (Percentage):** 6.04
- **Median 1965:** 250.5
- **Median 1997:** 267.2
- **Variance (Yards):** 16.7
- **Variance (Percentage):** 6.67

Augusta National has retained its par of 72 and generally the same layout throughout its Masters history. Certainly from 1965 through 1997 the layout was very similar, with the major exception being the conversion of its greens from bermuda to bentgrass in 1981. Upon excluding its four par-3 holes, the course is left with 14 par 4s and par 5s to which the above data can be applied.

Taking the average variance above of 16.8 yards per tee shot and multiplying it by 14, the resulting total yardage addition for driving alone is 235.2 in favor of Woods. And if the previously-referenced 55-yard course reduction (6,980 in 1965 vs. 6,925 in 1997) is factored in, the new total yardage favoring Woods is 290.2. Therefore, when analyzing the 17-under par score of 271 Nicklaus shot in 1965 compared to the 18-under par score of 270 achieved by Woods in 1997, a shorter Augusta National emerges based largely on increased driving distance and to a lesser degree, the course setup itself.

Obviously, the total yardage isn't literally 235.2 yards shorter for Woods. But based upon the difference technology made on equipment over the 32-year period, Woods was afforded an advantage over Nicklaus along with the respective median player in 1997 vs. his counterpart in 1965. But this does not tell the entire story. Were Nicklaus to average 16.8 yards more per drive at Augusta National in 1965, it would necessitate shorter irons for his approach shots into the greens. For Woods with this driving average in 1997 vs. Nicklaus at 278.0 yards in 1965, not only would he have shorter approach shots from a straight comparison, he would have even shorter distances with equipment advancements over 32 years. Lastly, the four par-3 holes have remained constant, so Woods again had shorter iron shots to each.

The preceding discussion is not meant to diminish Woods' accomplishment in the 1997 Masters. He still eclipsed Nicklaus' 72-hole score by one shot and his margin of victory was greater by three. Such variables as weather plus course severity nuances are not entirely observable nor quantifiable. My goal was to add some tangible perspective between the two players' performances.

The detail provided above confirms the impact technology has made and that it has outpaced course yardage expansions. To further supplement, let's review two unrelated players from 1980 through 2010.

Dan Pohl Driving Distance Historical Comparison			
Year	Driving Distance	Variance (Yards)	Variance (%)
1980	274.3	N/A	N/A
1985	272.0	(2.3)	(0.84%)
1991	275.7	3.7	1.36%
1996	275.9	0.2	0.07%
2005	300.5	24.6	8.92%

Fred Couples Driving Distance Historical Comparison			
Year	Driving Distance	Variance (Yards)	Variance (%)
1981	277.6	N/A	N/A
1985	276.9	(0.7)	(0.25%)
1990	272.6	(4.3)	(1.55%)
1995	276.3	3.7	1.36%
2000	284.7	8.4	3.04%
2005	296.4	11.7	4.11%
2010	292.8	(3.6)	(1.21%)

The above sets of driving distance histories and earlier site expansions elicit several findings.

- The leader in driving distance from 1980 through 2020 increased by 47.8 yards, while the median increased by 40.6 yards. Therefore, excluding par three holes, a player conceivably gained from 400 to 600 or more yards alone vs. an average course yardage increase of 341.55 above, which already factors in par three increases.
- From a percentage basis, Augusta National and Medinah expanded 9.12% and 7.52%, respectively. However, this pales in comparison to the driving distance leaders from 1980 through 2020 at 17.43% and the median of 15.82%. If projected further back, the distance leader increases would be greater, perhaps more for the median.
- Dan Pohl's average driving distance increased 26.2 yards from 1980 through 2005. Is he really more powerful at age 50 vs. age 25? Even the 1.6-yard average increase from 1980 through 1996 (ages 25 and 41, respectively) is unlikely without the help of technology.
- Fred Couples' average driving distance increased 18.8 yards from 1981 through 2005. Is he really more powerful at age 46 vs. age 22? As with Pohl, the impact of technology on Couples' recorded distance has been huge.

Hopefully, this has provided thoughtful perspective on player distances and analysis of course yardage variances relative to the effects of modern-day equipment. Even if the reader questions the calculations and/or inferences, it allows a method of analysis from which to build.

36-HOLE CUTS MADE & MISSED

"Every great player has learned the two Cs: how to concentrate and how to maintain composure." – Byron Nelson

Due to the increased amount of limited-field, no-cut events on the PGA Tour, the job of determining the true number of missed 36-hole cuts* and the number of consecutive cuts made has become time-consuming. What has been relayed over the years as "official" for Jack Nicklaus and Tiger Woods should not be taken at face value as the following will prove.

*It should be noted that the AT&T Pebble Beach Pro-Am has a 54-hole cut. For simplicity, it will be folded in the 36-hole cut scenarios, unless referenced otherwise.

36-hole Cuts Made – Primary Cut Streaks

Let's review the total number of consecutive cuts made for all eligible PGA-sanctioned events inclusive of the four major championships.

The first table below shows the official consecutive cuts made for Nicklaus and Woods.

Jack Nicklaus	Tiger Woods	Variance
105	142	(37)

Within each streak, tournaments with limited fields and no 36-hole cuts – including match play events – are included. The below graphic delineates these tournaments and the respective placements for Nicklaus and Woods.

Jack Nicklaus			Tiger Woods		
Year	Tournament	Placement	Year	Tournament	Placement
1971	Tournament of Champions	1	1998	NEC World Series of Golf	T-5
1971	National Team Championship	1	1998	The Tour Championship	20
1971	U.S. Professional Match Play Golf Championship	T-33	1999	Mercedes Championships	T-5
1972	Tournament of Champions	2	1999	WGC – Anderson Consulting Match Play Championship	T-5
1972	U.S. Professional Match Play Golf Championship	1	1999	WGC – NEC Invitational	1
1973	Tournament of Champions	1	1999	The Tour Championship	1
1973	U.S. Professional Match Play Golf Championship	T-5	1999	WGC – American Express Championship	1
1974	Tournament of Champions	T-9	2000	Mercedes Championships	1
1974	Walt Disney World National Team Championship	T-14	2000	WGC – Anderson Consulting Match Play Championship	2
1975	MONY Tournament of Champions	T-9	2000	WGC – NEC Invitational	1
1976	World Series of Golf	1	2000	The Tour Championship	2
			2000	WGC – American Express Championship	T-5
			2001	Mercedes Championships	T-8
			2001	WGC – NEC Invitational	1
			2001	The Tour Championship	T-13
			2002	Mercedes Championships	T-10

		2002	WGC – Accenture Match Play Championship	T-33
		2002	WGC – NEC Invitational	4
		2002	WGC – American Express Championship	1
		2002	The Tour Championship	T-7
		2003	WGC – Accenture Match Play Championship	1
		2003	WGC – NEC Invitational	T-4
		2003	WGC – American Express Championship	1
		2003	The Tour Championship	26
		2004	Mercedes Championships	T-4
		2004	WGC – Accenture Match Play Championship	1
		2004	WGC – NEC Invitational	T-2
		2004	WGC – American Express Championship	9
		2004	The Tour Championship	2
		2005	Mercedes Championships	T-3
		2005	WGC – Accenture Match Play Championship	T-17

Nicklaus competed in 11 events, while Woods competed in 31. Woods also played in the Sprint International during 1998 and 1999, finishing in a tie for fourth and a tie for 37th, respectively. These two events did not have a 36-hole cut, but they consisted of full-fields with elimination possible after each round, therefore they have been omitted. The listing also reflects a substantial increase in limited-field, no-cut tournaments over the years.

As referenced, the PGA Tour recognizes Woods having made 142 consecutive cuts. By its definition, making a cut means finishing "in the money."

Beginning with the 1998 Buick Invitational, Woods' streak was underway and continued through the 2005 Wachovia Championship. Woods then shot a one-over par score of 141 (69-72) to miss the 36-hole cut by one stroke at the 2005 EDS Byron Nelson Championship. What tournament immediately preceded Woods' run?

Amid rainy weather conditions, the AT&T Pebble Beach National Pro-Am having begun Thursday, 01/29/98 was temporarily washed out after only 36 holes. With continued weather problems and scheduling difficulties, the tournament was reduced to 54 holes and the third/final round was played on Monday, 08/17/98. Any player electing not to travel back to Pebble Beach in August was considered withdrawn and did not finish in the money. One such player was Woods.

Since when should a withdrawal impact a stretch of missed cuts? This tournament is not considered a missed cut from the perspective of Woods' total, so why does it have a bearing on the number of *consecutive* cuts he made? An added irony is the tournament generally has a 54-hole cut and not a 36-hole cut.

The bookend events surrounding Woods' consecutive cuts made likely should be the 1997 Bell Canadian Open when Woods shot a six-over par score of 146 (70-76) and as noted above, the 2005 EDS Byron Nelson Championship. By this criterion and with the 1998 AT&T Pebble Beach National Pro-Am excluded, Woods' consecutive cuts made would be 146.

Here is the new summary for Woods with the revised basis in place.

Jack Nicklaus	Tiger Woods	Variance
105	146	(41)

Yet, this streak is flawed. Upon examination of the tournaments comprising the original number of 142, there are 31 events that had no 36-hole cut. Likewise, when reviewing the 146 events alluded to, 33 had no 36-hole cut. Consequently, Woods' number of cuts made is reduced to 111 or 113, respectively, if the purity of true missed 36-hole cuts remains intact.

When Woods' list is drilled down further, 18 events immediately following the 1998 AT&T Pebble Beach Pro-Am from the 1998 Buick Invitational through his 11-over performance at the 1998 Tour Championship could be excluded, reducing the number of 142 to 124. If the 1998 AT&T Pebble Beach Pro-Am is removed altogether, 22 events from the 1997 Walt Disney World Classic through the 1998 Tour Championship could be excluded, again reducing the number of 146 to 124.

Why make the preceding deductions? While Woods played well in nearly all stroke-play events without a 36-hole cut in the ranges described, it is safe to say shooting 11-over par during the first two rounds of the 1998 Tour Championship would not have advanced to the weekend had a cut been a factor.

Relative to the new total of 124 consecutive cuts for Woods, there are also six WGC match play events included. Match play should never be factored into a 36-hole cut category where the basis is number of strokes. He won in 2003 and 2004, but he also had early exits in 2002 and 2005. Woods' cut series is then reduced to 118.

Here is the summary for Woods beginning with the 1997 Walt Disney World Classic up to the 2005 EDS Byron Nelson Championship with the following exclusions already denoted.

1. 22 tournaments concluding with the 1998 Tour Championship
2. Six match play events

Jack Nicklaus	Tiger Woods	Variance
105	118	(13)

If the same calculus applied to Woods is applied to Nicklaus, how do his numbers stack up?

Upon referral again to the PGA Tour, Nicklaus is credited with 105 consecutive cuts made. Immediately after missing the cut at the 1970 Kaiser International, this series began with the 1970 Sahara Invitational and concluded with the 1976 World Series of Golf. Nicklaus then shot a four-over par score of 146 (72-74) to miss the cut by one stroke at the 1976 World Open Golf Championship.

After closer inspection of the tournaments Nicklaus played during this span, he finished "in the money" in 111. This total includes six Open Championships from 1971 through 1976. In 1995, the PGA Tour retroactively made Open Championship victories official PGA Tour wins. By that logic, all placements in the Open Championship should count toward whatever applicable measurement.

As with Woods, Nicklaus competed in three match play events – the short-lived U.S. Match Play Championship – from 1971 through 1973. While he won once, finished tied for fifth once, and was eliminated in the first round in another, these events were not stroke-play and should not factor into a 36-hole cut streak based upon number of strokes. Furthermore, the 1971 National Team Championship Nicklaus won with Arnold Palmer along with the 1974 Walt Disney World National Team Championship he paired with Tom Weiskopf to finish tied for 14th should also be ineligible for inclusion in an individual player's consecutive cuts made.

With this rationale, the net effect for Nicklaus is an increase of one from the PGA Tour official number of cuts made of 105 to 106.

The updated total below for Nicklaus now incorporates the following changes.

1. Six Open Championships added
2. Three match play events deducted
3. Two team events deducted

Jack Nicklaus	Tiger Woods	Variance
106	118	(12)

Woods still leads Nicklaus, but the deficit is reduced from the original margin of 37 to a more realistic number of 12.

Let's examine consecutive cuts made for Nicklaus and Woods when all limited-field, no-cut events are deducted from each player.

For Nicklaus, the task is simple. After the calculations above are in place resulting in 106 consecutive cuts made, the remaining deductions are the Tournament of Champions events from 1971 through 1975 along with the 1976 World Series of Golf. These six adjustments leave him at an even 100 consecutive cuts made.

For Woods, the original number of 142 is magnified by 31 events detailed above, so the corresponding deduction reduces his total consecutive cut figure to 111.

The new summary and variance for the consecutive cut streaks of Nicklaus and Woods minus all limited-field tournaments without a 36-hole cut is below.

Jack Nicklaus	Tiger Woods	Variance
100	111	(11)

Woods leads this category by a narrower margin. This is the most direct listing relative to comparing the category of consecutive cuts being made as only tournaments with 36-hole cuts are included along with all four major championships for both players.

If Woods' consecutive cuts made commences with the 1997 Walt Disney World Classic and the 33 events with no cut referenced above plus the 1998 AT&T Pebble Beach Pro-Am are deducted, the tally is 113.

The updated total for Woods now incorporates the following exclusions.

1. 31 limited-field, no-cut events previously detailed
2. 1997 Tour Championship
3. 1998 Mercedes Championships
4. 1998 AT&T Pebble Beach Pro-Am (WD)

Jack Nicklaus	Tiger Woods	Variance
100	113	(13)

With this third variance between Nicklaus and Woods at 13, Woods leads by an average margin across the last three scenarios by 12.

As has been shown in the roster of limited-field, no-cut events that Nicklaus and Woods competed in, there is further room for modification. The following outlines the tournaments Nicklaus and Woods likely would have been cut if one existed and what impact, if any, their streaks would have realized.

Jack Nicklaus

- 1969 Tournament of Champions
  - ○ Opening 36-hole Rounds: 73, 80 (+9)
  - ○ **Impact:** None as was prior to the 1970 Kaiser International Open
- 1985 MONY Tournament of Champions
  - ○ Opening 36-hole Rounds: 74, 72 (+2)
  - ○ **Impact:** None as was after the 1976 World Open

Tiger Woods

- 1996 Tour Championship
  - ○ Opening 36-hole Rounds: 70, 78 (+8)
  - ○ **Impact:** None as was prior to the 1997 Bell Canadian Open
- 1998 Tour Championship
  - ○ Opening 36-hole Rounds: 75, 76 (+11)
  - ○ **Impact:** *23rd event played after the first official missed cut*
    - 1997 Bell Canadian Open
- 2010 WGC Bridgestone Invitational
  - ○ Opening 36-hole Rounds: 74, 72 (+6)
  - ○ **Impact:** None as was after the 2005 EDS Byron Nelson Championship
- 2012 WGC Bridgestone Invitational
  - ○ Opening 36-hole Rounds: 70, 72 (+2)
  - ○ **Impact:** None as was after the 2005 EDS Byron Nelson Championship
- 2013 Tour Championship
  - ○ Opening 36-hole Rounds: 73, 71 (+4)

- o **Impact:** None as was after the 2005 EDS Byron Nelson Championship
- 2014 WGC CA Championship
  - o Opening 36-hole Rounds: 73, 76 (+5)
  - o **Impact:** None as was after the 2005 EDS Byron Nelson Championship
- 2020 BMW Championship
  - o Opening 36-hole Rounds: 73, 75 (+8)
  - o **Impact:** None as was after the 2005 EDS Byron Nelson Championship
- 2020 Zozo Championship
  - o Opening 36-hole Rounds: 76, 66 (-2)
  - o **Impact:** None as was after the 2005 EDS Byron Nelson Championship

Based upon the above data, the only tournament impacting either player's respective cut streak was the 1998 Tour Championship. This event was the 23rd Woods played after his first missed cut in the 1997 Bell Canadian Open. At the end of 36 holes, Woods was 11-over par – last place in a field of 30, and 18 strokes behind leader Vijay Singh at seven-under par.

Thus, when all match play events for both players are excluded, the two team events for Nicklaus are excluded, Open Championships are included for Nicklaus as they are for Woods, and the 1998 Tour Championship for Woods is classified as a missed cut, the final version of consecutive cuts made for the two players reads as follows.

Jack Nicklaus	Tiger Woods	Variance
106	118	(12)

Woods leads in this 36-hole cut analysis by a margin of 12. With the above criteria incorporated, this may be the most equitable representation of the consecutive cut streaks for Nicklaus and Woods.

This study is not intended to suggest Nicklaus and/or Woods would have missed the cut in many of the limited-field, no-cut events if they were full-field tournaments with 36-hole cuts. Instead, the purpose is to propose that ineligible events should not be included in such a reference. And regardless of who the player is, the sizable increase in tournaments with smaller fields and no 36-hole cuts should not artificially augment that player's accomplishment when such a measurement (i.e. consecutive cuts made) is referenced. Lastly, the official PGA Tour records should be updated for consistency across all eras.

36-hole Cuts Made – Secondary Cut Streaks

While both cut streaks previously covered are impressive, it makes sense Nicklaus and Woods would have secondary listings of consecutive cuts made. The following provides the detail.

From the 1963 Portland Open and concluding with the 1967 Pensacola Open, Nicklaus competed in 80 consecutive, official PGA events; there was no PGA *Tour* at that time. In all, he did not miss a single 36-hole cut. However, during the fifth tournament, the 1964 Bing Crosby National Pro-Am, Nicklaus missed the **54**-hole cut.

Shooting rounds of 75-70-77 (six-over par 222) in difficult weather conditions, he did not qualify for the final round. Nevertheless, at one-over par through the first 36 holes, Nicklaus would have advanced to the weekend if the tournament reduced the field at the midway point.

Within these 80 events, there was no match play competition and only three limited-field, no-cut tournaments – the Tournament of Champions for 1964, 1965, and 1966 – in which Nicklaus finished first, 11th, and fifth, respectively. By virtue of his scores in these three tournaments, there was no danger of him missing the cut, had one existed.

Upon implementing the same logic used for the primary cut listing, Nicklaus either succeeded in making 80 consecutive 36-holes cuts – or by eliminating the 1964 Bing Crosby National Pro-Am, he was successful for 79.

How do the numbers line out for Woods in a secondary cut streak of his own?

Immediately following the 2006 U.S. Open wherein Woods missed the cut, he embarked on another succession of tournaments that began with the 2006

Cialis Western Open and concluded with the 2009 AT&T National. For these 38 events, he did not miss a 36-hole cut.

When these 38 tournaments are examined, the following emerges.

- **Full-field Events:** 27
- **Limited-field "No-cut" Stroke-play Events:** 8
- **Match Play Events:** 3

As with Nicklaus' secondary cut streak, Woods would not have been in danger of missing any cut in the eight limited-field, stroke-play events referenced as his worst finish was a tie for ninth. And with the earlier rationale to exclude match play events from all consecutive cuts made, Woods' number is adjusted to 35.

Therefore, with the secondary cut streaks for Nicklaus and Woods, three versions emerge with applicable descriptions for each.

Jack Nicklaus	Tiger Woods	Variance
80	35	45

Above includes all events for Nicklaus within the range first described. Since his scores through the first 36 holes in the 1964 Bing Crosby National Pro-Am would have advanced beyond a halfway cut, there is no interruption in the secondary streak. For Woods, his 38 events previously referenced only have the three match play competitions deducted and this is constant throughout all three aggregates.

Jack Nicklaus	Tiger Woods	Variance
79	35	44

For this second total, the 1964 Bing Crosby National Pro-Am is removed altogether from the 80 events since there was no 36-hole cut. However, there was a 54-hole cut that Nicklaus missed. Due to this scenario's ambiguity, the tournament is neither part of the series, nor does it adversely affect the series – it is simply excluded. Nicklaus' complete run is then abridged from 80 to 79 with Woods' total of 35 remaining constant.

Jack Nicklaus	Tiger Woods	Variance
75	35	40

This third version treats the 1964 Bing Crosby National Pro-Am like any other missed cut. Consequently, it renders the event along with the preceding four tournaments negated from the total of 80 in succession. The new aggregate of 75 for Nicklaus still dwarfs Woods' corresponding figure of 35.

36-hole Cuts Made – Primary Cut Streaks (Major Championships)

Let's examine consecutive cuts made in major championships. The task is very straightforward and even between the two players.

Jack Nicklaus	Tiger Woods	Variance
39	39	0

Nicklaus' above streak occurred after his missed cut in the 1968 PGA Championship through the 1978 Open Championship. For Woods, his streak occurred after his missed cut in the 1996 Masters (as an amateur) through the 2006 Masters. Since Woods was an amateur during the 1996 PGA Championship, he was ineligible to compete, so this event is not included in the applicable succession of majors.

Across the 39 major championships above for Nicklaus, his average finish was 6.49. For Woods, his average finish was 12.90. Both placements are very sound and for Woods, his includes the U.S. Open and Open Championships from 1996, when he was an amateur.

Incidentally, Gary Player is third in consecutive cuts made in major championships at 37. Player's streak began with the 1970 PGA Championship through the 1980 Masters, yet he did not compete in the 1973 Masters.

36-hole Cuts Made – Secondary Cut Streaks (Major Championships)

To add additional perspective to major championship performances by Nicklaus and Woods, a review of the secondary series of consecutive cuts made is necessary. The below graphic provides the number for each player, followed by supplemental detail.

Jack Nicklaus	Tiger Woods	Variance
24	10	14

Immediately following his missed cut in the 1978 PGA Championship, Nicklaus began a new campaign of major championship play with his fourth-place finish in the 1979 Masters. From that championship through the 1985 Masters, he navigated his way across 24 consecutive major championships without missing a 36-hole cut.

Yet, in the midst of this secondary streak, Nicklaus withdrew prior to his second round of the 1983 Masters, due to back problems. He shot a first-round 73 and was six shots adrift of three co-leaders. This was one shot lower than Nicklaus' first round of the 1986 Masters and the same number of shots behind the two first-round leaders.

After missing the cut in the 2006 U.S. Open, Woods won the 2006 Open Championship and proceeded to complete 10 major championships in succession without missing a 36-hole cut. While he did miss the Open Championship and PGA Championship in 2008 due to injury, it wasn't until the 2009 Open Championship that Woods had the weekend off.

Consecutive 36-hole Cuts Missed

With the scarcity of Nicklaus and Woods missing 36-hole cuts during the review period, another aspect up for study is the number of consecutive 36-hole cuts missed. The graphic below provides the occurrences for each player in regular PGA Tour events and major championships.

Consecutive 36-hole Cuts Missed – All PGA Tour Events		
	Jack Nicklaus	**Tiger Woods**
Tournament	1982 Honda Inverrary Classic	2014 PGA Championship
Age	42	38
Score	73 – 71 = 144	74 – 74 = 148
Tournament	1982 Players Championship	2015 Waste Management Phoenix Open
Age	42	39
Score	73 – 78 = 151	73 – 82 = 155

For Nicklaus, this took place during his 21st year as a playing professional. With Woods, this happened at the close of his 18th year and start of his 19th year on the PGA Tour. The fact this only occurred once for each player further illustrates their consistency.

How do the players stack up when this category is applied exclusively to major championships?

Consecutive 36-hole Cuts Missed – Major Championships		
	Jack Nicklaus	**Tiger Woods**
Tournament	1985 U.S. Open	2015 U.S. Open
Age	45	39
Score	76 – 73 = 149	80 – 76 = 156
Tournament	1985 Open Championship	2015 Open Championship
Age	45	39
Score	77 – 75 = 152	76 – 75 = 151
Tournament		2015 PGA Championship
Age		39
Score		75 – 73 = 148

Both Nicklaus and Woods launched their missed cut streaks in major championships with the U.S. Open. For Nicklaus, his opening missed cut was during his 24th year as a playing professional at age 45. The 1985 U.S. Open marked his 94th start in a major championship as a professional. He continued his substandard play in his 95th major at the Open Championship the subsequent month.

Woods began his missed cut stretch in the 2015 U.S. Open. At age 39, this major championship marked his 68th start as a touring professional during his 19th year on Tour. Woods then uncharacteristically followed up this missed cut with not one, but two in the final major championships of the year.

Cumulative 36-hole Cuts Missed

Finally, let's examine the true number of missed 36-hole cuts and their respective ratios in all PGA-sanctioned events and major championships for both players. The ratio of missed cuts to tournaments played for each player excludes all no-cut events under match play, stroke-play, and team play formats.

36-hole Cuts Missed as Professionals						
	Eligible PGA Tournaments Played	36-hole Cuts Missed	%	Major Championships Played	36-hole Cuts Missed	%
Nicklaus	447	26	5.82%	100	6	6.00%
Woods	277	22	7.94%	84	12	14.29%
Variance	170	4	(2.12%)	16	(6)	(8.29%)

Nicklaus played 447 PGA-sanctioned events with a 36-hole cut in each, including the four major championships, and missed a total of 26. His ratio equates to 5.82%. For Woods, he played 277 PGA Tour events inclusive of the four major championships with a 36-hole cut and missed 22. His ratio equates to 7.94%.

Within this data, Nicklaus played in 100 major championships as a professional and missed a total of six cuts, or 6.00%. When excluding the 1983 Masters, Nicklaus' missed cut ratio is 6/99, or 6.06%. When reviewing the same data for Woods, he played in 84 major championships having missed several due to injury and the 2020 Open Championship cancellation due to the coronavirus. He failed to qualify for the final 36 holes on 12 occasions rendering a 14.29% ratio, more than twice the percentage of Nicklaus.

Let's take a closer look at the respective cuts missed for Nicklaus and Woods in major championships to see how close each player was to advancing to the final 36 holes.

Year	Major Championship & Total	36-hole Cut Actual		Nicklaus Actual		Variances & Average
	Jack Nicklaus 36-hole Missed Cut Summary in Major Championships (1962 – 1986)					
		Score	To Par	Score	To Par	
1963	U.S. Open	152	+10	153	+11	1
1967	Masters	150	+6	151	+7	1
1968	PGA Championship	149	+9	150	+10	1
1978	PGA Championship	148	+6	153	+11	5
1985	U.S. Open	146	+6	149	+9	3
1985	Open Championship	149	+9	152	+12	3
	6		**+46**		**+60**	**2.33**

The above table is a great view of Nicklaus' six missed cuts in major championship play during the prescribed 25-year span as a professional. With a high 18-hole score of 79 shot three times, Nicklaus' average was 75.67 compared to a minimum required average of 74.50 to advance to the final 36 holes. Nicklaus' average 18-hole score was five-over par and the minimum required average for 18 holes was 3.83 strokes over par. Furthermore, between the PGA Championship bookends of 1968 and 1978 resides his record-setting 39 consecutive major championships played without missing a 36-hole cut. While six missed cuts out of 100 major championships is phenomenal consistency, the first three events each being a single shot away from advancing adds luster to the data.

Year	Major Championship & Total	36-hole Cut Actual		Woods Actual		Variances & Average
	Tiger Woods 36-hole Missed Cut Summary in Major Championships (1997 – 2022)					
		Score	To Par	Score	To Par	
2006	U.S. Open	149	+9	152	+12	3
2009	Open Championship	144	+4	145	+5	1
2011	PGA Championship	144	+4	150	+10	6

2014	PGA Championship	143	+1	148	+6	5
2015	U.S. Open	145	+5	156	+16	11
2015	Open Championship	144	0	151	+7	7
2015	PGA Championship	146	+2	148	+4	2
2018	U.S. Open	148	+8	150	+10	2
2019	Open Championship	143	+1	148	+6	5
2019	PGA Championship	144	+4	145	+5	1
2020	U.S. Open	146	+6	150	+10	4
2022	Open Championship	144	0	153	+9	9
	12		**+44**		**+100**	**4.67**

For Woods, his first missed cut in a major championship as a professional was at the 2006 U.S. Open, which concluded his record-tying effort of 39 consecutive 36-hole cuts made. With a maximum 18-hole score of 80, Woods' overall stroke average was 74.83 vs. the minimum required average of 72.50 necessary to progress to the weekend. The total of 44-over par translates to an average 18-hole score of 1.83 shots over par required to successfully navigate each 36-hole cut. In this context, Woods averaged 4.17 strokes over par per round. And like Nicklaus, Woods had events he only missed qualifying for the final 36 holes by one shot. However, as opposed to three of six for Nicklaus, Woods completed two of 12.

Lastly, even though Nicklaus leads Woods with fewer missed cuts and a narrower average stroke margin relative to the actual cut figures, Woods does not come up empty. As the data show, Woods scores almost one shot lower than Nicklaus per 18-hole round (74.83 vs. 75.67) and slightly better with respect to the average number of strokes over par per round (4.17 vs. 5.00). So, although Woods doubles Nicklaus in missed cuts across a fewer total number of major championships, the scores needed to advance to the final 36 holes improved by 2.00 total shots and 2.00 strokes relative to par, respectively.

COMPETITION

"When I came out, low 70 and ties made the cut and the low 50 places paid off. You had to play your ass off. Now a guy can make the cut and earn $1,500.00 for just walking around. You tell me which system is going to produce great players." – Tom Weiskopf **Golf Digest** *– March 1991*

"He doesn't need a challenge, I think that is the worst misconception going – that the No. 1 golfer needs a No. 2 golfer to push him. Tiger is pushed by history and by records and by his own goals. He doesn't need anybody pushing him." – Earl Woods

With scoring covered, it is time to review the competition in Jack Nicklaus' and Tiger Woods' eras who influenced their performances. Due to various limitations, the analysis on competition will focus on each player's top 10 opponents in major championships during their eras.

While the Woods era is one that has transpired over a more global arena, it is still a pretty straightforward task to identify 10 competitors to match up against the top 10 in Nicklaus' era. Realizing the lists of players are debatable, I tried to gather 20 who were active during our subjects' primes.

Nicklaus Era (1962 – 1986)	Woods Era (1997 – 2022)
Arnold Palmer	Jose Maria Olazabal
Billy Casper	Ernie Els
Gary Player	Vijay Singh
Lee Trevino	Retief Goosen
Raymond Floyd	David Duval

Johnny Miller	Jim Furyk
Tom Weiskopf	Phil Mickelson
Hale Irwin	Padraig Harrington
Tom Watson	Rory McIlroy
Seve Ballesteros	Adam Scott

Each player was selected based upon total performance in major championships while facing Nicklaus and Woods during their most effective years, number of PGA tournaments won, tournaments won overseas, and general consistency and longevity.

Top 10 Competitors – Major Championship Performances

Here are the players listed above segregated per era and the breakdown of their total top-10 finishes in major championships. The two charts are followed by a comparative review.

Jack Nicklaus Top 10 Competitors Major Championship Top-10 Placement Summary										
	1st	2nd	3rd	4th	5th	6th	7th	8th	9th	10th	Total
Palmer	7	10	2	3	4	2	5	1	2	2	38
Casper	3	4	1	5	2	2	2	2	2	1	24
Player	9	6	3	3	2	7	6	5	1	2	44
Trevino	6	2	1	4	2	0	2	1	1	3	22
Floyd	4	5	1	3	0	1	4	7	1	2	28
Miller	2	4	1	1	1	2	1	2	1	2	17
Weiskopf	1	5	3	3	0	2	2	2	1	2	21
Irwin	3	1	1	3	3	4	0	2	2	1	20
Watson	8	8	2	3	4	5	5	1	7	3	46
Ballesteros	5	3	2	2	3	2	1	0	1	1	20
Total	48	48	17	30	21	27	28	23	19	19	280

Tiger Woods Top 10 Competitors Major Championship Top-10 Placement Summary										
	1st	2nd	3rd	4th	5th	6th	7th	8th	9th	10th	Total
Olazabal	2	1	3	2	0	0	2	4	1	0	15
Els	4	6	5	3	5	4	3	2	2	1	35
Singh	3	1	1	1	3	5	3	3	1	2	23
Goosen	2	2	2	0	2	2	1	1	0	4	16
Duval	1	3	1	0	0	1	2	1	0	2	11
Furyk	1	4	0	7	4	2	1	1	1	2	23
Mickelson	6	11	7	2	2	3	4	1	1	2	39
Harrington	3	0	0	2	6	0	1	2	0	2	16
McIlroy	4	2	4	2	4	0	2	5	2	2	27
Scott	1	2	3	1	2	0	2	3	4	1	19
Total	27	32	26	20	28	17	21	23	12	18	224

Nicklaus' top 10 competitors beat Woods' competitors nearly across the board. In major championship victories alone, they have 48 compared to 27, with the peak individual being Gary Player having nine wins vs. Phil Mickelson at six wins. The total distribution of top-10 placements for Woods' 10 competitors is 224 compared to 280 for Nicklaus' 10 competitors – or 80.00%. Mickelson also leads the individual total top-10 placements for the Woods era at 39 vs. Tom Watson at 46 for the Nicklaus era.

Let's review the overall record summaries between the same sets of competitors including the span of years from their first major championship victory through their last.

Jack Nicklaus Top 10 Competitors Summary					
	Majors Championships Won	Year of First Major Victory	Year of Final Major Victory	Span of Years	Total PGA Victories
Palmer	7	1958	1964	7	62
Casper	3	1959	1970	12	51
Player	9	1959	1978	20	24
Trevino	6	1968	1984	17	29
Floyd	4	1969	1986	18	22

Miller		2	1973	1976	4	25
Weiskopf		1	1973	1973	1	16
Irwin		3	1974	1990	17	20
Watson		8	1975	1983	9	39
Ballesteros		5	1979	1988	10	9
Total		48			115	297

Tiger Woods Top 10 Competitors Summary					
	Majors Championships Won	Year of First Major Victory	Year of Final Major Victory	Span of Years	Total PGA Victories
Olazabal	2	1994	1999	6	6
Els	4	1994	2012	19	19
Singh	3	1998	2004	7	34
Goosen	2	2001	2004	4	7
Duval	1	2001	2001	1	13
Furyk	1	2003	2003	1	17
Mickelson	6	2004	2021	18	45
Harrington	3	2007	2008	2	6
McIlroy	4	2011	2014	4	21
Scott	1	2013	2013	1	14
Total	27			63	182

The same competitors again show 48 victories (Nicklaus era) compared to 27 in Woods' era. However, the average range of years from first to last victory for the Nicklaus era is 11.50 compared to 6.30 years for the competitors in the Woods era; the leaders are Player at 20 years and Ernie Els at 19 years, respectively. The total PGA wins for the top 10 from Nicklaus' era is 297 compared to 182 for the top 10 in Woods' era – a difference of 115.

Head-to-Head

The following shows key head-to-head results in major championships between Nicklaus and his top 10 competitors followed by Woods and his top 10 competitors. The basis for each matchup is when the two players were within four shots of one another after 54 holes and one or the other went on to tie after 72 holes and/or win the championship.

Arnold Palmer vs. Jack Nicklaus						
	Palmer (54)	Nicklaus (54)	Palmer Final Round	Nicklaus Final Round	Palmer (72)	Nicklaus (72)
1960 U.S. Open*	+2	-2	-6	0	-4	-2
1962 U.S. Open**	-1	+1	0	-2	-1	-1
1966 Masters	+2	0	0	0	+2	0
1966 U.S. Open***	-3	+1	+1	+4	-2	+5
1966 Open	+1	-1	+3	-1	+4	-2
1967 U.S. Open	0	0	-1	-5	-1	-5
1972 U.S. Open	+2	0	+4	+2	+6	+2

*Nicklaus was an amateur.

**Nicklaus and Palmer tied in regulation. Nicklaus defeated Palmer 71 to 74 in the following day's playoff.

***Palmer and Billy Casper tied in regulation. Casper defeated Palmer the next day 69 to 73 in the 18-hole playoff.

When including the 1962 U.S. Open playoff, Nicklaus and Palmer faced off on eight occasions. Nicklaus leads Palmer **5-2-1**. Also, Nicklaus leads in total final round scoring at **-2** to **+1**.

Billy Casper vs. Jack Nicklaus						
	Casper (54)	Nicklaus (54)	Casper Final Round	Nicklaus Final Round	Casper (72)	Nicklaus (72)
1966 U.S. Open	0	+1	-2	+4	-2	+5

1967 U.S. Open	0	0	+2	-5	+2	-5

Nicklaus and Casper were not known for great rivalries in major championships, but they did clash once in a while. Above shows the two occasions meeting the criteria. They are even at **1-1-0** and Nicklaus edges Casper in final round scoring at **-1** to **0**.

Gary Player vs. Jack Nicklaus						
	Player (54)	Nicklaus (54)	Player Final Round	Nicklaus Final Round	Player (72)	Nicklaus (72)
1962 U.S. Open	+1	+1	+3	-2	+4	-1
1968 Open	0	+2	+1	+1	+1	+3
1971 PGA	-4	-8	+1	+1	-3	-7
1974 Masters	-8	-4	-2	-3	-10	-7
1974 Open	-1	+3	-1	0	-2	+3
1978 Masters	-3	-2	-8	-5	-11	-7

During six instances, Nicklaus and Player battled under the criteria set up. Player leads Nicklaus **4-2-0**. However, Nicklaus' cumulative final rounds were **-8** compared to Player at **-6**.

Lee Trevino vs. Jack Nicklaus						
	Trevino (54)	Nicklaus (54)	Trevino Final Round	Nicklaus Final Round	Trevino (72)	Nicklaus (72)
1967 U.S. Open	+3	0	0	-5	+3	-5
1968 U.S. Open	-4	+2	-1	-3	-5	-1
1970 Open	-8	-6	+5	+1	-3	-5
1971 U.S. Open*	+1	-1	-1	+1	0	0

1972 U.S. Open	+1	0	+6	+2	+7	+2
1974 PGA	-3	-2	-1	-1	-4	-3

*Nicklaus and Trevino tied in regulation. Trevino defeated Nicklaus 68 to 71 in the following day's playoff.

When including the 1971 U.S. Open playoff, Nicklaus and Trevino faced off on seven occasions. Nicklaus is even with Trevino at **3-3-1**. However, Nicklaus leads in total final round scoring at **-5** to **+8**. One omission from the above is the 1972 Open Championship. Since Nicklaus was behind Trevino by six shots, it was outside the four-shot limit.

Raymond Floyd vs. Jack Nicklaus						
	Floyd (54)	Nicklaus (54)	Floyd Final Round	Nicklaus Final Round	Floyd (72)	Nicklaus (72)
1966 Masters	+3	0	+2	0	+5	0
1978 Open	-1	-4	-4	-3	-5	-7
1986 U.S. Open	+3	+6	-4	-2	-1	+4

Nicklaus and Floyd competed on three occasions under the parameters described. Although none were true "head-to-head" bouts, the results are Nicklaus leads Floyd **2-1-0** while coming up short in final rounds at **-5** to Floyd's **-6**.

Johnny Miller vs. Jack Nicklaus						
	Miller (54)	Nicklaus (54)	Miller Final Round	Nicklaus Final Round	Miller (72)	Nicklaus (72)
1972 U.S. Open	+2	0	+7	+2	+9	+2
1973 U.S. Open	+3	+1	-8	-3	-5	-2
1975 Masters	-5	-8	-6	-4	-11	-12

1976 Open		-3		0		-6		-3		-9		-3

Nicklaus and Miller met four times under the criteria established. They split at **2-2-0**. In addition, Miller was **-13** for his final round performances vs. Nicklaus at **-8**.

Tom Weiskopf vs. Jack Nicklaus						
	Weiskopf (54)	Nicklaus (54)	Weiskopf Final Round	Nicklaus Final Round	Weiskopf (72)	Nicklaus (72)
1972 Masters	-1	-4	+2	+2	+1	-2
1972 U.S. Open	+4	0	+6	+2	+10	+2
1973 PGA	-1	-5	0	-2	-1	-7
1975 Masters	-9	-8	-2	-4	-11	-12
1978 Open	-3	-4	+3	-3	0	-7

Nicklaus and Weiskopf went head-to-head under the above conditions on five instances. Nicklaus leads Weiskopf **5-0-0** and in final round scoring at **-5** to **+9**.

Hale Irwin vs. Jack Nicklaus						
	Irwin (54)	Nicklaus (54)	Irwin Final Round	Nicklaus Final Round	Irwin (72)	Nicklaus (72)
1990 U.S. Open	-3	-3	-5	+4	-8	+1

Nicklaus at age 50 and Irwin at age 45 crossed paths once under the criteria set up. Irwin leads by a **1-0-0** margin and his superb final round of **-5** that led him to victory in the 1990 U.S. Open significantly beat Nicklaus' substandard round of **+4**.

Tom Watson vs. Jack Nicklaus						
	Watson (54)	Nicklaus (54)	Watson Final Round	Nicklaus Final Round	Watson (72)	Nicklaus (72)
1975 Masters	-4	-8	+1	-4	-3	-12
1975 Open	-9	-8	0	0	-9	-8
1977 Masters	-7	-4	-5	-6	-12	-10
1977 Open	-7	-7	-5	-4	-12	-11
1978 Open	-5	-4	+4	-3	-1	-7
1980 U.S. Open	-4	-6	0	-2	-4	-8
1981 Masters	-7	-6	-1	0	-8	-6
1982 U.S. Open	-4	-1	-2	-3	-6	-4
1986 Masters	-4	-2	-1	-7	-5	-9

On nine occasions, Nicklaus and Watson battled one another under the criteria assigned. Watson leads Nicklaus **5-4-0**. However, when assessing each player's final round performances, Nicklaus leads Watson significantly at **-29** compared to **-9**. This is the most divergent reading for scoring on the comparative head-to-head analyses.

Seve Ballesteros vs. Jack Nicklaus						
	Ballesteros (54)	Nicklaus (54)	Ballesteros Final Round	Nicklaus Final Round	Ballesteros (72)	Nicklaus (72)
1978 Open	-1	-4	+1	-3	0	-7
1979 Open	0	+1	-1	+1	-1	+2
1986 Masters	-5	-2	-2	-7	-7	-9

Nicklaus and Ballesteros met during three instances under the prescribed criteria. Nicklaus leads Ballesteros **2-1-0** and with cumulative final round scoring of **-9** to **-2**.

The composite results for the above show that for the 48 head-to-head match ups, Nicklaus leads his top 10 competitors **26-20-2**. Nicklaus also outscored his top 10 competitors in final rounds by 45 shots at **-68** vs. **-23**.

Lee Trevino & Tom Watson

Of the 19 total runner-up finishes Nicklaus had in the majors, eight of them to two players is significant and would seem to entail Lee Trevino and Tom Watson had his number in competition. The following study should clear up any misconceptions.

Lee Trevino vs. Jack Nicklaus – 1968 U.S. Open			
Player	**54-hole Scores**	**Final Round Scores**	**72-hole Scores**
Nicklaus	212	67	279
Trevino	206	69	275
Variance	6	(2)	4

Lee Trevino vs. Jack Nicklaus – 1971 U.S. Open			
Player	**72-hole Scores**	**Playoff Scores**	**90-hole Scores**
Nicklaus	280	71	351
Trevino	280	68	348
Variance	0	3	3

Lee Trevino vs. Jack Nicklaus – 1972 Open Championship			
Player	**54-hole Scores**	**Final Round Scores**	**72-hole Scores**
Nicklaus	213	66	279
Trevino	207	71	278
Variance	6	(5)	1

Lee Trevino vs. Jack Nicklaus – 1974 PGA Championship			
Player	**54-hole Scores**	**Final Round Scores**	**72-hole Scores**
Nicklaus	208	69	279
Trevino	207	69	278
Variance	1	0	1

Lee Trevino vs. Jack Nicklaus – Aggregate		
Player	**Average Final Round/Playoff Scores**	**Championship Placements**
Nicklaus	68.25	2
Trevino	69.25	1
Variance	(1.00)	1

The above charts show the most notable major championship victories for Lee Trevino, largely due to Nicklaus having finished second.

Much has been made about the dramatic finishes wherein Trevino outdueled Nicklaus in the final rounds. Apart from the 1971 U.S. Open playoff, this is not entirely the case. Trevino did outduel Nicklaus in that playoff to win by three shots. However, when averaging the scores of all applicable rounds, Nicklaus was a shot lower than Trevino. While outdueling provides journalistic flair, generally speaking, Trevino was simply able to maintain championship leads during various charges by Nicklaus.

Tom Watson vs. Jack Nicklaus – 1977 Masters			
Player	**54-hole Scores**	**Final Round Scores**	**72-hole Scores**
Nicklaus	212	66	278
Watson	209	67	276
Variance	3	(1)	2

Tom Watson vs. Jack Nicklaus – 1977 Open Championship			
Player	**54-hole Scores**	**Final Round Scores**	**72-hole Scores**
Nicklaus	203	66	269
Watson	203	65	268
Variance	0	1	1

Tom Watson vs. Jack Nicklaus – 1981 Masters			
Player	**54-hole Scores**	**Final Round Scores**	**72-hole Scores**
Nicklaus	210	72	282
Watson	209	71	280
Variance	1	1	2

Tom Watson vs. Jack Nicklaus – 1982 U.S. Open			
Player	**54-hole Scores**	**Final Round Scores**	**72-hole Scores**
Nicklaus	215	69	284
Watson	212	70	282
Variance	3	(1)	2

Tom Watson vs. Jack Nicklaus – Aggregate		
Player	**Average Final Round/Playoff Scores**	**Championship Placements**
Nicklaus	68.25	2
Watson	68.25	1
Variance	0.00	1

Like Trevino, Tom Watson similarly emerged victorious over Nicklaus in four major championships. And the only true single round head-to-head duel was the 1977 Open Championship wherein Watson edged Nicklaus by a shot. However, Watson's stroke average for the final rounds was one shot better than Trevino's. Nicklaus' stroke average was the exact same against both players and equal to that of Watson.

These eight major championships show neither Trevino nor Watson wilted to challenges presented to them by Nicklaus. On just one occasion each did Trevino and Watson face Nicklaus over 18 holes where both began tied and they won. It also shows, on average, Nicklaus was either the equal or superior in scoring of his two opponents for the final rounds played – and he did so over a 15-year period from 1968 through 1982.

Jose Maria Olazabal vs. Tiger Woods						
			Olazabal Final Round	Woods Final Round		
	Olazabal (54)	Woods (54)			Olazabal (72)	Woods (72)

2000 PGA	-9	-13	-3	-5	-12	-18
2005 Open	-10	-12	+2	-2	-8	-14

On two occasions, Woods and Olazabal competed under the criteria established. Woods leads Olazabal **2-0-0** and scored a combined **-7** vs. **-1** in final rounds.

Ernie Els vs. Tiger Woods						
	Els (54)	Woods (54)	Els Final Round	Woods Final Round	Els (72)	Woods (72)
2001 Masters	-9	-12	0	-4	-9	-16
2002 Masters	-7	-11	+1	-1	-6	-12
2006 Open	-12	-13	-1	-5	-13	-18
2012 Open	-5	-6	-2	+3	-7	-3

Under the specifications set, Woods and Els battled four times. Woods leads Els **3-1-0** and in final round scoring at **-7** to **-2**.

Vijay Singh vs. Tiger Woods						
	Singh (54)	Woods (54)	Singh Final Round	Woods Final Round	Singh (72)	Woods (72)
2002 Masters	-9	-11	+4	-1	-5	-12

In just one instance did Woods and Singh meet under the parameters set forth. Woods leads Singh **1-0-0** and in final round scoring **-1** compared to **+4**.

Retief Goosen vs. Tiger Woods						
	Goosen (54)	Woods (54)	Goosen Final Round	Woods Final Round	Goosen (72)	Woods (72)
2002 Masters	-11	-11	+2	-1	-9	-12

2005 Open	-9	-12	+2	-2	-7	-14

Woods and Goosen competed twice under the set criteria. Woods leads Goosen **2-0-0** and in final round scoring at **-3** with Goosen at **+4**.

David Duval vs. Tiger Woods						
	Duval (54)	Woods (54)	Duval Final Round	Woods Final Round	Duval (72)	Woods (72)
2001 Masters	-9	-12	-5	-4	-14	-16

Surprisingly, only once did Woods and Duval coincide under the prescribed criteria. Woods leads Duval **1-0-0**, yet Duval's final round score was **-5** and Woods was **-4**.

Jim Furyk vs. Tiger Woods						
	Furyk (54)	Woods (54)	Furyk Final Round	Woods Final Round	Furyk (72)	Woods (72)
2006 Open	-11	-13	-1	-5	-12	-18

In just one instance did Woods and Furyk meet under the established parameters. Woods leads Furyk **1-0-0** and in final round scoring **-5** compared to **-1**.

Phil Mickelson vs. Tiger Woods						
	Mickelson (54)	Woods (54)	Mickelson Final Round	Woods Final Round	Mickelson (72)	Woods (72)
2001 Masters	-11	-12	-2	-4	-13	-16
2002 Masters	-7	-11	-1	-1	-8	-12
2006 Masters	-4	-2	-3	-2	-7	-4
2010 Masters	-11	-8	-5	-3	-16	-11

2013 Open	+2	-1	-5	+3	-3	+2

As shown, Woods and Mickelson met on five occasions under the criteria set. Mickelson leads Woods **3-2-0** and in combined final round scoring by a healthy margin of **-16** to **-7**.

Padraig Harrington vs. Tiger Woods						
	Harrington (54)	Woods (54)	Harrington Final Round	Woods Final Round	Harrington (72)	Woods (72)
2007 Open	-3	-1	-4	-1	-7	-2

Under the parameters set, Woods and Harrington crossed paths once. Harrington leads Woods **1-0-0** and with a final round score of **-4** vs. **-1**.

Rory McIlroy vs. Tiger Woods						
	McIlroy (54)	Woods (54)	McIlroy Final Round	Woods Final Round	McIlroy (72)	Woods (72)

There is no data.

Adam Scott vs. Tiger Woods						
	Scott (54)	Woods (54)	Scott Final Round	Woods Final Round	Scott (72)	Woods (72)
2006 Open	-9	-13	0	-5	-9	-18
2013 Masters	-6	-3	-3	-2	-9	-5
2019 Masters	-7	-11	+1	-2	-6	-13

Under the criteria established, Woods and Scott met three times. Woods leads the series at **2-1-0** and in total final round scoring by **-9** to **-2**.

The composite results for the above show that for the 20 head-to-head match ups, Woods leads his top 10 competitors **14-6-0**. In addition, Woods outscored his top 10 competitors in final rounds by 21 shots at **-44** to **-23**.

Let's expand the field of players to see how Nicklaus and Woods fare.

Combined Major Championship Victory & Top-10 Placement Leaders

At the time of this writing, there have been 36 professional golfers with 20 or more top-10 finishes in major championships (modern version). Below is the list:

Most Top-10 Placements in Major Championships	
Player	Total Placements
Jack Nicklaus	73
Sam Snead	48
Tom Watson	46
Gary Player	44
Tiger Woods	41
Ben Hogan	40
Phil Mickelson	39
Arnold Palmer	38
Gene Sarazen	36
Ernie Els	35
Walter Hagen	32
Greg Norman	30
Byron Nelson	28
Raymond Floyd	28
Ben Crenshaw	27
Rory McIlroy	27
Nick Faldo	26
Fred Couples	26
J. H. Taylor	24
Lloyd Mangrum	24
Billy Casper	24
Harry Vardon	23

Tom Kite	23
Vijay Singh	23
Jim Furyk	23
Julius Boros	22
Lee Trevino	22
Dustin Johnson	22
Tom Weiskopf	21
Nick Price	21
Davis Love III	21
Alex Herd	20
Peter Thomson	20
Gene Littler	20
Seve Ballesteros	20
Hale Irwin	20

In this graphic, Nicklaus completely dominates. His 73 top-10 finishes lead Sam Snead's total of 48 by an astounding 25. What makes this even more incredible is Snead's longevity of competitiveness in the game has thus far been unrivaled (i.e. winning the 1965 Greater Greensboro Open at age 52 and placing third in the 1974 PGA Championship at age 62 behind Trevino and Nicklaus, just to name a couple of latter-career accomplishments).

Below provides detail of the top 10 players on this listing:

	Masters	U.S. Open	Open	PGA	Total
Jack Nicklaus	22	18	18	15	73
Sam Snead	15	12	2	19	48
Tom Watson	15	11	10	10	46
Gary Player	15	9	12	8	44
Tiger Woods	14	8	10	9	41
Ben Hogan	17	15	1	7	40
Phil Mickelson	15	10	4	10	39
Arnold Palmer	12	13	7	6	38
Gene Sarazen	4	14	6	12	36
Ernie Els	6	10	13	6	35

118

Nicklaus is well ahead of Woods' impressive total of 41, which places the latter in fifth. Below isolates a comparative detail of the respective top-10 finishes for Nicklaus and Woods:

	Masters	U.S. Open	Open	PGA	Total
Nicklaus	22	18	18	15	73
Woods	14	8	10	9	41
Variance	8	10	8	6	32

The above two views are all of Nicklaus' finishes within the top 10. Focusing on the 25-year spans as professionals between him and Woods, the numbers reduce.

	Masters	U.S. Open	Open	PGA	Total
Nicklaus	18	16	18	15	67
Woods	14	8	10	9	41
Variance	4	8	8	6	26

In reference to the complete listing of 36 players, the next table shows which **34** players were chief competitors of Nicklaus, of Woods, and which were either marginal/neither. The results provide good insight to who Nicklaus and Woods faced.

Nicklaus Era	Woods Era	Marginal / Neither
Tom Watson (46)	Phil Mickelson (39)	Sam Snead (48)
Gary Player (44)	Ernie Els (35)	Ben Hogan (40)
Arnold Palmer (38)	Rory McIlroy (27)	Gene Sarazen (36)
Greg Norman (30)	Vijay Singh (23)	Walter Hagen (32)
Raymond Floyd (28)	Jim Furyk (23)	Byron Nelson (28)
Ben Crenshaw (27)	Dustin Johnson (22)	Fred Couples (26)
Nick Faldo (26)	Davis Love III (21)	J. H. Taylor (24)
Billy Casper (24)		Lloyd Mangrum (24)
Tom Kite (23)		Harry Vardon (23)
Julius Boros (22)		Nick Price (21)
Lee Trevino (22)		Alex Herd (20)
Tom Weiskopf (21)		Peter Thomson (20)

| Seve Ballesteros (20) |
| Hale Irwin (20) |
| Gene Littler (20) |

Total Players: 15	Total Players: 7	Total Players: 12
Total Top 10s: 411	Total Top 10s: 190	Total Top 10s: 342

Nicklaus competed against 15 players with a minimum of 20 top-10 finishes each in major championships. These 15 players achieved a total of 411 top-10 finishes, yet Nicklaus was still able to win 18 times and notch 73 top-10 placements of his own.

Woods won 15 major championships and accumulated 41 top-10 placements wherein seven competitors in his era garnered 190 top-10 finishes. This undoubtedly confirms the great play of Mickelson, Els, McIlroy, Singh, Furyk, Johnson, and Love III.

As a collective ratio between the Nicklaus competitors and Woods competitors, the number of players to top-10 placements is virtually the same. Yet, the total number on Nicklaus' side of the ledger is well over double. When Nicklaus' and Woods' individual top-10 finishes are factored in, Nicklaus's era leads Woods' era thus far by 484 to 231.

Below shows the same players and their respective numbers of major championships won:

Nicklaus Era	Woods Era	Marginal / Neither
Tom Watson (8)	Phil Mickelson (6)	Sam Snead (7)
Gary Player (9)	Ernie Els (4)	Ben Hogan (9)
Arnold Palmer (7)	Rory McIlroy (4)	Gene Sarazen (7)
Greg Norman (2)	Vijay Singh (3)	Walter Hagen (11)
Raymond Floyd (4)	Jim Furyk (1)	Byron Nelson (5)
Ben Crenshaw (2)	Dustin Johnson (2)	Fred Couples (1)
Nick Faldo (6)	Davis Love III (1)	J. H. Taylor (1)
Billy Casper (3)		Lloyd Mangrum (1)

Tom Kite (1)		Harry Vardon (7)
Julius Boros (3)		Nick Price (3)
Lee Trevino (6)		Alex Herd (1)
Tom Weiskopf (1)		Peter Thomson (5)
Seve Ballesteros (5)		
Hale Irwin (3)		
Gene Littler (1)		

Total Players: 15	Total Players: 7	Total Players: 12
Total Victories: 61	Total Victories: 21	Total Victories: 58

Almost by default, having more than twice the total players in Nicklaus' era should translate to more major championship wins than in Woods' era. The following illustrates the win totals on average, per player.

Average Victories: 4.07	Average Victories: 3.00	Average Victories: 4.83

The Nicklaus' competitor era average is noticeably higher than the Woods' competitor era average. When Nicklaus and Woods are added in, the numbers across all three segments change as follows.

Total Players: 16	Total Players: 8	Total Players: 12
Total Victories: 79	Total Victories: 36	Total Victories: 58
Average Victories: 4.94	Average Victories: 4.50	Average Victories: 4.83

Once the data for Nicklaus and Woods are added, it confirms how dominant Woods has been as the total wins increase by almost 75.00%. Nicklaus' 18 wins have less of an impact raising the previous total by nearly 30.00%. Finally, the average victory numbers across the three silos flatten out.

Number of Different Major Champions

During the 25-year period of 1962 through 1986, there were 100 major championships contested. Of these 100, there were 46 different champions. The following provides the detail per year.

Major Champions (1962 – 1986)				
Year	Masters	U.S. Open	Open	PGA
1962	Palmer	Nicklaus	Palmer	Player
1963	Nicklaus	Boros	Charles	Nicklaus
1964	Palmer	Venturi	Lema	Nichols
1965	Nicklaus	Player	Thomson	Marr
1966	Nicklaus	Casper	Nicklaus	Geiberger
1967	Brewer	Nicklaus	DeVicenzo	January
1968	Goalby	Trevino	Player	Boros
1969	Archer	Moody	Jacklin	Floyd
1970	Casper	Jacklin	Nicklaus	Stockton
1971	Coody	Trevino	Trevino	Nicklaus
1972	Nicklaus	Nicklaus	Trevino	Player
1973	Aaron	Miller	Weiskopf	Nicklaus
1974	Player	Irwin	Player	Trevino
1975	Nicklaus	L. Graham	T. Watson	Nicklaus
1976	Floyd	Pate	Miller	Stockton
1977	T. Watson	H. Green	T. Watson	Wadkins
1978	Player	North	Nicklaus	Mahaffey
1979	Zoeller	Irwin	Ballesteros	D. Graham
1980	Ballesteros	Nicklaus	T. Watson	Nicklaus
1981	T. Watson	D. Graham	Rogers	L. Nelson
1982	Stadler	T. Watson	T. Watson	Floyd
1983	Ballesteros	L. Nelson	T. Watson	Sutton
1984	Crenshaw	Zoeller	Ballesteros	Trevino
1985	Langer	North	Lyle	H. Green
1986	Nicklaus	Floyd	Norman	Tway

While these 46 players were victorious during this period, they won an additional 19 major championships throughout their careers bringing their cumulative total to 119. In addition, 23 of the 46 players were multiple major champions. These same 46 players won a combined 707 PGA tournaments as itemized below.

Major Champions (1962 – 1986)			
Player	**Majors Won (1962- 1986)**	**Career Majors Won**	**Career PGA Wins**
Nicklaus	18	18	73
T. Watson	8	8	39
Player	7	9	24
Trevino	6	6	29
Ballesteros	4	5	9
Floyd	4	4	22
Palmer	3	7	62
Casper	2	3	51
Irwin	2	3	20
Boros	2	3	18
L. Nelson	2	3	10
Miller	2	2	25
Green	2	2	19
Stockton	2	2	10
Zoeller	2	2	10
D. Graham	2	2	8
Jacklin	2	2	4
North	2	2	3
Thomson	1	5	6
Norman	1	2	20
Crenshaw	1	2	19
Lyle	1	2	6
Langer	1	2	3
Wadkins	1	1	21
Weiskopf	1	1	16
Venturi	1	1	14
Sutton	1	1	14
Stadler	1	1	13
Archer	1	1	12
Lema	1	1	12
Geiberger	1	1	11
Goalby	1	1	11

Nichols	1	1	11
Pate	1	1	11
Brewer	1	1	10
January	1	1	10
Mahaffey	1	1	10
Tway	1	1	8
Charles	1	1	6
L. Graham	1	1	6
Rogers	1	1	6
DeVicenzo	1	1	5
Aaron	1	1	3
Coody	1	1	3
Marr	1	1	3
Moody	1	1	1

Let's review the corresponding data for Woods and his competitors from 1997 through 2022.

Major Champions (1997 – 2022)				
Year	Masters	U.S. Open	Open	PGA
1997	Woods	Els	Leonard	Love III
1998	O'Meara	Janzen	O'Meara	Singh
1999	Olazabal	Stewart	Lawrie	Woods
2000	Singh	Woods	Woods	Woods
2001	Woods	Goosen	Duval	Toms
2002	Woods	Woods	Els	Beem
2003	Weir	Furyk	Curtis	Micheel
2004	Mickelson	Goosen	Hamilton	Singh
2005	Woods	Campbell	Woods	Mickelson
2006	Mickelson	Ogilvy	Woods	Woods
2007	Z. Johnson	Cabrera	Harrington	Woods
2008	Immelman	Woods	Harrington	Harrington
2009	Cabrera	Glover	Cink	Yang
2010	Mickelson	McDowell	Oosthuizen	Kaymer
2011	Schwartzel	McIlroy	Clarke	Bradley

2012	B. Watson	W. Simpson	Els	McIlroy
2013	Scott	Rose	Mickelson	Dufner
2014	B. Watson	Kaymer	McIlroy	McIlroy
2015	Spieth	Spieth	Z. Johnson	Day
2016	Willett	D. Johnson	Stenson	Walker
2017	Garcia	Koepka	Spieth	Thomas
2018	Reed	Koepka	Molinari	Koepka
2019	Woods	Woodland	Lowry	Koepka
2020	D. Johnson	DeChambeau	DNP	Morikawa
2021	Matsuyama	Rahm	Morikawa	Mickelson
2022	Scheffler	Fitzpatrick	Smith	Thomas

For these 103 majors contested, 61 different champions emerge. The players were victorious in five other major championships bringing their cumulative total to 108. Also, 20 of the 61 players were multiple major champions. Lastly, these players have a total PGA victory number of 606. The following graphic shows the detail per year in the same format.

Major Champions (1997 – 2022)			
Player	Majors Won (1997- 2022)	Career Majors Won	Career PGA Wins
Woods	15	15	82
Mickelson	6	6	45
McIlroy	4	4	21
Koepka	4	4	8
Els	3	4	19
Singh	3	3	34
Spieth	3	3	13
Harrington	3	3	6
D. Johnson	2	2	24
O'Meara	2	2	16
Thomas	2	2	15
B. Watson	2	2	12
Z. Johnson	2	2	12
Goosen	2	2	7
Morikawa	2	2	5

Cabrera	2	2	3
Kaymer	2	2	3
Stewart	1	3	11
Janzen	1	2	8
Olazabal	1	2	6
Love III	1	1	21
Furyk	1	1	17
Scott	1	1	14
Duval	1	1	13
Toms	1	1	13
Day	1	1	12
Leonard	1	1	12
Garcia	1	1	11
Rose	1	1	10
Reed	1	1	9
Cink	1	1	8
DeChambeau	1	1	8
Matsuyama	1	1	8
Ogilvy	1	1	8
Weir	1	1	8
Rahm	1	1	7
W. Simpson	1	1	7
Smith	1	1	6
Stenson	1	1	6
Walker	1	1	6
Dufner	1	1	5
Bradley	1	1	4
Curtis	1	1	4
McDowell	1	1	4
Scheffler	1	1	4
Woodland	1	1	4
Beem	1	1	3
Clarke	1	1	3
Glover	1	1	3

Molinari		1	1	3
Immelman		1	1	2
Lowry		1	1	2
Schwartzel		1	1	2
Yang		1	1	2
Campbell		1	1	1
Fitzpatrick		1	1	1
Hamilton		1	1	1
Lawrie		1	1	1
Micheel		1	1	1
Oosthuizen		1	1	1
Willett		1	1	1

With the preceding information, below is a high-level comparative summary. As a reminder, there is one extra year (three major championships) factored in the "Woods Era" data.

	Total Different Major Champions	Total Major Championships Won	Total PGA Tournaments Won
Nicklaus Era (1962 – 1986)	46	119	707
Woods Era (1997 – 2022)	61	108	606
Variance	(15)	11	101

It should be noted for specific verifiability, only *PGA Tournaments Won* have been included for the above tables. While many players listed in the Woods era have won numerous events overseas (i.e. Ernie Els, Angel Cabrera, Jose Maria Olazabal, etc.), the same is also true for the Nicklaus era (i.e. Gary Player, Seve Ballesteros, Roberto DeVicenzo, etc.). For this segue, the Nicklaus era would likely outpace the Woods era.

Having gathered and presented the above information in detail and summary, the following items should now be included.

Foreign Invasion

Another element to review when considering competitors in Nicklaus' and Woods' eras is the impact of non-U.S. players. With the game of golf expanding, it makes sense the competition of non-U.S. players would be greater for Woods. Let's see to what degree that is the case.

	Total Non-U.S. Major Champions	Majors Won Per Era	Total Majors Won	Total PGA Tournaments Won
Nicklaus Era (1962 – 1986)	10	21	31	91
Woods Era (1997 – 2022)	30	42	44	212
Variance	(20)	(21)	(13)	(121)
% Increase	200.00%	100.00%	41.94%	132.97%

The preceding graphic confirms the significant growth in non-U.S. player competition. Below expands on this concept:

Nicklaus Era Top-5 Distribution in Major Championships			
	(1962 – 1969)	(1970 – 1979)	(1980 – 1986)
Total Players	184	230	157
Total Non – U.S. Players	50	38	49
Non – U.S. Player %	27.17%	16.52%	31.21%
Total Champions	32	40	28
Total Non – U.S. Champions	7	7	7
Non – U.S. Champion %	21.88%	17.50%	25.00%

For the 25-year, 100-major championship era above, 21 champions – or 21.00%, were non-U.S. players. Of the players finishing in the top-five for this period totaling 571, 137 – or 23.99%, were non-U.S. competitors.

Woods Era Top-5 Distribution in Major Championships			
	(1997 – 1999)	(2000 – 2009)	(2010 – 2019)	(2020 – 2022)
Total Players	70	236	235	66
Total Non – U.S. Players	23	124	120	33

Non – U.S. Player %	32.86%	52.54%	51.06%	50.00%
Total Champions	12	40	40	11
Total Non – U.S. Champions	4	15	19	4
Non – U.S. Champion %	33.33%	37.50%	47.50%	36.36%

In the Woods era above, the 2020 Open Championship (coronavirus) is deducted. Therefore, the timeframe consists of 103 major championships to summarize. For this era, 42 champions – or 40.78%, were non-U.S. players. Of the players finishing in the top-five for this period totaling 607, 300 – or 49.42%, were non-U.S. The increase of non-U.S. players is substantial.

Average Age of Major Champions Per Era

As the game of golf grows, players are becoming accomplished at younger ages. How has this impacted the Nicklaus and Woods eras for major champions?

- **Nicklaus Era (1962 – 1986) Average Age:** 31.74
- **Woods Era (1997 – 2022) Average Age:** 31.17

The figures prove there has been a minimal reduction in the average age of major champions.

Major Championship Runner-up Finishes

In addition to the record number of 18 major championship victories, Jack Nicklaus has an even more unique record – 19 second-place finishes (includes the 1960 U.S. Open as an amateur). Below is the breakdown:

- **Masters:**   4
- **U.S. Open:**   4
- **Open Championship:**   7
- **PGA Championship:**   4

For Tiger Woods, his 15 major championship victories are supplemented by seven second-place finishes. Below is the breakdown:

- **Masters:**   2
- **U.S. Open:**   2
- **Open Championship:** 0
- **PGA Championship:**   3

Let's review in detail the distribution of each player's second-place finishes.

Jack Nicklaus Major Championship Runner-up Finishes				
Year	Championship	Champion	Total Majors Over Nicklaus	Total Majors Won
1960	U.S. Open	Arnold Palmer	2	7
1964	Masters	Arnold Palmer		
1964	Open	Tony Lema	1	1
1964	PGA	Bobby Nichols	1	1
1965	PGA	Dave Marr	1	1
1967	Open	Roberto DeVicenzo	1	1
1968	U.S. Open	Lee Trevino	4	6
1968	Open	Gary Player	1	9
1971	Masters	Charles Coody	1	1
1971	U.S. Open	Lee Trevino		
1972	Open	Lee Trevino		
1974	PGA	Lee Trevino		
1976	Open	Johnny Miller	1	2
1977	Masters	Tom Watson	4	8
1977	Open	Tom Watson		
1979	Open	Seve Ballesteros	1	5
1981	Masters	Tom Watson		
1982	U.S. Open	Tom Watson		
1983	PGA	Hal Sutton	1	1

Nicklaus finished second on 19 occasions to 12 different players who won a total of 43 major championships. Nicklaus' second-place finishes are distributed below by decade.

- **1960s:**   8
- **1970s:**   8
- **1980s:**   3

With Nicklaus' first second-place finish in the 1960 U.S. Open as a 20-year-old amateur and his final in the 1983 PGA Championship at age 43, this 24-year all-inclusive range nearly equals his 25-year victory range from the 1962 U.S. Open through the 1986 Masters.

Adding to the volume of second place finishes, Nicklaus missed playoffs for victory by one shot on five separate occasions as noted.

- **1963 Open Championship – Third Place**
    - Bob Charles defeated Phil Rodgers
- **1967 PGA Championship – Third Place**
    - Don January defeated Don Massengale
- **1975 Open Championship – Third Place**
    - Tom Watson defeated Jack Newton
- **1977 PGA Championship – Third Place**
    - Lanny Wadkins defeated Gene Littler
- **1979 Masters – Fourth Place**
    - Fuzzy Zoeller defeated Ed Sneed and Tom Watson

The expression "no one remembers who finished second" does have relevance. However, along with Nicklaus' victories in major championships, the above further illustrates an incredible level of consistency and longevity in the most difficult arenas.

This does not imply all of Nicklaus' 19 second-place finishes were close calls. Some were distant (i.e. 1964 Masters, 1964 Open, 1968 U.S. Open, and the 1976 Open). Yet on 24 occasions, he was either second alone, tied for second, or missed tying for first by one shot. Along with 18 wins, this is an astounding 42 major championships. Moreover, second-place (and other top-tier) finishes are important as they mean more money, more FedEx Cup points, more Presidents Cup points, more Ryder Cup points, and more World Ranking points.

Tiger Woods Major Championship Runner-up Finishes				
Year	Championship	Champion	Total Majors Over Woods	Total Majors Won
2002	PGA	Rich Beem	1	1
2005	U.S. Open	Michael Campbell	1	1
2007	Masters	Zach Johnson	1	2
2007	U.S. Open	Angel Cabrera	1	2
2008	Masters	Trevor Immelman	1	1
2009	PGA	Y.E. Yang	1	1
2018	PGA	Brooks Koepka	1	4

Woods finished second seven times in major championships to seven different players. These players won a total of 12 major championships. Woods' second place finishes occurred over a 17-year period from 2002 through 2018, all-inclusive. While Woods' major championship victories spanned 23 years from 1997 through 2019, his runner-up range lasted nearly as long.

In line with Nicklaus, Woods had one third-place finish a single shot out of a playoff.

- **1998 Open Championship – Third Place**
  - o   Mark O'Meara defeated Brian Watts

Though not as voluminous as Nicklaus, Woods' record in major championships of 15 wins and seven runner-up finishes in his first 84 as a professional shows a 26.19% combined placement rate, which is remarkable.

Major Championship Final Round Performance When Leading After 54 Holes

Tiger Woods has proven himself the greatest front-runner in the history of professional golf when leading after 54 holes. He has won 54 of 58 events when either leading outright or holding a share of the lead – a 93.10% conversion rate. However, as both Woods and Jack Nicklaus have declared major championships are the standard by which players should be remembered. How do the two compare in this category?

Jack Nicklaus & Tiger Woods Victory Rate When Leading/Co-leading After 54 Holes			
	Solo & Co-leads	Victories	Conversion %
Nicklaus	12	10	83.33%
Woods	15	14	93.33%

Nicklaus either led alone or was tied for the lead in major championships on 12 occasions heading into the final round. While he won 10, below provides detail of the two he did not.

- **1971 Masters – Charles Coody, Champion**
  - 54-hole Co-leaders
    - Jack Nicklaus & Charles Coody
  - Final Round Score – Nicklaus
    - 72 (even par)
  - Final Round Score – Coody
    - 70 (2-under par)
- **1977 Open Championship – Tom Watson, Champion**
  - 54-hole Co-leaders
    - Jack Nicklaus & Tom Watson
  - Final Round Score – Nicklaus
    - 66 (4-under par)
  - Final Round Score – Watson
    - 65 (5-under par)

For Woods, 14 of his 15 major championship victories came when leading after 54 holes. However, when he led after 54 holes for a 15th time, he was unsuccessful. Here is the summary of that unexpected loss.

- **2009 PGA – Y.E. Yang, Champion**
  - 54-hole Leader
    - Tiger Woods
      - 2 Shots
  - Final Round Score – Woods
    - 75 (3-over par)

o   Final Round Score – Yang
  ▪   70 (2-under par)

Even though Nicklaus did not win the 1971 Masters or the 1977 Open Championship, his final rounds were sound. Shooting even par at Augusta is somewhat flat, it just happened that Coody shot two-under. As for shooting a four-under par 66 in the final round of the Open Championship, that is exceptional. However, Watson was able to go five-under the same day. The latter is arguably the greatest head-to-head battle in professional golf with Watson shooting 65-65 to Nicklaus' 65-66 during the last 36 holes of play. With Hubert Green finishing in third place 10 shots behind Nicklaus, it lives up to the hype.

Conversely, Woods' three-over par 75 during the final round of the 2009 PGA Championship was uncharacteristic. Yang was able to win by shooting a solid two-under par 70.

Jack Nicklaus & Tiger Woods Victory Rate When Leading Alone After 54 Holes			
	Solo Leads Only	**Victories**	**Conversion %**
Nicklaus	8	8	100.00%
Woods	12	11	91.67%

Nicklaus attained the outright 54-hole lead on eight occasions by a total of 22 shots for an average margin of 2.75 shots per event. He was successful in converting all eight solo leads to victories. In Woods' case, he held the outright lead on 12 occasions by a total of 43 shots, or 3.58 shots per event. He was successful in converting 11 of these leads to victories; a synopsis of the loss (2009 PGA Championship) was previously outlined.

Major Championship Final Round Performance When Trailing After 54 Holes

Once again using a four-shot threshold, the following study delineates how Jack Nicklaus and Tiger Woods performed relative to their competition when trailing the 54-hole leaders from one to four shots in all applicable major championships as professionals.

Jack Nicklaus Trailing Status After 54 Holes			
Championship	54-hole Leader(s)	Shots Trailing	54-hole Placement
1962 U.S. Open	Bobby Nichols, Arnold Palmer	2	T-5
1963 Open	Bob Charles	2	T-3
1963 PGA	Bruce Crampton	3	3
1965 PGA	Tommy Aaron, Dave Marr	2	T-4
1966 U.S. Open	Arnold Palmer	4	3
1966 Open	Phil Rodgers	2	2
1967 U.S. Open	Marty Fleckman	1	T-2
1967 Open	Roberto DeVicenzo	3	3
1967 PGA	Dan Sikes	2	T-2
1968 Masters	Gary Player	4	T-11
1968 Open	Billy Casper	4	4
1970 Open	Lee Trevino	2	T-2
1971 U.S. Open	Jim Simons	2	2
1973 U.S. Open	Julius Boros, Jerry Heard, Arnold Palmer, John Schlee	4	T-9
1974 Open	Gary Player	4	3
1974 PGA	Lee Trevino	1	2
1975 Masters	Tom Weiskopf	1	2
1975 Open	Bobby Coles	4	T-5
1976 PGA	Charles Coody	2	T-2
1977 Masters	Tom Watson	3	4
1977 PGA	Gene Littler	4	2
1978 Open	Peter Oosterhuis, Tom Watson	1	T-3
1979 Open	Hale Irwin	3	T-3
1981 Masters	Tom Watson	1	2
1982 U.S. Open	Bill Rogers, Tom Watson	3	T-7
1986 Masters	Greg Norman	4	T-9

Nicklaus was behind in 26 events after 54 holes from one to four strokes. While he was four shots behind on eight occasions, his average deficit was 2.62 shots with a corresponding average placement of 3.81 and maximum of 11th place once. Let's review how Nicklaus capitalized.

Jack Nicklaus Performance When Trailing After 54 Holes						
	Final Round Score (Nicklaus)		Final Placement (Nicklaus)		Final Round Score (Champ)	
Championship	Gross	To Par		Champion	Gross	To Par
1962 U.S. Open	69	-2	1	Nicklaus	69	-2
1963 Open	70	0	3	Charles	71	+1
1963 PGA	68	-3	1	Nicklaus	68	-3
1965 PGA	71	0	T-2	Marr	71	0
1966 U.S. Open	74	4	3	Casper	68	-2
1966 Open	70	-1	1	Nicklaus	70	-1
1967 U.S. Open	65	-5	1	Nicklaus	65	-5
1967 Open	69	-3	2	DeVicenzo	70	-2
1967 PGA	71	-1	T-3	January	71	-1
1968 Masters	67	-5	T-5	Goalby	66	-6
1968 Open	73	+1	2	Player	73	+1
1970 Open	73	+1	1	Nicklaus	73	+1
1971 U.S. Open	71	+1	2	Trevino	69	-1
1973 U.S. Open	68	-3	T-4	Miller	63	-8
1974 Open	71	0	3	Player	70	-1
1974 PGA	69	-1	2	Trevino	69	-1
1975 Masters	68	-4	1	Nicklaus	68	-4
1975 Open	72	0	T-3	T. Watson	72	0
1976 PGA	74	+4	T-4	Stockton	70	0
1977 Masters	66	-6	2	T. Watson	67	-5
1977 PGA	73	+1	3	Wadkins	70	-2
1978 Open	69	-3	1	Nicklaus	69	-3
1979 Open	72	+1	T-2	Ballesteros	70	-1
1981 Masters	72	0	T-2	T. Watson	71	-1
1982 U.S. Open	69	-3	2	T. Watson	70	-2
1986 Masters	65	-7	1	Nicklaus	65	-7

Nicklaus was able to win on eight of the 26 occasions, or 30.77%. For the eight wins, he was behind an average of 2.62 strokes and shot an average final round of 68.38 or three-under par. Regarding the entire 26 final rounds, Nicklaus shot in the 60s 12 times, was under par 14 times, and averaged 69.96

per round or 1.31-under par. His scores moved him from an average position after 54 holes of 3.81 to 2.15 after 72 holes. All champions of these 26 majors averaged 69.15 or 2.12-under par for their final rounds – this includes the wins by Nicklaus. When Nicklaus is factored out, the average final round score is 69.50 or 1.72-under par.

Tiger Woods Trailing Status After 54 Holes			
Championship	54-hole Leader(s)	Shots Trailing	54-hole Placement
1999 U.S. Open	Payne Stewart	2	T-3
2003 Masters	Jeff Maggert	4	T-5
2003 Open	Thomas Bjorn	2	T-3
2004 Open	Todd Hamilton	4	T-7
2006 Masters	Phil Mickelson	2	T-4
2007 Masters	Stuart Appleby	1	T-2
2007 U.S. Open	Aaron Baddeley	2	2
2010 Masters	Lee Westwood	4	T-3
2013 Masters	Angel Cabrera, Brandt Snedeker	4	T-7
2013 Open	Lee Westwood	2	T-2
2018 Open	Kevin Kisner, Xander Schauffele, Jordan Spieth	4	T-6
2018 PGA	Brooks Koepka	4	T-6
2019 Masters	Francesco Molinari	2	T-2

In 13 major championships as a professional, Woods was behind after 54 holes from one to four strokes. While he was four shots behind on six occasions, his average deficit was 2.85 shots with a corresponding average placement of 4.08 and maximum of seventh place twice. Let's review how Woods capitalized.

Tiger Woods Performance When Trailing After 54 Holes						
	Final Round Score (Woods)		Final Placement		Final Round Score (Champ)	
Championship	Gross	To Par	(Woods)	Champion	Gross	To Par
1999 U.S. Open	70	0	T-3	Stewart	70	0
2003 Masters	75	+3	T-15	Weir	68	-4
2003 Open	71	0	T-4	Curtis	69	-2

2004 Open	72	+1	T-9	Hamilton	69	-2
2006 Masters	70	-2	T-3	Mickelson	69	-3
2007 Masters	72	0	T-2	Z. Johnson	69	-3
2007 U.S. Open	72	+2	T-2	Cabrera	69	-1
2010 Masters	69	-3	T-4	Mickelson	67	-5
2013 Masters	70	-2	T-4	Scott	69	-3
2013 Open	74	+3	T-6	Mickelson	66	-5
2018 Open	71	0	T-6	Molinari	69	-2
2018 PGA	64	-6	2	Koepka	66	-4
2019 Masters	70	-2	1	Woods	70	-2

Woods was able to win once out of 13 occasions. He averaged 70.77 or 0.46-under par in final round scoring which moved him from an average starting position of 4.08 to 4.69 at the conclusion of 72 holes. Woods shot in the 60s twice and was under par five times. All champions of these 13 majors, including Woods averaged 68.46 or 2.77-under par for their final rounds. For Woods' competitors, their average score was 68.33 and were under par by 2.83 strokes.

Below provides a comparative tabular summary:

Jack Nicklaus & Tiger Woods Summary When Trailing After 54 Holes							
	Average Shot Deficit	Total Major Championships	Average Final Round Score		Rounds in the 60s	Rounds Under Par	Wins
			Gross	To Par			
Nicklaus	2.62	26	69.96	(1.31)	12	14	8
Woods	2.85	13	70.77	(0.46)	2	5	1
Variance	(0.23)	13	(0.81)	(0.85)	10	9	7

Nicklaus' performance when entering the final rounds of major championships trailing the 54-four-hole leader surpasses that of Woods.

As a corollary to Nicklaus and Woods for their final round performances in major championship play, the following is noted.

During 20 final rounds for Nicklaus which include his 18 victories – 10 when leading/co-leading after 54 holes plus the eight he won when entering the final round behind the leader(s) – he is a combined 30-under par with 11 of 20 rounds in the 60s. His stroke average is 69.80 or 1.50-under par with a low round of 65 (twice) and high of 74 (twice). His lowest under par round is -7 and highest over par round is +2 (twice).

Woods registered 15 final rounds when leading/co-leading after 54 holes plus one round under a two-shot deficit position encompassing his 15 victories. He was a combined 28-under par with eight of 16 rounds in the 60s. Woods' stroke average was 69.88 or 1.75-under par with a low round of 67 (three times) and a high of 75. His lowest under par score was -5 (twice) and highest over par was +3.

Playoff Records

Relative to the total number of playoffs Tiger Woods participated in, he has the greatest win-loss percentage in professional golf. Jack Nicklaus has been involved in more playoffs and also has a winning record. However, there is a significant gap between the two players when the numbers are examined closely.

Jack Nicklaus Playoff Record				
Year	Event	Opponent	Win	Loss
1962	Houston Classic	Bobby Nichols		X
1962	U.S. Open	Arnold Palmer	X	
1963	Palm Springs Golf Classic	Gary Player	X	
1963	Western Open	Arnold Palmer		X
1964	Australian Open	Bruce Devlin	X	
1965	Pensacola Open	Doug Sanders		X
1965	Memphis Open	Johnny Pott	X	
1966	Masters	Gay Brewer, Tommy Jacobs	X	
1968	American Golf Classic	Frank Beard, Lee Elder	X	
1969	Kaiser International	George Archer, Billy Casper, Don January	X	
1970	Byron Nelson Classic	Arnold Palmer	X	
1970	Open Championship	Doug Sanders	X	
1971	Atlanta Golf Classic	Gardner Dickinson		X

1971	U.S. Open	Lee Trevino		X
1972	Bing Crosby National Pro-Am	Johnny Miller	X	
1972	Tournament of Champions	Bobby Mitchell		X
1973	Bing Crosby National Pro-Am	Raymond Floyd, Orville Moody	X	
1973	Greater New Orleans Open	Miller Barber	X	
1974	World Open	Johnny Miller		X
1975	Canadian Open	Tom Weiskopf		X
1975	World Open	Billy Casper	X	
1977	Tournament of Champions	Bruce Lietzke	X	
1980	Doral-Eastern Open	Raymond Floyd		X
1982	Bay Hill Classic	Tom Kite		X
1984	Memorial Tournament	Andy Bean	X	

Tiger Woods Playoff Record				
Year	**Event**	**Opponent**	**Win**	**Loss**
1996	Las Vegas Invitational	Davis Love III	X	
1997	Mercedes Championships	Tom Lehman	X	
1998	Johnnie Walker Classic	Ernie Els	X	
1998	Nissan Open	Billy Mayfair		X
1998	Nedbank Golf Challenge	Nick Price		X
1999	American Express Championship	Miguel Angel-Jimenez	X	
2000	Mercedes Championships	Ernie Els	X	
2000	PGA Championship	Bob May	X	
2001	NEC Invitational	Jim Furyk	X	
2002	Deutsche Bank - SAP Open	Colin Montgomerie	X	
2005	Masters	Chris DiMarco	X	
2005	American Express Championship	John Daly	X	
2006	Dubai Desert Classic	Ernie Els	X	
2006	Buick Invitational	Nathan Green, Jose Maria Olazabal	X	
2006	Bridgestone Invitational	Stewart Cink	X	

2006	Dunlop Phoenix Open	Padraig Harrington		X
2008	U.S. Open	Rocco Mediate	X	
2010	Chevron World Challenge	Graeme McDowell		X
2013	Northwestern Mutual World Challenge	Zach Johnson		X

Now, let review each player's record in greater detail.

Jack Nicklaus Playoff Record					
Major Championships		Official PGA Events		Worldwide & Unofficial	
Win	Loss	Win	Loss	Win	Loss
3	1	15	10	15	10

The following will supplement the above illustration of Nicklaus' playoff results.

- **Major Championships**
  - Record
    - 3-1
  - Win Percentage
    - 75.00%
  - Winning Opponent(s)
    - Lee Trevino
      - 1971 U.S. Open
- **Official PGA Events**
  - Record
    - 15-10
  - Win Percentage
    - 60.00%
  - Winning Opponent(s)
    - Bobby Nichols
    - Arnold Palmer
    - Doug Sanders
    - Gardner Dickinson
    - Lee Trevino
    - Bobby Mitchell
    - Johnny Miller

- Tom Weiskopf
    - Raymond Floyd
    - Tom Kite
- **Worldwide & Unofficial**
    - Record
        - See "Official PGA Events."
    - Win Percentage
        - See "Official PGA Events."
    - Winning Opponent(s)
        - See "Official PGA Events."

Nicklaus' playoff record is sound. Is it one to match his other achievements? No. Of the four majors he played off for, he lost only once and that was to Lee Trevino during the greatest run of the latter player's career. Of the 10 players he lost to, five are Hall of Fame members – Palmer, Trevino, Miller, Floyd, and Kite. Yet, while it would be natural to assume Nicklaus to have a higher win percentage in playoffs, the 10 players to whom he lost won a total of 214 PGA tournaments including 22 major championships. What about the 18 players he won against in the 15 playoff victories? They include five Hall of Fame members and combined for 305 PGA wins including 29 major championships.

Tiger Woods Playoff Record					
Major Championships		**Official PGA Events**		**Worldwide & Unofficial**	
Win	**Loss**	**Win**	**Loss**	**Win**	**Loss**
3	0	11	1	14	5

The following will supplement the above illustration of Woods' playoff results.

- **Major Championships**
    - Record
        - 3-0
    - Win Percentage
        - 100.00%
    - Winning Opponent(s)
        - None
- **Official PGA Events**
    - Record

- 11-1
  - ○ Win Percentage
    - 91.67%
  - ○ Winning Opponent(s)
    - Billy Mayfair
- **Worldwide & Unofficial**
  - ○ Record
    - 14-5
  - ○ Win Percentage
    - 73.68%
  - ○ Winning Opponent(s)
    - Billy Mayfair
    - Nick Price
    - Padraig Harrington
    - Graeme McDowell
    - Zach Johnson

While the five players Woods lost to do not have the credentials the 10 had to whom Nicklaus lost, Price is already in the Hall of Fame, while Harrington and Johnson will be elected in the future. These five players have won 45 PGA events including nine major championships. What about the 13 players he won against in the 14 playoff victories? They include three Hall of Fame members and combined for 91 PGA wins including 12 major championships.

Below provides a comparison of Nicklaus' and Woods' playoff opponents:

	Losing Opponents' Total PGA Victories	Losing Opponents' Major Championship Victories	Winning Opponents' Total PGA Victories	Winning Opponents' Major Championship Victories
Nicklaus Era (1962 – 1986)	305	29	214	22
Woods Era (1997 – 2022)	91	12	45	9
Variance	214	17	169	13

Major Championship Absences

When speaking of the Nicklaus era (1962 – 1986) and the Woods era (1997 – 2022), injuries were inevitable for both players. The following shows how each player was affected and previous best finish(es) ***to that point*** at the location the championship was conducted. Due to the coronavirus, the Open Championship of 2020 was canceled.

- **1983 Masters – Augusta National Golf Club**
  - Nicklaus withdrew prior to the start of the second round due to back spasms.
    - First round one-over par 73
  - Best Finish(es)
    - 1st in 1963, 1965, 1966, 1972, and 1975
- **2008 Open Championship – Royal Birkdale Golf Club**
  - Woods was unable to play due to knee surgery.
  - Best Finish(es)
    - 3rd in 1998
- **2008 PGA Championship – Oakland Hills Country Club**
  - Woods was unable to play due to knee surgery.
  - Best Finish(es)
    - T-82 (as amateur) in the 1996 U.S. Open
- **2011 U.S. Open – Congressional Country Club**
  - Woods was unable to play due to knee problems.
  - Best Finish(es)
    - T-19 in 1997
      - 1st in 2009 (AT&T National)
- **2011 Open Championship – Royal St. George's Golf Club**
  - Woods was unable to play due to knee problems.
  - Best Finish(es)
    - T-4 in 2003
- **2014 Masters – Augusta National Golf Club**
  - Woods was unable to play due to back surgery.
  - Best Finish(es)
    - 1st in 1997, 2001, 2002, and 2005
- **2014 U.S. Open – Pinehurst Number 2**
  - Woods was unable to play due to back surgery.
  - Best Finish(es)

- ▪ T-3 in 1999
- ▪ 2nd in 2005
- **2020 Open Championship – Royal St. George's Golf Club**
  - ○ Woods was unable to play due to the coronavirus pandemic.
  - ○ Best Finish(es)
    - ▪ T-4 in 2003

For Nicklaus, his one-over par 73 was six shots back of three first-round leaders' 67s. This is the exact number he was adrift in 1986 when he won his sixth green jacket having shot a first-round two-over par 74 with the two leaders at four-under par 68. Yet, there is no way to know how he would have finished even though he had won five Masters' titles to that point and had an overall good year in 1983.

For Woods, there would also be no way to reliably predict how he would have placed in any of his absences. In 2008, he was playing very well prior to his knee surgery having placed second in the Masters and winning the U.S. Open. Though in 2011, Woods was not playing up to the same caliber. Likewise, in 2014, he was playing at a much lower standard.

Having missed the entire season of 2016, nearly all of 2017, and all of 2021, Woods was unable to compete in the corresponding 12 major championships. These are not listed in detail due to an inability to predict his performance based on results in close proximity during the same years.

MONEY LEADERS

"He always said, 'I never played for the money. I always played for the title.' He wanted the trophies. He wanted to be in the history books." – *Dan Jenkins on Jack Nicklaus*

"If money titles meant anything, I'd play more tournaments. The only thing that means a lot to me is winning. If I have more wins than anybody else and win more majors than anybody else in the same year, then it's been a good year." – *Tiger Woods*

Throughout most of their careers, Jack Nicklaus and Tiger Woods played less than a full schedule annually in the U.S., which makes their repeated frequency at or near the top of the PGA money leaders quite impressive.

Below displays the regularity with which each player attained a position within the top 10 of their respective yearly PGA money lists:

Jack Nicklaus (1962 – 1986)		Tiger Woods (1997 – 2022)	
Position	Frequency	Position	Frequency
1	8	1	10
2	7*	2	3
3	2	3	0
4	0	4	2
5	0	5	0
6	0	6	0
7	0	7	0
8	0	8	1
9	0	9	0

10	2*	10	0
Total	**19**	**Total**	**16**

*Open Championship winnings were not part of the official PGA earnings during the years for Nicklaus. Once factored in, they improve his position on the money list during the following years. The results for three of the four years are included in the above chart.

- **1970** – $12,600 would increase Nicklaus' official earnings from $142,149 to $154,749 and result in a ranking change from fourth to second behind Lee Trevino.
- **1978** – $22,500 would increase Nicklaus' official earnings from $256,672 to $279,172 and result in a ranking change from fourth to second behind Tom Watson.
- **1979** – $25,740 would increase Nicklaus' official earnings from $59,434 to $85,174 and result in a ranking change from 71st to 43rd.
- **1980** – $21,623 would increase Nicklaus' official earnings from $172,386 to $194,009 and result in a ranking change from 13th to 10th.

While Open Championship prize money would have also affected Nicklaus in all years under review, except for his missed cut in 1985, they would have had no appreciable bearing on his money list position in the top 10 beyond what has been updated.

Any impact for each year in the entire eras reviewed is outlined in the below chart. The detail corresponds with the above summary.

Jack Nicklaus & Tiger Woods PGA Money List Rank Per Year				
Nicklaus (1962 – 1986)			Woods (1997 – 2022)	
Year	Position (Without Open Championship)	Position (With Open Championship)	Year	Position
1962	3	3	1997	1
1963	2	2	1998	4
1964	1	1	1999	1

1965	1	1	2000	1
1966	2	2	2001	1
1967	1	1	2002	1
1968	2	2	2003	2
1969	3	3	2004	4
1970	4	2	2005	1
1971	1	1	2006	1
1972	1	1	2007	1
1973	1	1	2008	2
1974	2	2	2009	1
1975	1	1	2010	68
1976	1	1	2011	128
1977	2	2	2012	2
1978	4	2	2013	1
1979	71	43	2014	201
1980	13	10	2015	162
1981	16	16	2016	X
1982	12	11	2017	X
1983	10	10	2018	8
1984	15	15	2019	24
1985	43	43	2020	38
1986	34	33	2021	X
			2022	X

During the course of 25 years, Nicklaus averaged a ranking of 9.84 when the Open Championship earnings were excluded and 8.36 when included.

Woods' average all-inclusive rank was 29.68*. But this includes the two years (2010 and 2011) immediately following issues from late 2009. This also includes 2014 where Woods had back surgery during the middle part of the season followed by a dismal 2015. And finally, 2022 is only through the Open Championship in July.

The following provides a summary analysis of both players' money list position during their 20s and 30s.

Jack Nicklaus (1962 – 1979)		Tiger Woods (1997 – 2015)	
Age Range	**Average Position**	**Age Range**	**Average Position**
20s	1.88	20s	1.78
30s	8.80	30s	56.70
30s	5.80	30s	1.14

For this representation, the row of data for the age range of 20s is a straight average from the official money lists for both players. Although Open Championship winnings were not included for Nicklaus, they have no bearing on the actual annual rankings he attained.

When reviewing Nicklaus and Woods during their 30s, the following caveats are taken into consideration.

The second row shows Nicklaus' average position during his 30s without Open Championship prize money added. This includes two fourth place finishes and one 71st-place finish as noted earlier. For Woods, the average position includes one 68th-place finish, one 128th-place finish, one 201st-place finish, and one 162nd-place finish. Again, these latter rankings are anomalies.

The final row shows their respective positions again during their 30s. However, for Nicklaus, Open Championship prize money has been included, thus his average has improved as alluded to by three spots to 5.80. For Woods, his results for 2010, 2011, 2014, and 2015 have been omitted to obtain an average position of 1.14. It is anybody's guess where he would have legitimately ranked had the issues from late 2009 and the back injury from 2014 not occurred, but it is likely he would have been in the top 10 each year. Although 1.14 is probably too low of an average, 56.70 is definitely too high.

*The 1996 season was not included for Woods since he was only able to compete in a partial number of tournaments near its end – he finished 24th. Furthermore, as Woods' 2008 season was abbreviated due to knee surgery, it is likely he would have led the money list based on his performance through the conclusion of the U.S. Open.

PLAYER OF THE YEAR

"The first time I ever saw Arnold Palmer, I said, 'There's a star.'
The first time I saw Jack Nicklaus, I said, 'Superstar.' I feel the
same way about Tiger Woods." – Gary Player

"Finally, I matured to the point where I understood my game
well enough to make my own corrections during the course of a
tournament, and that's when I'd say I became a good golfer." –
Bobby Jones

There are two Player of the Year awards given annually. The first was
established in 1948 by the PGA of America and the second in 1990 by the
PGA Tour. Until 1982, there was no in-depth, standardized set of criteria (i.e.
point system) to rate players eligible for the PGA of America's version. For
purposes of this analysis, the focus will be on the former award as the latter
is irrelevant for Jack Nicklaus because of its recent inception.

Nicklaus began his professional playing career in January of 1962 and under
the current PGA of America guidelines, was not immediately eligible for Player
of the Year honors. He declared his professional status in November of 1961
when securing PGA of America membership – a "Class A" PGA member –
took five years. Therefore, Nicklaus was not eligible until November of 1966,
or January of 1967 at the start of that season's play. For the 10 years beginning
in 1967 through 1976, he won the award five times.

With no qualification restrictions, Tiger Woods amassed 11 Player of the Year
awards beginning with his first full season of 1997.

Below shows the breakdown for each player:

Jack Nicklaus		Tiger Woods	
Year	Award Status	Year	Award Status
1962	Ineligible	1997	Won
1963	Ineligible	1999	Won
1964	Ineligible	2000	Won
1965	Ineligible	2001	Won
1966	Ineligible	2002	Won
1967	Won	2003	Won
1972	Won	2005	Won
1973	Won	2006	Won
1975	Won	2007	Won
1976	Won	2009	Won
		2013	Won

While Nicklaus did win Rookie of the Year honors in 1962 having captured the U.S. Open and two other titles, plus finishing third on the money list, Arnold Palmer was named Player of the Year. With eight victories, including the Masters and Open Championship – along with leading the money list and scoring – he was more than justified.

Let's review the Player of the Year winners from 1963 through 1966 compared to Nicklaus. The winners are listed below followed by a tabular summary of their seasons' highlights along with those of Nicklaus.

1963   Julius Boros
1964   Ken Venturi
1965   Dave Marr
1966   Billy Casper

Jack Nicklaus Summary Performance vs. Player of the Year Winners 1963 – 1966							
	Masters	U.S. Open	Open	PGA	Total Wins	Money Rank	Scoring Average (Rank)
1963							
Nicklaus	1	MC	3	1	5	2	70.42 (2)

Boros	T-3	1	DNP	T-13	3	3	70.73 (5)
1964							
Nicklaus	T-2	T-23	2	T-2	4	1	69.96 (1)
Venturi	DNP	1	DNP	T-5	3	6	70.94 (7)
1965							
Nicklaus	1	T-31	T-12	T-2	5	1	70.09 (1)
Marr	MC	MC	DNP	1	1	7	70.98 (7)
1966							
Nicklaus	1	3	1	T-22	3	2	70.58 (2)
Casper	T-10	1	DNP	T-3	4	1	70.16 (1)

In all four years, Nicklaus had Player of the Year-caliber seasons. When compared to the winners Julius Boros, Ken Venturi, and Dave Marr for the first three years, Nicklaus was clearly superior. He led each in overall performance in major championships, total victories, money rankings, and average score.

The distinction in 1966 between Nicklaus and Billy Casper is somewhat blurred. Nicklaus had an overall better year in the major championships than Casper having won two, including a successful defense at the Masters, vs. one. And both players had three top 10 finishes in the events, but Casper did not compete in the Open Championship.

But Casper led the money list, scoring average, and in total victories. While the margins were small, these are still significant categories. Although debatable who had the better season in 1966, with Nicklaus being ineligible, the point was moot at the time.

Keeping the scenario for 1966 in mind, let's extrapolate further for the year 1980. The following is a high-level snapshot of Nicklaus and Player of the Year, Tom Watson.

					Total Wins	Money Rank	Scoring Average (Rank)
Jack Nicklaus Summary Performance vs. Player of the Year Tom Watson 1980							
	Masters	U.S. Open	Open	PGA			
Nicklaus	T-33	1	T-4	1	2	9	70.79 (7)
Watson	T-12	T-3	1	T-10	7	1	69.86 (2)

Like Casper in 1966, Watson led Nicklaus in total number of victories, scoring average, and money rank, but the margins for each were greater.

Yet, Nicklaus had a unique year punctuated by two major championship wins. The below highlights show why his performance deserves consideration.

- Shot the then-record aggregate and relation to par scores of eight-under 272 in the U.S. Open. This U.S. Open win was Nicklaus' fourth tying him with Willie Anderson, Bobby Jones, and Ben Hogan for the most victories.
- Won the PGA Championship by a then-record margin of seven shots. This PGA Championship win was Nicklaus' fifth tying him with Walter Hagen for the most victories. This was also the most titles in the stroke-play era.
- Nicklaus became only the third player, at the time, behind Gene Sarazen and Hogan to win the U.S. Open and PGA Championship in the same year.
- Nicklaus became the first player since Hogan in 1953 to win multiple major championships in one season after the age of 40.

Keeping the above for 1966 and 1980 in mind, let's fast-forward to the year 1998 and its Player of the Year, Mark O'Meara compared to his closest competitor, David Duval.

David Duval Summary Performance vs. Player of the Year Mark O'Meara 1998							
	Masters	U.S. Open	Open	PGA	Total Wins	Money Rank	Scoring Average (Rank)
Duval	T-2	T-7	T-11	MC	4	1	69.60 (1)
O'Meara	1	T-32	1	T-4	2	7	70.40 (12)

Duval led the Tour in total numbers of wins, earnings, and scoring average, yet did not win a major championship. Despite twice as many wins and wider placement disparities in earnings and scoring favoring Duval, O'Meara's Masters and Open Championship victories clinched both Player of the Year awards for 1998.

The purpose of this review is to show if the same criteria used today were previously in place, Nicklaus would have definitely attained three, likely four, and *possibly* five additional Player of the Year awards bringing his total from eight to 10.

As for Woods, injury interrupted his campaign of 2008. Otherwise, he likely would have captured a 12th Player of the Year award. The proceeding graphic provides a comparison of Woods' abbreviated season highlights compared to those of the official Player of the Year, Padraig Harrington.

Tiger Woods Summary Performance vs. Player of the Year Padraig Harrington 2008							
	Masters	U.S. Open	Open	PGA	Total Wins	Money Rank	Scoring Average (Rank)*
Woods	2	1	DNP	DNP	4	2	69.00 (1)
Harrington	T-5	T-36	1	1	2	8	70.70 (35)

*Non-adjusted average

In six events, Woods completed 27 rounds. Due to the lack of play relative to the Vardon Trophy requirements, only his non-adjusted scoring average is referenced. Yet, Woods' raw scoring average was still lower than Vardon Trophy winner Sergio Garcia's adjusted average of 69.12 and Harrington's third-place adjusted average of 69.28. Woods also outpaced Bob Tway's leading non-adjusted average for the year of 69.94. Harrington placed in a tie for 35th with a non-adjusted scoring average of 70.70.

Lastly, in the six events Woods played, he won four, finished second in one, and fifth in one. Woods was still able to place second on the money list.

Regardless of the conjecture above for a twelfth award for Woods, with 11 titles, he is still superior to Nicklaus in this category.

WORLD RANKING

"I feel that neither money winnings nor stroke averages alone afford a good comparison on ability, that current ability spans more than a single calendar year, that the importance of a tournament and the overall ability of the field play a part and that victory deserves a bonus." – Mark H. McCormack

Upon conclusion of the 1968 season, attorney and sports agent Mark McCormack implemented a performance ranking system for professional golfers. It was then known as the "Mark H. McCormack Proficiency Rating System." The methodology of this system was used through the 1985 season.

Below lists the tournament "classes," point allocations for the current year, previous year, and two years previous. This is followed by the five top-ranked players at the end of each year with the total number of major championships each player won in their careers.

Class 1: Masters, U.S. Open, Open Championship, and PGA Championship

Class 2: U.S. Tour events in which at least 13 of the 15 leading money-winners of that particular year competed

Class 3: U.S. Tour events in which from 10 to 12 of the leading money-winners competed

Class 4: All other U.S. Tour events of regular status*

*Includes non-U.S. tournaments excluding purely domestic or satellite events as well as the Open Championship noted in Class 1 above.

Current Year

Class 1: Top 10 Finishers – 30 points for winner, 24 for second, down to 16 for 10th

Class 2: Top 8 Finishers – 25 points for winner, 19 for second, down to 13 for 8th

Class 3: Top 6 Finishers – 20 points for winner, 14 for second, down to 10 for 6th

Class 4: Top 3 Finishers – 12 points for winner, 6 for second, 5 for third

One Year Prior

Class 1: Top 10 Finishers – 25, 19, to 11 points

Class 2: Top 8 Finishers – 20, 14, to 8 points

Class 3: Top 6 Finishers – 15, 9, to 5 points

Class 4: Top 3 Finishers – 10, 4, to 3 points

Two Years Prior

Class 1: Top 10 Finishers – 20, 14, to 6 points

Class 2: Top 8 Finishers – 15, 9, to 3 points

Class 3: Top 6 Finishers – 11, 5, to 1 point

Class 4: Top 3 Finishers – 8, 2, to 1 point

Mark H. McCormack Proficiency Rating System Top Five Players Per Year									
Year	Player / Rank					Major Championships Won			
1968	Nicklaus	Palmer	Casper	Player	Charles	18	7	3	9	1
1969	Nicklaus	Player	Casper	Palmer	Charles	18	9	3	7	1
1970	Nicklaus	Player	Casper	Trevino	Charles	18	9	3	6	1
1971	Nicklaus	Trevino	Player	Palmer	Casper	18	6	9	7	3
1972	Nicklaus	Player	Trevino	Crampton	Palmer	18	9	6	0	7
1973	Nicklaus	Weiskopf	Trevino	Player	Crampton	18	1	6	9	0
1974	Nicklaus	Miller	Player	Weiskopf	Trevino	18	2	9	1	6
1975	Nicklaus	Miller	Weiskopf	Irwin	Player	18	2	1	3	9
1976	Nicklaus	Irwin	Miller	Player	Green	18	3	2	9	2
1977	Nicklaus	T. Watson	Green	Irwin	Crenshaw	18	8	2	3	2
1978	T. Watson	Nicklaus	Irwin	Green	Player	8	18	3	2	9
1979	T. Watson	Nicklaus	Irwin	Trevino	Player	8	18	3	6	9
1980	T. Watson	Trevino	Aoki	Crenshaw	Nicklaus	8	6	0	2	18
1981	T. Watson	Rogers	Aoki	J. Pate	Trevino	8	1	0	1	6
1982	T. Watson	Floyd	Ballesteros	Kite	Stadler	8	4	5	1	1
1983	Ballesteros	T. Watson	Floyd	Norman	Kite	5	8	4	2	1
1984	Ballesteros	T. Watson	Norman	Wadkins	Langer	5	8	2	1	2
1985	Ballesteros	Langer	Norman	T. Watson	Nakajima	5	2	2	8	0

For 10 straight years beginning at the conclusion of a relatively flat year for Nicklaus, he led the rankings. It is also likely he would have led three, if not four previous years, had the system been in place. This would have been a total of 13 or 14 years in succession leading the forerunner to the Official World Rankings.

A more globalized system was instituted in 1986 known as the Sony Ranking to better incorporate the growth of the game outside the United States. This system further evolved over the succeeding years into the Official World Golf Rankings.

Similar to the above chart, the following lists the five top-ranked players in the Official World Golf Rankings at the end of each year with the total number of major championships each competitor won in their careers.

	Official World Golf Ranking Top Five Players Per Year									
Year	Player / Rank					Major Championships Won				
1986	Norman	Langer	Ballesteros	Nakajima	Bean	2	2	5	0	0
1987	Norman	Ballesteros	Langer	Lyle	Strange	2	5	2	2	2
1988	Ballesteros	Norman	Lyle	Faldo	Strange	5	2	2	6	2
1989	Norman	Faldo	Ballesteros	Strange	Stewart	2	6	5	2	3
1990	Norman	Faldo	Olazabal	Woosnam	Stewart	2	6	2	1	3
1991	Woosnam	Faldo	Olazabal	Ballesteros	Norman	1	6	2	5	2
1992	Faldo	Couples	Woosnam	Olazabal	Norman	6	1	1	2	2
1993	Faldo	Norman	Langer	Price	Couples	6	2	2	3	1
1994	Price	Norman	Faldo	Langer	Olazabal	3	2	6	2	2
1995	Norman	Price	Langer	Els	Montgomerie	2	3	2	4	0
1996	Norman	Lehman	Montgomerie	Els	Couples	2	1	0	4	1
1997	Norman	Woods	Price	Els	Love III	2	15	3	4	1
1998	Woods	O'Meara	Duval	Love III	Els	15	2	1	1	4
1999	Woods	Duval	Montgomerie	Love III	Els	15	1	0	1	4
2000	Woods	Els	Duval	Mickelson	Westwood	15	4	1	6	0
2001	Woods	Mickelson	Duval	Els	Love III	15	6	1	4	1
2002	Woods	Mickelson	Els	Garcia	Goosen	15	6	4	1	2
2003	Woods	Singh	Els	Love III	Furyk	15	3	4	1	1
2004	Singh	Woods	Els	Goosen	Mickelson	3	15	4	2	6
2005	Woods	Singh	Mickelson	Goosen	Els	15	3	6	2	4
2006	Woods	Furyk	Mickelson	Scott	Els	15	1	6	1	4
2007	Woods	Mickelson	Furyk	Els	Stricker	15	6	1	4	0
2008	Woods	Garcia	Mickelson	Harrington	Singh	15	1	6	3	3
2009	Woods	Mickelson	Stricker	Casey	Westwood	15	6	0	0	0
2010	Westwood	Woods	Kaymer	Mickelson	Furyk	0	15	2	6	1
2011	Donald	Westwood	McIlroy	Kaymer	Scott	0	0	4	2	1
2012	McIlroy	Donald	Woods	Rose	Scott	4	0	15	1	1
2013	Woods	Scott	Stenson	Rose	Mickelson	15	1	1	1	6
2014	McIlroy	Scott	Stenson	Garcia	Rose	4	1	1	1	1
2015	Spieth	Day	McIlroy	B. Watson	Stenson	3	1	4	2	1
2016	Day	D. Johnson	McIlroy	Spieth	Stenson	1	2	4	3	1
2017	D. Johnson	Spieth	Thomas	Rahm	Matsuyama	2	3	2	1	1
2018	D. Johnson	Rose	Koepka	Thomas	Molinari	2	1	4	2	1
2019	Koepka	McIlroy	D. Johnson	Rose	Thomas	4	4	2	1	2
2020	D. Johnson	Rahm	Thomas	McIlroy	Morikawa	2	1	2	4	2
2021	Rahm	Morikawa	D. Johnson	Cantlay	DeChambeau	1	2	2	0	1
2022	Scheffler	Smith	McIlroy	Cantlay	Rahm	1	1	4	0	1

From the first number one player in the world, Bernhard Langer, to the first year's designate and owner of 331 weeks as the top-ranked player, Greg Norman, the list criteria evolves periodically as the game grows.

While Norman's 331-week run (6.36 years) is amazing, Woods' run at 683 weeks (13.13 years) is staggering. The subsequent chart shows the top 10 players who have held the number one ranking based upon duration along with their total major championship victories.

Player	Weeks at Number One	Major Championships Won
Tiger Woods	683	15
Greg Norman	331	2
Dustin Johnson	135	2
Rory McIlroy	106	4
Nick Faldo	97	6
Seve Ballesteros	61	5
Luke Donald	56	0
Jason Day	51	1
Ian Woosnam	50	1
Brooks Koepka	47	4

The above graphic confirms Woods' dominance. What this also shows is achieving and sustaining the number one ranking is not solely based upon winning major championships. This is verified when reviewing Norman and Nick Faldo. Norman's consistency of great play is superior to Faldo's. Yet, Faldo's major championship victories of six lead most historians to regard him ahead of Norman and his two Open Championships in an overall player rank.

This brings the discussion back to Nicklaus and Woods. As seen in the earlier "Mark H. McCormack Proficiency Rating System," Nicklaus led for 10 consecutive years. While these 10 years included his prime of the early and mid-1970s, great performances from 1962 through 1967 are omitted. When factoring in these six years, it is possible Nicklaus would have surpassed Woods' 683 weeks as the number one-ranked professional.

While Woods has 82 PGA wins compared to Nicklaus at 73, Nicklaus' greater major championship total and consistent, top-level positions in majors for a longer period of time would play a role in elevating him to the top of a uniformly-based world ranking system.

LIMITED-FIELD PGA TOURNAMENTS WITH NO 36-HOLE CUT

*"Tiger has someone to compare his greatness. Jack just went out and played. Every time Jack won, it was his record. If he had had what Tiger has, he might have been better." – Hubert Green **Golf Digest** – December 2002*

PGA tournaments with smaller fields and no 36-hole cuts have existed as long as professional golf has been played under its heading. With the inception of the World Golf Championships in 1999 and the FedEx Cup Playoffs in 2007, their presence has grown considerably. As such, it is necessary to identify these events and how they have impacted the records of Jack Nicklaus and Tiger Woods.

Below is a complete listing of the applicable PGA-sanctioned tournaments Nicklaus and Woods played along with their respective results:

Jack Nicklaus Limited-field PGA Tournaments with no 36-hole Cut									
Tournament	Win	2nd	3rd	4th	5th	6 - 10	11 - 20	20 +	WD
National Team Championship	2	0	0	0	0	0	0	0	0
Tournament of Champions	5	1	0	2	1	3	5	1	0
U.S. Match Play Championship	1	0	0	0	1	0	0	1	0
Walt Disney World National Team Championship	0	0	0	0	0	0	1	0	0
World Series of Golf	1	1	0	0	1	5	0	0	1

Tiger Woods Limited-field PGA Tournaments with no 36-hole Cut									
Tournament	**Win**	**2nd**	**3rd**	**4th**	**5th**	**6 - 10**	**11 - 20**	**20 +**	**WD**
BMW Championship	2	0	0	1	0	1	2	2	0
Hyundai Tournament of Championships	2	1	1	1	1	2	0	0	0
Tour Championship	3	4	0	0	0	2	3	3	0
WGC American Express Championship	5	0	0	0	1	1	0	0	0
WGC-Bridgestone Invitational	4	0	0	0	0	1	0	3	1
WGC-CA/Mexico Championship	2	0	0	0	1	3	0	1	1
WGC Match Play Championship	3	1	0	0	2	2	3	3	0
WGC NEC Invitational	4	0	0	3	0	0	0	0	0
World Series of Golf	0	0	1	0	1	0	0	0	0
Zozo Championship	1	0	0	0	0	0	0	1	0

For Nicklaus during 1962 through 1986, he competed in five official PGA-sanctioned tournaments designated as limited-field, no 36-hole cut events as follows.

- **National Team Championship (1968, 1970 – 1972)**
  - Competed in this event (with Arnold Palmer) twice and won twice.
  - Considered an official PGA event from 1968 through 1972, no tournament was held during 1969.
- **Tournament of Champions (1962 – 1986)**
  - Competed in this event 18 times and won five.
- **U.S. Match Play Championship (1971 – 1973)**
  - Competed in this event three times and won once.
- **Walt Disney World National Team Championship (1974 – 1981)**
  - Competed in this event (with Tom Weiskopf) once and finished T-14.

- **World Series of Golf (1976 – 1986)**
  - Competed in this event nine times and won once.
  - Began when Nicklaus was 36 years old.
    - Expanded from the four-person tournament played from 1962 – 1975.
    - Won the inaugural, expanded-field edition.
  - Forerunner to the WGC-NEC/Bridgestone Invitational.

For Woods during his career beginning in late 1996, he competed in 10 different PGA tournaments designated as limited-field, no 36-hole cut events as noted below.

- **BMW Championship (2007 – 2022)**
  - Competed in this event eight times and won twice.
  - Formerly the (full-field) Western Open (1899 – 2006).
    - Won the Western Open in 1997, 1999, and 2003.
- **Hyundai Tournament of Champions (1997 – 2022)**
  - Competed in this event eight times and won twice.
  - Began as the Tournament of Champions in 1953.
- **Tour Championship (1996 – 2022)**
  - Competed in this event 15 times and won three.
- **WGC-American Express Championship (1999 – 2006)**
  - Competed in this event seven times and won five.
  - Change of site and sponsor in 2007 to the WGC-CA Championship.
- **WGC-Bridgestone Invitational (2006 – 2018)**
  - Competed in this event nine times and won four.
  - Formerly the WGC-NEC Invitational (1999 – 2005)
- **WGC-Mexico Championship (2007 – 2021)**
  - Competed in this event eight times and won twice.
  - Formerly the WGC-Cadillac Championship (2011 – 2016)
  - Formerly the WGC-CA Championship (2007 – 2010)
  - Formerly the Doral Open (1962 – 2006).
    - Also won the Doral Open in 2005 and 2006.
- **WGC-Match Play Championship (1999 – 2022)**
  - Competed in this event 14 times and won three.
- **WGC-NEC Invitational (1999 – 2005)**
  - Competed in this event seven times and won four.

        o   Forerunner to the WGC-Bridgestone Invitational.
- **World Series of Golf (1997 – 1998)**
  - o   Competed in this event twice and did not win either.
  - o   See "World Series of Golf" above.
  - o   Forerunner to the WGC-NEC Invitational.
- **Zozo Championship (2019 – 2022)**
  - o   Competed in this event twice and won once.

Woods' PGA victory total of 82 includes 26 limited-field, no 36-hole cut events (31.71%) as opposed to Nicklaus' 73 total PGA wins comprised of nine (12.33%). Therefore, Nicklaus leads Woods in full-field wins by 64 to 56.

When reviewing these events on their own, Woods' superior win rate is 26 of 80 or 32.50% compared to Nicklaus at nine of 33 or 27.27%.

MAJOR CHAMPIONSHIP VICTORY MARGINS & WIRE-TO-WIRE WINS

*"Jack just wanted to win. Tiger likes to rub it in." – Hubert Green **Golf Digest** – December 2002*

It is common knowledge Jack Nicklaus won 18 major championships and Tiger Woods won 15. When reviewing these victories, the aspects of victory margins and wire-to-wire wins should be considered. Below is a summary breakdown of each player's wins by number of shots. A zero-shot margin indicates victory in a playoff.

	Masters	U.S. Open	Open	PGA
Jack Nicklaus Major Championship Margins of Victory				
1962		0		
1963	1			2
1965	9			
1966	0		1	
1967		4		
1970			0	
1971				2
1972	3	3		
1973				4
1975	1			2
1978			2	
1980		2		7
1986	1			

- **Total Victories: 18**
  - ○ Masters: 6
  - ○ U.S. Open: 4
  - ○ Open Championship: 3
  - ○ PGA: 5
- **Total Victory Margins: 44**
  - ○ Masters: 15
  - ○ U.S. Open: 9
  - ○ Open Championship: 3
  - ○ PGA: 17
- **Average Victory Margin: 2.44**
  - ○ Masters: 2.50
  - ○ U.S. Open: 2.25
  - ○ Open Championship: 1.00
  - ○ PGA: 3.40

Tiger Woods Major Championship Margins of Victory				
	Masters	**U.S. Open**	**Open**	**PGA**
1997	12			
1999				1
2000		15	8	0
2001	2			
2002	3	3		
2005	0		5	
2006			2	5
2007				2
2008		0		
2019	1			

- **Total Victories: 15**
  - ○ Masters: 5
  - ○ U.S. Open: 3
  - ○ Open Championship: 3
  - ○ PGA: 4
- **Total Victory Margins: 59**
  - ○ Masters: 18
  - ○ U.S. Open: 18

○ Open Championship: 15
○ PGA: 8
• **Average Victory Margin: 3.93**
    ○ Masters: 3.60
    ○ U.S. Open: 6.00
    ○ Open Championship: 5.00
    ○ PGA: 2.00

Although Woods won three fewer titles than Nicklaus, his wins were more dominant having an average margin of victory of 3.93 shots compared to Nicklaus' 2.44. Nicklaus' 18 wins were more consistent over a time span of 25 years compared to Woods' 23 years. Thus, while the field of players in Woods' era may have been deeper, Nicklaus faced a varied pool of top-level competition due to his longevity of winning throughout.

This consistency/longevity offsets much of the scrutiny Nicklaus now seems to get for competing against "weaker" fields. In effect during his 25-year victory span, Nicklaus was contending and winning major championships during the close of the Hogan/Snead era, in the heart of the Palmer/Player/Casper era, on to the Trevino/Floyd/Miller era, and into the Watson/Ballesteros/Norman era.

Dominance

Below is a chart specific to Nicklaus and Woods and their largest victory margins in each of the four major championships:

Jack Nicklaus Largest Victory Margins in Major Championships			Tiger Woods Largest Victory Margins in Major Championships		
Year	Championship	Victory Margin	Year	Championship	Victory Margin
1965	Masters	9	1997	Masters	12
1967	U.S. Open	4	2000	U.S. Open	15
1978	Open	2	2000	Open	8
1980	PGA	7	2006	PGA	5

Woods leads Nicklaus considerably in total number of shots at 40 compared to 22; an average of 10.00 shots per event vs. 5.50. In addition, Woods leads in three of the four majors compared to Nicklaus. Two of Woods' three victory margins remain the record, while Nicklaus' seven-shot PGA Championship win in 1980 was broken by Rory McIlroy in 2012 with his eight-shot triumph. Finally, Woods' margin was completed over a 10-year span where Nicklaus' was completed over a 16-year span.

Nicklaus finished 10 shots ahead of Hubert Green in the 1977 Open Championship but was runner-up to Tom Watson by one. Similarly, Woods was pressed by Bob May in the 2000 PGA Championship, where he ultimately won in a playoff, yet Thomas Bjorn finished in third place five shots behind.

Wire-to-Wire

With respect to wire-to-wire victories (including ties), Nicklaus and Woods are uncannily similar in distribution. The following is a summary of their wins.

Jack Nicklaus Wire-to-Wire Victories in Major Championships			Tiger Woods Wire-to-Wire Victories in Major Championships		
Year	Championship	Victory Margin	Year	Championship	Victory Margin
1971	PGA	2	2000	U.S. Open	15
1972	Masters	3	2000	PGA	Playoff
1972	U.S. Open	3	2002	U.S. Open	3
1980	U.S. Open	2	2005	Open	5

Each player accomplished the task four times during three years across three of the four major championships. While Nicklaus did not achieve this feat in the Open Championship and Tiger did not achieve it in the Masters, both were able to convert twice in the U.S. Open.

This is arguably the most significant accomplishment and similarity since the U.S. Open is regarded as the most arduous test of championship golf.

In addition, Nicklaus won two of the four championships with no ties – the 1971 PGA Championship and the 1972 Masters. Woods was able to win three – the 2000 U.S. Open, the 2002 U.S. Open, and the 2005 Open Championship with no ties.

Thanks largely to his 15-shot win in the 2000 U.S. Open, Woods' total victory margin for the same number of wins is greater than Nicklaus at 23 shots vs. 10, while capturing these titles over six years compared to Nicklaus' span of 10 years.

MAJOR CHAMPIONSHIP DETAIL

*"It never entered my mind that there was any such thing as destiny. The only thing that was in my mind was that I had a major championship to prepare for, and if I wanted to win it, I better prepare." – Jack Nicklaus **Golf Digest** – December 2002*

"Any time you are in a final pairing it's fun, but I tell you, it's even more fun winning in that final pairing in a major championship. That's why you play, why you practice, that's why you dream as a kid, and that's why you put in all of those long hours." – Tiger Woods Interview Augusta National – April 2005

Whether Bobby Jones, Jack Nicklaus, Tiger Woods, or as referred to in the introduction, Jimmy Connors, most top-level players in their respective sport agree that performance in the major championships is the defining aspect of a competitor's career. This chapter will provide comparative detail on Nicklaus and Woods in major championship play.

When the subject of major championships in golf arises, four names typically surface – Walter Hagen, Jones, Nicklaus, and Woods. Below are snapshots of the number of titles they each won in the old and new compositions:

Major Championship Victories – Includes Amateur Championships							
	Masters	U.S. Open	Open	PGA	U.S. Amateur	British Amateur	Total
Jack Nicklaus	6	4	3	5	2	0	20
Tiger Woods	5	3	3	4	3	0	18
Bobby Jones	0	4	3	0	5	1	13

Walter Hagen	0	2	4	5	0	0	11

Throughout the early part of Nicklaus' career, the major championship standard was Jones' tally of 13. With the Masters yet to be established (by Jones in 1934) and his ineligibility for the PGA Championship, Jones' record was exceptional across the board.

In the old-style major championship amalgamation, the U.S. Open and Amateur Championships and the British Open (Open Championship) and Amateur Championships comprised the four titles. Jones claimed the most U.S. Amateur wins with five, tied Willie Anderson for the most U.S. Open victories with four, won three Open Championships, and in three appearances, attained one British Amateur Championship. He also completed the calendar-year Grand Slam, or Impregnable Quadrilateral, in 1930.

As the professional game grew into greater prominence, the Masters and PGA Championship supplanted the two amateur events to form the modern-day version of the Grand Slam. It is under this combination of "old" and "new" championships that explains Nicklaus having 20 titles vs. 18. Therefore, Nicklaus passed Jones with his win in the 1973 PGA Championship for victory number 14. By virtue of Woods' unprecedented three consecutive U.S. Amateur Championship wins in 1994 through 1996, he is one title closer to Nicklaus at 18.

Major Championship Victories – Professional Only					
	Masters	U.S. Open	Open	PGA	Total
Jack Nicklaus	6	4	3	5	18
Tiger Woods	5	3	3	4	15
Walter Hagen	0	2	4	5	11
Bobby Jones	0	4	3	0	7

The above table is the most recognizable composition of major championship titles and victory distribution of the subject four players. In this case, Jones lags due to the inability to compete in the PGA Championship and the Masters; the latter he established after his prime playing years.

However, due to a superb record in the PGA Championship, Hagen elevates past Jones without amateur titles included. Hagen as well was unable to compete in the Masters during his prime to contribute to his overall victory total. It should be noted Hagen won five Western Open titles in an era when that event was perhaps second only in prestige to the U.S. Open in the United States. If recognized as a major championship, that would give him 16 titles and changed Nicklaus' and Woods' approach and level of participation in the event.

Multiple Major Champions Per Event

For the record, the following lists all multiple champions of each professional major to date with the ranking order by number of wins and if any ties, by chronology of achievement.

Masters – Champions of Multiple Events 17 Different Champions		
Player	**Number of Wins**	**Rank**
Jack Nicklaus	6	1
Tiger Woods	5	2
Arnold Palmer	4	3
Jimmy Demaret	3	4
Sam Snead	3	4
Gary Player	3	4
Nick Faldo	3	4
Phil Mickelson	3	4
Horton Smith	2	9
Byron Nelson	2	9
Ben Hogan	2	9
Tom Watson	2	9
Seve Ballesteros	2	9
Bernhard Langer	2	9
Ben Crenshaw	2	9
Jose Maria Olazabal	2	9
Bubba Watson	2	9

U.S. Open – Champions of Multiple Events 21 Different Champions		
Player	**Number of Wins**	**Rank**
Willie Anderson	4	1
Bobby Jones	4	1
Ben Hogan	4	1
Jack Nicklaus	4	1
Hale Irwin	3	5
Tiger Woods	3	5
Alex Smith	2	7
John McDermott	2	7
Walter Hagen	2	7
Gene Sarazen	2	7
Ralph Guldahl	2	7
Cary Middlecoff	2	7
Julius Boros	2	7
Billy Casper	2	7
Andy North	2	7
Curtis Strange	2	7
Ernie Els	2	7
Lee Janzen	2	7
Payne Stewart	2	7
Retief Goosen	2	7
Brooks Koepka	2	7

Open Championship – Champions of Multiple Events 25 Different Champions		
Player	**Number of Wins**	**Rank**
Harry Vardon	6	1
J. H. Taylor	5	2
James Braid	5	2
Peter Thomson	5	2
Tom Watson	5	2
Willie Park, Sr.	4	6
Tom Morris, Sr.	4	6

Tom Morris, Jr.	4	6
Walter Hagen	4	6
Bobby Locke	4	6
Jamie Anderson	3	11
Bob Ferguson	3	11
Bobby Jones	3	11
Henry Cotton	3	11
Gary Player	3	11
Jack Nicklaus	3	11
Seve Ballesteros	3	11
Nick Faldo	3	11
Tiger Woods	3	11
Bob Martin	2	20
Harold Hilton	2	20
Arnold Palmer	2	20
Greg Norman	2	20
Padraig Harrington	2	20
Ernie Els	2	20

PGA Championship – Champions of Multiple Events 22 Different Champions		
Player	**Number of Wins**	**Rank**
Walter Hagen	5	1
Jack Nicklaus	5	1
Tiger Woods	4	3
Gene Sarazen	3	4
Sam Snead	3	4
Jim Barnes	2	6
Leo Diegel	2	6
Paul Runyan	2	6
Denny Shute	2	6
Byron Nelson	2	6
Ben Hogan	2	6
Gary Player	2	6

Dave Stockton	2	6
Raymond Floyd	2	6
Lee Trevino	2	6
Larry Nelson	2	6
Nick Price	2	6
Vijay Singh	2	6
Rory McIlroy	2	6
Brooks Koepka	2	6
Phil Mickelson	2	6
Justin Thomas	2	6

It makes sense in the above listings that the most numerous different winners would congregate in the Open Championship. It is the oldest by 35 years to the U.S. Open (1860 vs. 1895) and occurred for many years with smaller, localized fields. Conversely, the fewest number of different champions resides in the Masters. With its establishment in 1934, it is the newest by 18 years when compared to the inception of the PGA Championship in 1916.

Regardless of these bits of information, both Nicklaus and Woods figure heavily in all four of the major championships with no less than three victories in any. As has been provided earlier in the book, if their immediate placements were carried out, their performance level would be more dominant compared to the other players listed.

Multiple Major Champions Per Year

In a concentrated version of multiple major champions, the following depicts the roster of 20 players who won more than one per year in the professional era. Nicklaus and Woods factor prominently with record-setting and/or tying performances.

Winners of Multiple Professional Major Championships Per Year 20 Different Champions			
Player	Number Won Per Year(s)	Championships Won Per Year	Year(s) Achieved
Ben Hogan	3 (1)	Masters, U.S. Open, Open	1953

Tiger Woods	3 (1)	U.S. Open, Open, PGA	2000
Jack Nicklaus	2 (1)	Masters, PGA	1963
Jack Nicklaus	2 (2)	Masters, Open	1966
Jack Nicklaus	2 (3)	Masters, U.S. Open	1972
Jack Nicklaus	2 (4)	Masters, PGA	1975
Jack Nicklaus	2 (5)	U.S. Open, PGA	1980
Tiger Woods	2 (1)	Masters. U.S. Open	2002
Tiger Woods	2 (2)	Masters, Open	2005
Tiger Woods	2 (3)	Open, PGA	2006
Gene Sarazen	2 (1)	U.S. Open, PGA	1922
Gene Sarazen	2 (2)	U.S. Open, Open	1932
Bobby Jones	2 (1)	U.S. Open, Open	1926
Bobby Jones	2 (2)	U.S. Open, Open	1930
Ben Hogan	2 (1)	U.S. Open, PGA	1948
Ben Hogan	2 (2)	Masters, U.S. Open	1951
Arnold Palmer	2 (1)	Masters, U.S. Open	1960
Arnold Palmer	2 (2)	Masters, Open	1962
Tom Watson	2 (1)	Masters, Open	1977
Tom Watson	2 (2)	U.S. Open, Open	1982
Walter Hagen	2 (1)	Open, PGA	1924
Craig Wood	2 (1)	Masters, U.S. Open	1941
Sam Snead	2 (1)	Masters, PGA	1949
Jackie Burke	2 (1)	Masters, PGA	1956
Lee Trevino	2 (1)	U.S. Open, Open	1971
Gary Player	2 (1)	Masters, Open	1974
Nick Faldo	2 (1)	Masters, Open	1990
Nick Price	2 (1)	Open, PGA	1994
Mark O'Meara	2 (1)	Masters, Open	1998
Padraig Harrington	2 (1)	Open, PGA	2008
Rory McIlroy	2 (1)	Open, PGA	2014
Jordan Spieth	2 (1)	Masters, U.S. Open	2015
Brooks Koepka	2 (1)	U.S. Open, PGA	2018

With Ben Hogan's Triple Crown in 1953, he was the first player to win three professional major championships in a calendar year, capturing the first three and in his case, the only three majors he competed in. This lasted until Woods won the final three majors in 2000 after a solo fifth-place finish in the Masters.

Even though Nicklaus did not win three major championships in one year, he leads in having the largest number of years with two victories apiece. Nicklaus' five years of achieving this is two ahead of Woods' three-year run.

Major Championship Victories by Age & Number of Attempts

Another aspect of the performances in major championships by Nicklaus and Woods is how quickly they achieved their victories. Not only are they the two youngest players to complete the career Grand Slam, they are also the only two players to complete that feat twice and three times. The upcoming graphics examine their proficiency in attaining career Grand Slams by age and number of attempts.

Jack Nicklaus & Tiger Woods Career Grand Slams by Age			
	Age (1)	**Age (2)**	**Age (3)**
Nicklaus	26	31	38
Woods	24	29	30
Variance	2	2	8

While Woods' first *full* season as a professional began when he was 21 and Nicklaus' first professional season commenced at age 22, he was able to achieve his three career Grand Slam milestones much earlier. When Nicklaus completed his first career Grand Slam at age 26, he was the youngest of four players to do so. Since there was no precedent for a second and third time around, Nicklaus set his record at his own pace. A likely motivator for Woods was to complete multiple career Grand Slams faster than Nicklaus.

Jack Nicklaus & Tiger Woods Career Grand Slams by Total Number of Majors Played			
	Attempts (1)	**Attempts (2)**	**Attempts (3)**
Nicklaus	27	45	75

Woods	21	41	52
Variance	6	4	23

Beginning with his first U.S. Open in 1957 at age 17, Nicklaus competed in eight major championships prior to turning professional; excluding the U.S. Amateur. For Woods, he competed in six major championships (minus the U.S. Amateur) as an amateur beginning with the 1995 Masters at age 19. Woods was still able to complete his first career Grand Slam in fewer attempts. And while Woods finalized the second and third career Grand Slams faster, Nicklaus had a narrower gap between completing his first and second career Grand Slams and Woods was much quicker between his second and third.

Jack Nicklaus & Tiger Woods Career Grand Slams by Number of Majors Played as Professionals			
	Attempts (1)	**Attempts (2)**	**Attempts (3)**
Nicklaus	19	37	67
Woods	15	35	46
Variance	4	2	21

The above reflects much the same as the previous chart minus Nicklaus' and Woods' amateur efforts. The relative gaps between the two players are similar with a reduction of two across the board bringing their record closer, yet Nicklaus' relatively late win at age 38 in the Open Championship is the main disparity.

Let's review each player under the three scenarios above for each major championship.

Jack Nicklaus & Tiger Woods Masters Victories by Age						
	Age (1)	**Age (2)**	**Age (3)**	**Age (4)**	**Age (5)**	**Age (6)**
Nicklaus	23	25	26	32	35	46
Woods	21	25	26	29	43	N/A
Variance	2	0	0	3	(8)	N/A

Jack Nicklaus & Tiger Woods Masters Victories by Total Number of Attempts						
	Attempts (1)	Attempts (2)	Attempts (3)	Attempts (4)	Attempts (5)	Attempts (6)
Nicklaus	5	7	8	14	17	28
Woods	3	7	8	11	22	N/A
Variance	2	0	0	3	(5)	N/A

Jack Nicklaus & Tiger Woods Masters Victories by Number of Attempts as Professionals						
	Attempts (1)	Attempts (2)	Attempts (3)	Attempts (4)	Attempts (5)	Attempts (6)
Nicklaus	2	4	5	11	14	25
Woods	1	5	6	9	20	N/A
Variance	1	(1)	(1)	2	(6)	N/A

Although Nicklaus has six green jackets vs. Woods at five, the above data confirms their win rates based on age and number of attempts were similar. Woods leads, but only marginally through his fourth win. The gap between victories four and five for Woods is substantial, somewhat akin to Nicklaus' fifth and sixth wins.

Jack Nicklaus & Tiger Woods U.S. Open Victories by Age			
	Age (1)	Age (2)	Age (3)	Age (4)
Nicklaus	22	27	32	40
Woods	24	26	32	N/A
Variance	(2)	1	0	N/A

Jack Nicklaus & Tiger Woods U.S. Open Victories by Total Number of Attempts			
	Attempts (1)	Attempts (2)	Attempts (3)	Attempts (4)
Nicklaus	6	11	16	24
Woods	6	8	14	N/A
Variance	0	3	2	N/A

Jack Nicklaus & Tiger Woods U.S. Open Victories by Number of Attempts as Professionals				
	Attempts (1)	Attempts (2)	Attempts (3)	Attempts (4)
Nicklaus	1	6	11	19
Woods	4	6	12	N/A
Variance	(3)	0	(1)	N/A

For the U.S. Open, the data are also close. Nicklaus leads Woods in total victories by one, but both players' ability to win their titles at early ages and based upon number of attempts is virtually identical. Nicklaus qualified at age 17 to Woods at age 19 and this works to the former's disadvantage in the second table.

Jack Nicklaus & Tiger Woods Open Championship Victories by Age			
	Age (1)	Age (2)	Age (3)
Nicklaus	26	30	38
Woods	24	29	30
Variance	2	1	8

Jack Nicklaus & Tiger Woods Open Championship Victories by Total Number of Attempts			
	Attempts (1)	Attempts (2)	Attempts (3)
Nicklaus	5	9	17
Woods	6	11	12
Variance	(1)	(2)	5

Jack Nicklaus & Tiger Woods Open Championship Victories by Number of Attempts as Professionals			
	Attempts (1)	Attempts (2)	Attempts (3)
Nicklaus	5	9	17
Woods	4	9	10
Variance	1	0	7

For the Open Championship, both players have three wins, so the focus is specifically on how quickly each were able to secure their titles. It is in this championship where some real separation develops. Woods leads Nicklaus across the board by age of wins. Yet, while each player is nearly exact on their first two wins with respect to number of attempts, Woods' third win came much earlier than it did for Nicklaus.

Jack Nicklaus & Tiger Woods PGA Championship Victories by Age					
	Age (1)	Age (2)	Age (3)	Age (4)	Age (5)
Nicklaus	23	31	33	35	40
Woods	23	24	30	31	N/A
Variance	0	7	3	4	N/A

Jack Nicklaus & Tiger Woods PGA Championship Victories by Total Number of Attempts					
	Attempts (1)	Attempts (2)	Attempts (3)	Attempts (4)	Attempts (5)
Nicklaus	2	10	12	14	19
Woods	3	4	10	11	N/A
Variance	(1)	6	2	3	N/A

Due to amateurs being excluded from the PGA Championship, only two views of Nicklaus' and Woods' performances apply. Except for the opening victories, Woods leads Nicklaus in fewer attempts to achieve wins two, three, and four – as well as doing so at younger ages. Woods successfully defended his title on two occasions, an unprecedented accomplishment in the stroke-play era and second only to Hagen winning four straight match-play formats from 1924 through 1927. However, Nicklaus with five victories exceeds Woods by one.

When reviewing all tables listed under this section, Nicklaus shows his consistency and longevity with more major titles over a greater expanse of years – consistently winning from age 22 through age 46. No one has come close to that number in winning major championships routinely throughout. Woods won from age 21 through age 43, which is also remarkable. Yet, the victory gap between his win in the 2008 U.S. Open to the 2019 Masters hurts his case for consistency over time. As of this writing, Gary Player's 20-year range from the 1959 Open Championship through the 1978 Masters is next in line. Player was also able to win his nine championships at a relatively consistent rate during the span.

However, it does again show how dominant Woods was from 1997 through 2008 including an unprecedented four successful title defenses. To recap, Nicklaus completed his title defense of the Masters in 1966, yet Woods was successful in defending titles for one Masters (2002), one Open Championship (2006), and two PGA Championships (2000 and 2007).

Major Championship Comparison Summaries as Professionals

As a final review for this chapter, below are condensed, high-level comparative placement summaries of Nicklaus and Woods in each major championship as professionals in the date ranges specified. These are followed by the same graphic for the four major championships combined and finally a composite snapshot of both players for all. Tom Weiskopf's quote, *"Going head-to-head against Jack Nicklaus in a major was like trying to drain the Pacific Ocean with a teacup,"* isn't far from the truth. Woods' contemporaries might say the same thing about him.

Jack Nicklaus (1962 – 1986) & Tiger Woods (1997 – 2022) Masters – Discrete Placement Summary									
	Wins	2nds	3rds	4ths	5ths	6 - 10	11 - 15	16 - 20	21 - 25
Nicklaus	6	4	2	2	1	3	2	1	1
Woods	5	2	1	3	1	2	1	2	1
Variance	1	2	1	(1)	0	1	1	(1)	0

Jack Nicklaus (1962 – 1986) & Tiger Woods (1997 – 2022) Masters – Cumulative Placement Summary									
	Wins	Top-2	Top-3	Top-4	Top-5	Top-10	Top-15	Top-20	Top-25
Nicklaus	6	10	12	14	15	18	20	21	22
Woods	5	7	8	11	12	14	15	17	18
Variance	1	3	4	3	3	4	5	4	4

Jack Nicklaus (1962 – 1986) & Tiger Woods (1997 – 2022) U.S. Open – Discrete Placement Summary									
	Wins	2nds	3rds	4ths	5ths	6 - 10	11 - 15	16 - 20	21 - 25
Nicklaus	4	3	1	1	0	7	1	0	3
Woods	3	2	1	1	0	1	1	4	2
Variance	1	1	0	0	0	6	0	(4)	1

Jack Nicklaus (1962 – 1986) & Tiger Woods (1997 – 2022) U.S. Open – Cumulative Placement Summary									
	Wins	Top-2	Top-3	Top-4	Top-5	Top-10	Top-15	Top-20	Top-25
Nicklaus	4	7	8	9	9	16	17	17	20
Woods	3	5	6	7	7	8	9	13	15
Variance	1	2	2	2	2	8	8	4	5

Jack Nicklaus (1962 – 1986) & Tiger Woods (1997 – 2022) Open Championship – Discrete Placement Summary									
	Wins	2nds	3rds	4ths	5ths	6 - 10	11 - 15	16 - 20	21 - 25
Nicklaus	3	7	3	2	1	2	1	0	1
Woods	3	0	2	1	0	4	1	0	3
Variance	0	7	1	1	1	(2)	0	0	(2)

Jack Nicklaus (1962 – 1986) & Tiger Woods (1997 – 2022) Open Championship – Cumulative Placement Summary									
	Wins	Top-2	Top-3	Top-4	Top-5	Top-10	Top-15	Top-20	Top-25
Nicklaus	3	10	13	15	16	18	19	19	20
Woods	3	3	5	6	6	10	11	11	14
Variance	0	7	8	9	10	8	8	8	6

Jack Nicklaus (1962 – 1986) & Tiger Woods (1997 – 2022) PGA Championship – Discrete Placement Summary									
	Wins	2nds	3rds	4ths	5ths	6 - 10	11 - 15	16 - 20	21 - 25
Nicklaus	5	4	3	2	0	1	2	2	2
Woods	4	3	0	1	0	1	1	0	1
Variance	1	1	3	1	0	0	1	2	1

Jack Nicklaus (1962 – 1986) & Tiger Woods (1997 – 2022) PGA Championship – Cumulative Placement Summary									
	Wins	Top-2	Top-3	Top-4	Top-5	Top-10	Top-15	Top-20	Top-25
Nicklaus	5	9	12	14	14	15	17	19	21
Woods	4	7	7	8	8	9	10	10	11
Variance	1	2	5	6	6	6	7	9	10

Jack Nicklaus (1962 – 1986) & Tiger Woods (1997 – 2022) Major Championship – Discrete Placement Summary									
	Wins	2nds	3rds	4ths	5ths	6 - 10	11 - 15	16 - 20	21 - 25
Nicklaus	18	18	9	7	2	13	6	3	7
Woods	15	7	4	6	1	8	4	6	7
Variance	3	11	5	1	1	5	2	(3)	0

Jack Nicklaus (1962 – 1986) & Tiger Woods (1997 – 2022) Major Championship – Cumulative Placement Summary									
	Wins	Top-2	Top-3	Top-4	Top-5	Top-10	Top-15	Top-20	Top-25
Nicklaus	18	36	45	52	54	67	73	76	83
Woods	15	22	26	32	33	41	45	51	58
Variance	3	14	19	20	21	26	28	25	25

With placements in major championships to be covered in detail later in the book, the previous series of graphics were a succinct, meaningful comparison within the context of the chapter. Realizing no other player comes close to the totality of either Nicklaus or Woods in major championship excellence, it is clear Nicklaus exceeds Woods from a high-level placement perspective nearly across the board. Although Woods achieved significant milestones in major championships earlier than Nicklaus, there is no doubt that Nicklaus' consistency and longevity stand well above all others.

Jack Nicklaus (1962 – 1986) & Tiger Woods (1997 – 2022) Major Championship Summary					
	Nicklaus	%	Woods	%	Variance
Wins	18	18.00%	15	17.86%	3
Playoff Losses	1		0		1
One Shot Losses	9		3		6
Two Shot Losses	10		6		4
Three Shot Losses	5		5		0

Four Shot Losses	8		6		2
Top Two	36	36.00%	22	26.19%	14
Top Three	45	45.00%	26	30.95%	19
Top Four	52	52.00%	32	38.10%	20
Top Five	54	54.00%	33	39.29%	21
Top 10	67	67.00%	41	48.81%	26
Top 20	76	76.00%	51	60.71%	25
Wire-To-Wire Wins (With Ties)	4	22.22%	4	26.67%	0
Wire-To-Wire Wins (No Ties)	2	11.11%	3	20.00%	(1)
36-hole Lead / Win (Total)	9	81.82%	8	72.73%	9.09%
54-hole Lead / Win (Solo)	8	100.00%	11	91.67%	8.33%
54-hole Lead / Win (Tied)	2	50.00%	3	100.00%	(50.00%)
54-hole Lead / Win (Total)	10	83.33%	14	93.33%	(10.00%)
Final Round from Behind Wins	8	44.44%	1	6.67%	7
Low 18 (Aggregate)	63		63		0
Low 18 (To Par)	-8		-7		1
Low 72 (Aggregate)	269		266		(3)
Low 72 (To Par)	-17		-19		(2)
Avg 72-hole Victory Score (Aggregate)	279.94		273.53		(6.41)
Avg 72-hole Victory Score (To Par)	-5.67		-12.87		(7.20)
Avg Margin of Victory	2.44		3.93		(1.49)
Cumulative Under Par Victory Scores	-102		-193		(91)
Rounds in the 60s – Masters	32	33.33%	26	29.55%	6
Rounds Under Par – Masters	53	55.21%	51	57.95%	2
Rounds in the 60s – U.S. Open	22	22.45%	20	27.40%	2
Rounds Under Par – U.S. Open	27	27.55%	22	30.14%	5
Rounds in the 60s – Open	28	28.28%	25	34.72%	3
Rounds Under Par – Open	45	45.45%	32	44.44%	13
Rounds in the 60s – PGA	38	39.58%	30	37.97%	8
Rounds Under Par – PGA	47	48.96%	38	48.10%	9
Missed Cuts	6	6.00%	12	14.29%	(6)
Withdrawals	1	1.00%	1	1.19%	0

The above is a great view of Nicklaus and Woods in the major championships as professionals. The two records independent of one another are the greatest the game has produced to date. When aligning them with one another, several key elements arise.

- **Placements**
  - Nicklaus completely dominates in this category. Not only does he lead Woods in victories, but his consistency is unmatched by anyone in total finishes within four shots of the winning score. To achieve this 51 times in 100 consecutive major championships is unique and leads Woods' 35 finishes.
  - When reviewing discrete placements, Nicklaus again leads by significant margins from first place through the top 20. On two out of three occasions for these 100 major championships in succession, Nicklaus was no worse than tied for 10th, and no worse than tied for fifth 54.00% of the time.

- **Closing Ability**
  - As established earlier in the book, Woods is the greatest front-runner in the history of professional golf. Yet, in major championships, he and Nicklaus emerge virtually equal. Woods' fifteen major championship wins occurred fourteen times as either an outright or co-leader heading into the final round and once when trailing by two shots. However, he was unable to convert the two-shot lead after 54 holes in the 2009 PGA Championship by shooting a three-over 75 in the final round and lost to Y.E. Yang, thus rendering a 93.33% success rate. Nicklaus won 10 of 12 major championships (83.33%) when leading or tied for the lead after three rounds. He won eight of eight when leading alone. And while Nicklaus only converted two of four co-leads after 54 holes, his final rounds were an even par 72 and a four-under par 66 to lose the 1971 Masters and 1977 Open Championship, respectively.
  - Nicklaus and Woods exhibited success in wire-to-wire major championship victories having four apiece with ties and two and three, respectively, without ties.
  - Regarding winning major championships when trailing the leader(s) after three rounds, Nicklaus was successful eight times, while Woods accomplished this feat once. These eight come-from-behind victories for Nicklaus comprise 44.44%

of his 18 titles with Woods' lone victory in the 2019 Masters occupying 6.67% of his 15 wins.

- **Scoring**
    - ○ Woods' ability to score in major championships goes hand-in-hand with his dominating performances (i.e. 1997 Masters, 2000 U.S. Open, 2000 Open Championship). When referring to Woods' fifteen wins achieved at an average margin of 3.93 shots vs. Nicklaus' 18 wins at an average of 2.44 shots, the disparity of 1.49 shots per victory does not appear that significant. It is only when the numbers are examined further that Woods' dominance is really on display. Woods' average victory score of 12.87-under par more than doubles Nicklaus' average of 5.67-under. The corresponding average aggregates are 273.53 and 279.94. And when these scores are placed in the context of each player's major championship wins, Nicklaus level of 102-under par is superb, but Woods at 193-under is phenomenal.
    - ○ When reviewing Nicklaus' and Woods' ability to score in major championships, it is necessary to examine another angle. During the 25-year span noted, Nicklaus leads with the total number of rounds in the 60s in major championships at 120 and number of rounds under par at 172. In comparison, Woods recorded 101 total rounds in the 60s and 143 rounds under par. Both players tied the previous 18-hole record of 63 (each at seven under par) and have four-round aggregate scores under 270; Nicklaus once at 269 and Woods once at 266 and once at 269. Finally, in relation to par, Nicklaus shot 17-under in the 1965 Masters, while Woods shot 19-under in the 2000 Open Championship for their respective lows.

- **Missed Cuts**
    - ○ The lack of missed cuts for both players is staggering. For Nicklaus to have missed only six cuts in 100 major championships is significantly better than Woods' level of 12 missed cuts in 84, or 6.00% and 14.29%, respectively. However, these are the two greatest players ever to play the game, so while both are remarkable achievements, they are expected.

Throughout this chapter, there have been detailed examples placing the records of Nicklaus and Woods in greater perspective. This can apply as a standalone review of each player's major championship record and also provide insight when comparing the two records under a variety of scenarios with sufficient depth to appreciate what each player accomplished.

PERCENT OF PURSE

"I never thought anyone would ever put Hogan in the shadows, but he did." – Gene Sarazen on Jack Nicklaus

"I have been fortunate to have my game peak at the right times."–Tiger Woods

In the 1989 book <u>The History of The PGA Tour</u>, author Al Barkow introduced a player ranking system called the "Percent of Purse." This methodology awards points to finishes from first to 25th throughout a player's career in all events (including major championships) sanctioned by the PGA of America or later, the PGA Tour.

Each event is awarded 10,000 points, therefore 1,800 goes to the winner and reduced denominations are subsequent in accordance with their placement. Although 10,000 points would comprise placements further down the leaderboard than 25th, this evaluation system concludes at 25th place and ties.

In that book, the top five players were ranked as follows:

1. Sam Snead
2. Jack Nicklaus
3. Arnold Palmer
4. Ben Hogan
5. Billy Casper

With over 30 years having elapsed since the book was published, I decided to apply the same point system to Jack Nicklaus and Tiger Woods for the periods under review. The results are shown for three scenarios.

- **Percent of Purse – PGA/PGA Tour-sanctioned Events; includes Major Championships**
  - o Jack Nicklaus
    - ▪ 1962 through 1986
  - o Tiger Woods
    - ▪ 1996 through 2022
- **Percent of Purse – Major Championships only**
  - o Jack Nicklaus
    - ▪ 1962 through 1986
  - o Tiger Woods
    - ▪ 1997 through 2022
- **Percent of Purse – Major Championships; most prolific decades**
  - o Jack Nicklaus
    - ▪ 1970 through 1979
  - o Tiger Woods
    - ▪ 2000 through 2009

Jack Nicklaus (1962 – 1986) & Tiger Woods (1996 – 2022) Percent of Purse Results (All)							
Jack Nicklaus				Tiger Woods			
Placement	Points	Finishes	Points Earned	Placement	Points	Finishes	Points Earned
1	1,800	73	131,400	1	1,800	82	147,600
2	1,080	65	70,200	2	1,080	31	33,480
3	680	38	25,840	3	680	19	12,920
4	480	29	13,920	4	480	19	9,120
5	400	23	9,200	5	400	12	4,800
6	360	19	6,840	6	360	6	2,160
7	335	13	4,355	7	335	7	2,345
8	310	12	3,720	8	310	6	1,860
9	290	15	4,350	9	290	10	2,900
10	270	12	3,240	10	270	7	1,890
11	250	17	4,250	11	250	9	2,250
12	230	6	1,380	12	230	7	1,610
13	210	6	1,260	13	210	6	1,260
14	190	7	1,330	14	190	1	190
15	180	9	1,620	15	180	5	900
16	170	8	1,360	16	170	3	510

17	160	8	1,280	17	160	5	800
18	150	6	900	18	150	6	900
19	140	4	560	19	140	2	280
20	130	3	390	20	130	6	780
21	120	4	480	21	120	3	360
22	112	2	224	22	112	5	560
23	104	7	728	23	104	6	624
24	96	4	384	24	96	4	384
25	88	4	352	25	88	2	176
Total	8,335	394	289,563	Total	8,335	269	230,659

Above is another look at both players' performances from the established timelines. While Woods has nine more wins in fewer efforts and leads with a weighted average point value of 857.47 compared to 734.93, the remainder of high-level placements is dominated by Nicklaus.

Jack Nicklaus (1962 – 1986) & Tiger Woods (1997 – 2022) Percent of Purse Results (All Major Championships)							
Jack Nicklaus				Tiger Woods			
Placement	Points	Finishes	Points Earned	Placement	Points	Finishes	Points Earned
1	1,800	18	32.400	1	1,800	15	27,000
2	1,080	18	19,440	2	1,080	7	7,560
3	680	9	6,120	3	680	4	2,720
4	480	7	3,360	4	480	6	2,880
5	400	2	800	5	400	1	400
6	360	5	1,800	6	360	4	1,440
7	335	2	670	7	335	1	335
8	310	2	620	8	310	1	310
9	290	1	290	9	290	1	290
10	270	3	810	10	270	1	270
11	250	2	500	11	250	1	250
12	230	1	230	12	230	2	460
13	210	1	210	13	210	0	0
14	190	0	0	14	190	0	0
15	180	2	360	15	180	1	180
16	170	2	340	16	170	0	170
17	160	0	0	17	160	2	320

18	150	1	150	18	150	2	300
19	140	0	0	19	140	1	140
20	130	0	0	20	130	1	130
21	120	1	120	21	120	2	240
22	112	1	112	22	112	1	112
23	104	2	208	23	104	1	104
24	96	1	96	24	96	2	192
25	88	2	176	25	88	1	88
Total	8,335	83	68,812	Total	8,335	58	45,891

Per the above chart, in major championship play for the timeline under review, Nicklaus' performance is superior to that of Woods with a weighted average of 829.06 vs. 791.22. From number of wins through top-10 placements, Nicklaus leads in all but ninth place finishes, where the two are even.

Jack Nicklaus (1970 – 1979) & Tiger Woods (2000 – 2009*) Percent of Purse Results Per Decade (Major Championships)							
Jack Nicklaus				Tiger Woods			
Placement	Points	Finishes	Points Earned	Placement	Points	Finishes	Points Earned
1	1,800	8	14,400	1	1,800	12	21,600
2	1,080	8	8,640	2	1,080	6	6,480
3	680	5	3,400	3	680	1	680
4	480	5	2,400	4	480	4	1,920
5	400	1	400	5	400	1	400
6	360	2	720	6	360	2	720
7	335	2	670	7	335	0	0
8	310	1	310	8	310	0	0
9	290	1	290	9	290	1	290
10	270	2	540	10	270	0	0
11	250	1	250	11	250	0	0
12	230	0	0	12	230	2	460
13	210	1	210	13	210	0	0
14	190	0	0	14	190	0	0
15	180	0	0	15	180	1	180
16	170	0	0	16	170	0	0
17	160	0	0	17	160	1	160
18	150	0	0	18	150	0	0

19	140	0	0	19	140	0	0
20	130	0	0	20	130	1	130
21	120	0	0	21	120	0	0
22	112	0	0	22	112	1	112
23	104	0	0	23	104	0	0
24	96	0	0	24	96	1	96
25	88	0	0	25	88	1	88
Total	**8,335**	**37**	**32,230**	**Total**	**8,335**	**35**	**33,316**

*In fairness to Woods, due to his missing the 2008 Open Championship and the 2008 PGA Championship, and to balance the number of major championships played between him and Nicklaus, I added the 2010 Masters and U.S. Open finishes. In each championship, Woods tied for fourth place. The weighted average point value for Woods was 951.89 vs. Nicklaus' corresponding number of 871.08.

For the decades referenced, the following provides a high-level summary that again delineates Nicklaus' consistency and Woods' dominance.

- **Victories**
  - Nicklaus   8
  - Woods   12
- **Top-5 Placements**
  - Nicklaus   27
  - Woods   24
- **Top-10 Placements**
  - Nicklaus   35
  - Woods   27
- **Top-25 Placements**
  - Nicklaus   37
  - Woods   35
- **Missed Cuts**
  - Nicklaus   1
  - Woods   2

Masterful Masters Mettle

As another element of the above decade study, I selected the most similar major championship for a review of each player's performance. The below data provides a summary of Nicklaus and Woods at the Masters.

Jack Nicklaus (1970 – 1979) & Tiger Woods (2000 – 2009) Masters Summary								
Jack Nicklaus				Tiger Woods				
Year	Score (Aggregate)	Score (To Par)	Placement	Year	Score (Aggregate)	Score (To Par)	Placement
1970	284	-4	8	2000	284	-4	5
1971	281	-7	T-2	2001	272	-16	1
1972	286	-2	1	2002	276	-12	1
1973	285	-3	T-3	2003	290	+2	T-15
1974	281	-7	T-4	2004	290	+2	T-22
1975	276	-12	1	2005	276	-12	1
1976	282	-6	T-3	2006	284	-4	T-3
1977	278	-10	2	2007	291	+3	T-2
1978	281	-7	7	2008	283	-5	2
1979	281	-7	4	2009	280	-8	T-6
AVG	281.50	-6.50	3.50	AVG	282.60	-5.40	5.80

Here are the highlights.

- **Victories**
  - Nicklaus   2   20.00%
    - Average Margin: 2.00
  - Woods   3   30.00%
    - Average Margin: 1.67
- **Top-5 Placements**
  - Nicklaus   8   80.00%
  - Woods   7   70.00%
- **Top-10 Placements**
  - Nicklaus   10   100.00%
  - Woods   8   80.00%

- **Missed Cuts**
  - o Nicklaus   0
  - o Woods   0

For consistency, Nicklaus again leads the way, but Woods has one more victory. There have been players who completed more consecutive top-10 finishes at the Masters as noted below.

- **Consecutive Top-10 Placements**
  - o Ben Hogan   14
    - ▪ 1939 – 1956
      - • Excludes 1943 – 1945, and 1949
  - o Byron Nelson   12
    - ▪ 1937 – 1951
      - • Excludes 1943 – 1945
  - o Arnold Palmer   11
    - ▪ 1957 – 1967

However, in the above three cases, none were able to complete each event under par for their aggregate scores. In seven of the 14 years for Hogan (1939, 1940, 1948, 1950, 1952, 1954, and 1956), he was unable to break par. For Nelson, he was unable to break par in six of his 12 years (1938, 1946, 1948, 1949, 1950, and 1951). Finally, Palmer was deficient in three years (1957, 1963, and 1966) in breaking par during his run of 11 years; the latter two years consisting of difficult scoring conditions wherein Nicklaus won both at two-under par and even, respectively, at the end of regulation. Nicklaus followed up with a two-under 70 in the playoff in 1966.

In the Woods' era, Phil Mickelson completed nine straight Masters from 1998 through 2006 under par and was in the top 10 eight times from 1999 through 2006.

The best series for Woods occurred during the seven years from 2005 through 2011. While he was in the top 10 in each event, he was unable to break par during the tough scoring conditions in 2007, where the winning score by Zach Johnson was a shot over par.

Yet, in referring to the decades for Nicklaus and Woods described above, Woods leads Nicklaus with three victories to two. While Nicklaus has an impressive total of 65-under par for the 10 years and eclipses Woods' total of 54-under by 11 shots, Woods' three wins stand out.

Woods' three victories total 40 strokes under par. What makes this even more noteworthy is his average margin of victory is less than two shots. Therefore, not only did Woods play well, his competitors pushed him along.

These great performances by Nicklaus and Woods throughout the 10 years specified do not include their dominant, record-setting weeks at the Masters during 1965 and 1997, respectively.

To further examine the similarities between Nicklaus and Woods in the Masters, the following is a snapshot of their records during the first 20 each played as professionals.

Jack Nicklaus & Tiger Woods Masters Summary – First 20 Attempts as Professionals		
	Nicklaus (aged 22 – 41)	Woods (aged 21 – 43)
Victories/Attempts	5/14 = 35.71%	5/20 = 25.00%
Largest Victory Margin	9	12
Average Victory Margin	2.80	3.60
Top-5 Finishes/Attempts	14/20 = 70.00%	12/20 = 60.00%
Top-10 Finishes/Attempts	16/20 = 80.00%	14/20 = 70.00%
Scoring Average	70.87	70.60
Sub-par Rounds/Attempts	44/79 = 55.70%	48/80 = 60.00%
Sub-70 Rounds/Attempts	28/79 = 35.44%	25/80 = 31.25%
Early Win Ratios	3/5 = 60.00%	3/6 = 50.00%
Ages of Title Defenses	26	26
Missed Cuts	1	0
Withdrawals	0	0

With the respective age ranges, Nicklaus completed his first 20 Masters competitions as a professional in uninterrupted succession. Woods was sidetracked in years 2014, 2016, and 2017 due to injuries, therefore his first 20 concluded at age 43 vs. 41 for Nicklaus. Had Woods competed in 2014 and won, his fifth victory would have occurred in his 18th attempt vs. the 14th attempt for Nicklaus.

Thanks in large part to Woods' 12-shot win in 1997 vs. Nicklaus' win in 1965 by nine, his total performance in victory is more dominant. Coincidentally, each captured the green jacket once in a playoff – Nicklaus over 18 holes (1966) and Woods in sudden death (2005).

Nicklaus was more consistent with a greater number of higher-level finishes, while Woods' scoring average was a bit lower. The one blemish contributing to Nicklaus' higher scoring average was the 79 he shot in 1967 leading to his single missed cut vs. Woods at zero missed cuts; this was the highest score shot by either player.

Another coincidence is Nicklaus and Woods successfully defended their second Masters titles at age 26. These third wins represented hot starts for both players relative to the total tournaments played to that point.

It would be interesting to know how the data would vary if Woods had not missed the three aforementioned years. Regardless, when the two records are juxtaposed, the results are remarkable with striking parallels.

PLACEMENT SUMMARY

"Jack's strength is his swing tempo. It rarely changes." – *Tom Watson*
Golf Digest – *"Weighing in for the U.S. Open" June 1983*

*"Tiger does things that are just not normal by any stretch of the
imagination."* – *Rocco Mediate*

The following is a placement comparison/summary of Jack Nicklaus and
Tiger Woods for PGA-sanctioned events **during the periods under review**.
This includes itemized victories, second-, third-, fourth-, and fifth-place
finishes, as well as top-five and top-10 composite finishes. Also, the impacts
of major championships along with full-field vs. limited-field, no 36-hole cut
tournaments* are noted.

*Although the Masters generally has around 90 participants, due to its status
as a major championship and having a 36-hole cut, it is not included in any
limited-field category.

Jack Nicklaus & Tiger Woods All Top-Five Placement Summary						
	Win	**Second**	**Third**	**Fourth**	**Fifth**	**Total**
Nicklaus	73	65	38	29	23	228
Woods	82	31	19	19	12	163
Variance	(9)	34	19	10	11	65

Jack Nicklaus & Tiger Woods Major Championships Top-Five Placement Summary						
	Win	Second	Third	Fourth	Fifth	Total
Nicklaus	18	18	9	7	2	54
Woods	15	7	4	6	1	33
Variance	3	11	5	1	1	21

Jack Nicklaus & Tiger Woods Full-field Events Top-Five Placement Summary						
	Win	Second	Third	Fourth	Fifth	Total
Nicklaus	64	63	38	27	20	212
Woods	56	25	16	14	6	117
Variance	8	38	22	13	14	95

Jack Nicklaus & Tiger Woods Limited-field Events Top-Five Placement Summary						
	Win	Second	Third	Fourth	Fifth	Total
Nicklaus	9	2	0	2	3	16
Woods	26	6	3	5	6	46
Variance	(17)	(4)	(3)	(3)	(3)	(30)

Woods leads Nicklaus in total PGA victories at 82 compared to 73. When factoring out the total limited-field, no 36-hole cut wins of 26 and nine, respectively, Nicklaus leads Woods in full-field wins at 64 to 56. Furthermore, 87.67% of Nicklaus' total PGA wins was in full-field events, with Woods' full-field ratio of PGA wins to his total at 68.29%.

While Woods leads Nicklaus by nine total victories, Nicklaus' placements of second, third, fourth, and fifth lead Woods by 34, 19, 10, and 11, respectively. Therefore, the composite of top-five PGA finishes for Nicklaus is 228 vs. 163 for Woods – a difference of 65.

In major championships, Nicklaus leads Woods in all placements from first through fifth. His total top-five placements in major championships are 54 compared to Woods' 33.

However, when calculating the number of full-field PGA wins as a percentage of the full-field top-five finishes, Woods leads Nicklaus 47.86% to 30.19%. In other words, of the 117 top-five finishes for Woods, he won on 56 occasions vs. 64 wins of the 212 top-five finishes for Nicklaus.

For the same years, Woods also leads Nicklaus when determining the percentage of total top-10 finishes within the top five at 81.91% vs. 76.25%. Or of Woods' total top-10 placements of 199, 163 of them were within the top five, while Nicklaus finished in the top five 228 times out of 299 total top-10 finishes.

As a point of reference, below are 20 leading players and their top-10 placements in all PGA events (includes the Open Championship). The list is led by Sam Snead and for Nicklaus includes all tournament finishes in the top-10 from his amateur years through 1998 plus the 299 strictly for the years 1962 through 1986.

- Sam Snead: 332
- ***Jack Nicklaus:***   311 (all)   299 (1962 – 1986)
- Arnold Palmer: 252
- Billy Casper: 238
- Ben Hogan: 230
- Tom Watson: 229
- Tom Kite: 214
- Gene Littler: 213
- Byron Nelson: 207
- ***Tiger Woods:***   199
- Phil Mickelson: 197
- Gary Player: 189
- Jim Furyk: 188
- Vijay Singh: 185
- Lee Trevino: 173
- Raymond Floyd: 168
- Hale Irwin: 168
- Ernie Els: 126

- Rory McIlroy: 102
- David Duval: 68

Nicklaus' total includes 12 additional top-10 finishes in PGA-sanctioned events and major championships before 1962 and after 1986 and is second only to Sam Snead's total of 332. Although Snead's record and longevity are impressive, many of these events were small fields during the early days of the professional circuit. Woods' total top-10 finishes is at 199 – a difference from Nicklaus of 112 or 100, as applicable.

When these numbers are examined further, Nicklaus' *total* top-five finishes of 231 is 74.28% of his total of 311. And again, Woods' 163 top-five finishes is 81.91% of his total of 199. Therefore, just fewer than three out of every four times Nicklaus finished in the top-10, he was actually in the top five, while slightly more than four out of every five times Woods finished in the top-10, he was actually in the top five.

These are impressive statistics for both players as it shows they were generally "in the hunt" at an exceedingly high rate in both full-field events and when combined with all tournaments. For Nicklaus and Woods, this reflects well as opposed to sliding into the top 10 by way of player attrition or having closed with an unusual amount of low final rounds.

PLACEMENT DETAIL

"The battle is to believe in yourself." – Jack Nicklaus **Golf Digest** *– "Weighing in for the U.S. Open" June 1983*

"Your senses are heightened when you're in a clutch situation. You just feel if you believe in something so hard, if you truly believe...the ball will go in." – Tiger Woods **Golf Digest** *– December 2002*

Since the previous chapter relayed placement summaries for Jack Nicklaus and Tiger Woods, this chapter will expand on that topic. Woods may be the most dominant player in history based upon victory margins and overall win percentage. So, how does Nicklaus measure up?

Major Championship Placement Distribution as Professionals

For the 25-year period beginning in 1962 and running through 1986, at four major championships per year, there were a total of 100 major championships contested and Nicklaus competed in them all. The following is a snapshot of his performance. Subsequent to this, Woods' record in the major championships beginning in 1997 will be shown. Due to various injuries and the coronavirus outbreak in 2020, he only competed in 84 events.

Jack Nicklaus Major Championship Placements (1962 – 1986)		
Total Championships Played	100	
Total Wins & Percentage	18	18.00%
Total Runner-up Finishes & Percentage	18	18.00%

Total Third Place Finishes & Percentage	9	9.00%
Total Fourth Place Finishes & Percentage	7	7.00%
Total Fifth Place Finishes & Percentage	2	2.00%
Total Top-10 Finishes & Percentage	67	67.00%
Total Top-20 Finishes & Percentage	76	76.00%
Missed Cuts & Percentage	6	6.00%
Withdrawals & Percentage	1	1.00%

Besides a record 18 victories, there are other impressive aspects of this graphic not as well-known. The number of second place finishes at 18 is unbelievable. But when referring to the earlier data provided, Nicklaus was one shot out of a playoff in five other major championships. So, out of 100 major championships played, he won, was in second place/tied for second place, or finished one shot from tying for first place in 41. More than half the time (52.00%), Nicklaus finished no worse than fourth. Regardless of any debate about competition, the depth of his record is prodigious.

Tiger Woods Major Championship Placements (1997 – 2022)		
Total Championships Played	84	
Total Wins & Percentage	15	17.86%
Total Runner-up Finishes & Percentage	7	8.33%
Total Third Place Finishes & Percentage	4	4.76%
Total Fourth Place Finishes & Percentage	6	7.14%
Total Fifth Place Finishes & Percentage	1	1.19%
Total Top-10 Finishes & Percentage	41	48.81%
Total Top-20 Finishes & Percentage	51	60.71%
Missed Cuts & Percentage	12	14.29%
Withdrawals & Percentage	1	1.19%

In winning 15 major championships, Woods not only placed himself second behind Nicklaus and solidly ahead of Walter Hagen's total of 11, he further proved his dominance in the way he achieved his victories. In his first 46 major championships played as a professional, Woods won 14, which equates to a 30.43% conversion rate. The total stroke differential for the 15 wins was 59, or an average winning margin of 3.93 shots. From his win in the 1999

PGA Championship through his 2002 U.S. Open victory, Woods won a mind-boggling seven of 11 major championships played, or 63.64%. While Woods' other placements are solid, this win percentage is the highest in the modern era.

Major Championship Wins & Top Placements in Succession

Subsequent to the above data, the below table provides detail on Nicklaus and Woods when they were able to win, place in the top five, and place in the top 10 in major championships in consecutive starts.

Jack Nicklaus & Tiger Woods Major Championship Discrete Victories in Succession		
	4 Consecutive Wins	**3 Consecutive Wins**	**2 Consecutive Wins**
Nicklaus	0	0	1
Woods	1	0	2
Variance	(1)	0	(1)

Woods' dominance is on full display supplemented by his record-setting year of 2000. Woods began his "Tiger Slam" by winning the 2000 U.S. Open followed by the Open Championship and the PGA Championship. However, he finished in fifth place, six shots behind Vijay Singh in the Masters earlier in the year. By winning the 2001 Masters, he was able to win four major championships in succession. While not the Grand Slam due to the victories occurring over two years, it is the closest to it in the modern era. Woods was also able to win the 2002 Masters and U.S. Open followed by the 2006 Open Championship and PGA Championship as the final times he won at least two major championships in a row.

Nicklaus was only able to win two major championships in succession once. In 1972, he won the Masters followed by the U.S. Open. However, a one-shot runner-up to Lee Trevino in the 1972 Open Championship prevented Nicklaus from further advancement. While Nicklaus had a total of five years with two major championship victories each, no more were won consecutively.

Jack Nicklaus & Tiger Woods Major Championship Discrete Top-5 Placements in Succession						
	7	6	5	4	3	2
Nicklaus	1	1	1	2	5	2
Woods	0	1	1	1	2	2
Variance	1	0	0	1	3	0

The above are each discrete successive top-five streaks in major championships for Nicklaus and Woods. There is no overlap. Nicklaus leads significantly in this measure, which again is attributable to his consistency and longevity. At 45 major championships compared to Woods at 25, he has nearly twice the performance. Woods' level of consistency is remarkable, but Nicklaus is far superior in this area.

Jack Nicklaus & Tiger Woods Major Championship Discrete Top-10 Placements in Succession											
	13	12	11	10	9	8	7	6	5	4	3	2
Nicklaus	1	0	0	0	2	0	0	1	1	1	3	4
Woods	0	0	0	0	0	1	0	0	1	1	3	3
Variance	1	0	0	0	2	(1)	0	1	0	0	0	1

As with the preceding chart, the above top-10 placements for each player are all discrete efforts with no overlap. Woods is again impressive with 32, but Nicklaus exceeds this number by 31 for a total of 63 major championships, nearly double.

When reviewing the data in both displays, it should be noted that of the 63 top-10 placements for Nicklaus, 49 were within the top five, or 77.78%. Woods' relative tally is higher with 27 of his 32 top-10 finishes within the top five, or 84.38%. This shows while each top-10 placement total will automatically include top-five finishes, the majority for each player was in the upper half.

Major Championship Finishes Within Four Shots

To expand on Nicklaus' and Woods' ability to win and contend in major championships, the following summarizes their distribution of 72-hole finishes when both players won or were within four shots of the winning score. The objective is provide the full record for each player and not just the 25-year performances as professionals. This measurement is significant enough that I included all placements for Nicklaus to further illustrate his longevity. Subsequent placements by Woods can be added post-2022. Or if the reader prefers only the years previously defined, the deductions for Nicklaus can be made easily.

The four additions to Nicklaus' 25-year record are noted here.

- **Masters**
  - 1987
    - Nicklaus finished tied for seventh place, four shots behind.
  - 1998
    - Nicklaus finished tied for sixth place, four shots behind.
- **U.S. Open**
  - 1960
    - Nicklaus finished second, two shots behind.
      - Amateur
  - 1961
    - Nicklaus finished tied for fourth place, three shots behind.
      - Amateur

Jack Nicklaus & Tiger Woods Masters Finishes Within 4 Shots of the 72-hole Winning Score – All							
	Win	0	1	2	3	4	Total
Nicklaus	6	0	1	4	1	5	17
Woods	5	0	0	1	2	3	11
Variance	1	0	1	3	(1)	2	6

This chart reflects exceptional performances by both players. Ironically, for Nicklaus his next closest championship placement outside of winning was his fourth-place finish in 1979. This is a good example for reviewing the number of shots vs. simply placements as none of his four second- place finishes were closer than two shots (1971, 1977, and 1981), while in 1964, he was six shots adrift of Arnold Palmer. Similarly, Woods either won or was not less than two shots from the champion; his closest finish being two shots short of Zach Johnson in 2007. However, from the perspective of frequency within the range, Nicklaus leads Woods convincingly.

Jack Nicklaus & Tiger Woods U.S. Open Finishes Within 4 Shots of the 72-hole Winning Score – All							
	Win	0	1	2	3	4	Total
Nicklaus	4	1	0	3	2	2	12
Woods	3	0	1	2	1	1	8
Variance	1	1	(1)	1	1	1	4

As noted, two of the placements for Nicklaus occurred when he was an amateur. The placement at zero refers to the 1971 U.S. Open where he tied with Trevino in regulation, but lost the 18-hole playoff. Woods also displays a solid record in this championship, yet without the "anomalies" Nicklaus registered.

Jack Nicklaus & Tiger Woods Open Championship Finishes Within 4 Shots of the 72-hole Winning Score – All							
	Win	0	1	2	3	4	Total
Nicklaus	3	0	4	2	1	2	12
Woods	3	0	1	1	1	2	8
Variance	0	0	3	1	0	0	4

This is the one major championship Nicklaus and Woods are equal in number of victories. However, Nicklaus' record of consistency in this event may be the greatest of anyone ever to play. Woods has also been quite consistent in this event, especially in his first 10 years as a professional with seven top-10 placements including three wins.

Jack Nicklaus & Tiger Woods PGA Championship Finishes Within 4 Shots of the 72-hole Winning Score – All							
	Win	0	1	2	3	4	Total
Nicklaus	5	0	4	2	2	1	14
Woods	4	0	1	2	1	0	8
Variance	1	0	3	0	1	1	6

Nicklaus nearly doubles Woods' total of 72-hole placements within four shots of the winning score. What is most significant for Nicklaus is that on nine occasions he either won or was one shot from tying the winning score. In Woods' case, his four victories represent successfully defending his title on two occasions, which has never been done before in the stroke-play era and may never happen again.

	Jack Nicklaus & Tiger Woods Total Major Championship Finishes Within 4 Shots of the 72-hole Winning Score – All						
	Win	0	1	2	3	4	Total
Nicklaus	18	1	9	11	6	10	55
Woods	15	0	3	6	5	6	35
Variance	3	1	6	5	1	4	20

By calculating the number of strokes vs. discrete placements, this study reflects more accurately the frequency of contention Nicklaus and Woods were able to achieve in major championships throughout their careers.

For example, when Nicklaus finished tied for second in the 1964 Masters by six shots, second alone in the 1964 Open Championship by five shots, tied for third in the 1976 Masters by 11 shots, and tied for fourth in the 1980 Open Championship by nine shots, these are properly credited, yet he wasn't in serious contention. Conversely, the data quells the argument that many of Nicklaus' second-place finishes like the two listed above were overrated by providing a better balance not directly tied to specific placements. By including such instances as the 1975 U.S. Open where Nicklaus finished in a tie for seventh place, we get a clearer reflection of performance. On that occasion, he was in contention the final day and came up short by two shots. Due to the leaderboard being bunched up, he finished further down, placement-wise.

Nicklaus either won or finished no worse than four shots behind the champion on 55 occasions, which closely resembles his complete top-5 major championship placement total of 56.

This also better conveys Woods' record vs. simply stating he had seven second-place finishes. Instead, he completed 35 major championships by either winning or being no worse than four shots back. This number again aligns itself to the 33 top-five finishes Woods garnered.

PGA Tour Placement Distribution as Professionals (All Events)

Once turning professional, Nicklaus and Woods built their schedules around the four major championships. To succeed, they also had to compete in non-major events to assist in preparing. The following shows how each fared across all PGA-sanctioned tournaments with no distinction between major championships, full-field, or limited-field events.

Jack Nicklaus PGA Tour Placements All Events (1962 – 1986)		
Total Events Played	480	
Total Wins & Percentage	73	15.21%
Total Runner-up Finishes & Percentage	65	13.54%
Total Third Place Finishes & Percentage	38	7.92%
Total Fourth Place Finishes & Percentage	29	6.04%
Total Fifth Place Finishes & Percentage	23	4.79%
Total Top-10 Finishes & Percentage	299	62.29%
Total Top-20 Finishes & Percentage	373	77.71%
Missed Cuts & Percentage	26	5.42%
Withdrawals & Percentage	4	0.83%

At first glance, the win percentage for Nicklaus seems low. Upon further review, the entirety of the record corresponds similarly in proportion to his performance shown earlier in the major championships. With his second-place finishes nearly equal the number of wins, that is a noteworthy achievement. And when all top-five placements are tallied, they occupy 47.50%. So, nearly half the time Nicklaus was fifth or better while in nearly two out of every three tournaments played, he finished in the top 10. This is an unmatched consistency and ability to contend for 25 years.

Tiger Woods PGA Tour Placements All Events (1996 – 2022)		
Total Events Played	357	
Total Wins & Percentage	82	22.97%
Total Runner-up Finishes & Percentage	31	8.68%
Total Third Place Finishes & Percentage	19	5.32%
Total Fourth Place Finishes & Percentage	19	5.32%
Total Fifth Place Finishes & Percentage	12	3.36%
Total Top-10 Finishes & Percentage	199	55.74%
Total Top-20 Finishes & Percentage	249	69.75%
Missed Cuts & Percentage	22	6.16%
Withdrawals & Percentage	10	2.80%

Woods' win percentage confirms the greatness of his career. He has been able to *win* more than one out of every five events played. With this amazing statistic over a long period, it would be expected that the next immediate placements would drop off sharply. However, when reviewing the percentage of top-10 and top-20 finishes, Woods shows a great ability to contend with over half the placements in the former and just under seven out of 10 placements for the latter.

PGA Tour Placement Distribution as Professionals (Full-field Events)

As the PGA Tour has progressed, so has the number of limited-field events. For Nicklaus, the number of full-field events at 447 represents 93.13% of the total 480 official PGA tournaments he played from 1962 through 1986. This segment is significantly lower for Woods whose 264 full-field events comprise 73.95% of his total 357. In this review, both the Masters and Open Championship are included.

Jack Nicklaus PGA Tour Placements Full-field Events (1962 – 1986)		
Total Events Played	447	
Total Wins & Percentage	64	14.32%
Total Runner-up Finishes & Percentage	63	14.09%

Total Third Place Finishes & Percentage	38	8.50%
Total Fourth Place Finishes & Percentage	27	6.04%
Total Fifth Place Finishes & Percentage	20	4.47%
Total Top-10 Finishes & Percentage	275	61.52%
Total Top-20 Finishes & Percentage	343	76.73%
Missed Cuts & Percentage	26	5.82%
Withdrawals & Percentage	3	0.67%

Once again, Nicklaus' win percentage and runner-up percentage are almost identical. Due to his relative lack of limited-field events during the 25-year review period, the percentages have not varied greatly. The numbers of missed cuts and withdrawals were weighed more heavily once Nicklaus hit age 40 with 10 of 26 and two of three, respectively during the seven years from 1980 through 1986.

Tiger Woods PGA Tour Placements Full-field Events (1996 – 2022)		
Total Events Played	264	
Total Wins & Percentage	56	21.21%
Total Runner-up Finishes & Percentage	22	8.33%
Total Third Place Finishes & Percentage	16	6.06%
Total Fourth Place Finishes & Percentage	14	5.30%
Total Fifth Place Finishes & Percentage	6	2.27%
Total Top-10 Finishes & Percentage	138	52.27%
Total Top-20 Finishes & Percentage	177	67.05%
Missed Cuts & Percentage	22	8.33%
Withdrawals & Percentage	7	2.65%

Woods has similar percentage ratios again exist across the board. The win rate Woods accomplished is still greater than a one in five success. Due to the larger fields, the percentages are just slightly down on average, but still quite good. And similar to Nicklaus, Woods' missed cuts accelerated in his later years.

PGA Tour Placement Distribution as Professionals (Limited-field Events)

Although limited-field tournaments occupy a larger percentage of the PGA Tour schedule in Woods' era than in Nicklaus' era, it is noteworthy to review each player's applicable record. Even with a disparity in the total number, the ratios should still be examined.

Jack Nicklaus PGA Tour Placements Limited-field Events (1962 – 1986)		
Total Events Played	33	
Total Wins & Percentage	9	27.27%
Total Runner-up Finishes & Percentage	2	6.06%
Total Third Place Finishes & Percentage	0	0.00%
Total Fourth Place Finishes & Percentage	2	6.06%
Total Fifth Place Finishes & Percentage	3	9.09%
Total Top-10 Finishes & Percentage	24	72.73%
Total Top-20 Finishes & Percentage	30	90.91%
Missed Cuts & Percentage	0	0.00%
Withdrawals & Percentage	1	3.03%

Nicklaus only played in 33 limited-field events sanctioned by the PGA during the 25-year period of review. Two were the National Four-ball Championship in 1970 and again in 1971 as the National Team Championship, which the PGA Tour counts as wins. Also, the 1974 Walt Disney World National Team Championship, where Nicklaus and Tom Weiskopf finished in a tie for 14th, is added. However, he did win five Tournament of Champions titles, which is a record.

Tiger Woods PGA Tour Placements Limited-field Events (1996 – 2022)		
Total Events Played	93	
Total Wins & Percentage	26	27.96%
Total Runner-up Finishes & Percentage	9	9.68%
Total Third Place Finishes & Percentage	3	3.23%
Total Fourth Place Finishes & Percentage	5	5.38%
Total Fifth Place Finishes & Percentage	6	6.45%

Total Top-10 Finishes & Percentage	61	65.59%
Total Top-20 Finishes & Percentage	72	77.42%
Missed Cuts & Percentage	0	0.00%
Withdrawals & Percentage	3	3.23%

With the advent of the World Golf Championship ("WGC") events, Woods has not only competed in more limited-field tournaments, he has won more. Having won 18 WGC events, he established a record for the total plus individual titles for each – Bridgestone Invitational (eight), WGC Championship (seven), and the Accenture Match Play Championship (three). Woods' numbers across the board are excellent.

PGA Tour Placement Distribution as Amateurs (Includes Major Championships)

Nicklaus and Woods competed as amateurs at early ages in several tournaments and major championships alongside touring professionals. Below summarizes how each handled the experience:

Jack Nicklaus PGA Tour Placements Amateur (1957 – 1961)		
Total Events Played	15	
Total Wins & Percentage	0	0.00%
Total Runner-up Finishes & Percentage	1	6.67%
Total Third Place Finishes & Percentage	0	0.00%
Total Fourth Place Finishes & Percentage	1	6.67%
Total Fifth Place Finishes & Percentage	0	0.00%
Total Top-10 Finishes & Percentage	3	20.00%
Total Top-20 Finishes & Percentage	6	40.00%
Missed Cuts & Percentage	3	20.00%
Withdrawals & Percentage	0	0.00%

Nicklaus first qualified for the U.S. Open Championship in 1957 at age 17. In total, he competed in eight major championships before turning professional – five U.S. Opens and three Masters. For the 15 events Nicklaus played, he made the 36-hole cut 12 times or 80.00%. While his three top-10 finishes were in major championships (second in the 1960 U.S. Open, tied for seventh in the 1961 Masters, and tied for fourth in the 1961 U.S. Open), his three missed cuts were also in two U.S. Opens and one Masters prior to 1960. Nicklaus finished as Low Amateur in the 1960 Masters, the 1960 U.S. Open, and the 1961 U.S. Open. His two-under par score of 282 in the 1960 U.S. Open remained the record by an amateur until 2019, when Viktor Hovland shot a four-under par score of 280 and tied for 12th at Pebble Beach. However, Nicklaus was unable to crack the top-10 in any of the seven non-major tournaments. His best finish was 12th place in the 1958 Rubber City Open.

It should be mentioned that Nicklaus also won the 1956 Ohio Open at age 16 against professionals. This was not an official PGA-sanctioned event at the time, but had been previously and a tournament Byron Nelson won on three occasions.

Tiger Woods PGA Tour Placements Amateur (1992 – 1996)		
Total Events Played	14	
Total Wins & Percentage	0	0.00%
Total Runner-up Finishes & Percentage	0	0.00%
Total Third Place Finishes & Percentage	0	0.00%
Total Fourth Place Finishes & Percentage	0	0.00%
Total Fifth Place Finishes & Percentage	0	0.00%
Total Top-10 Finishes & Percentage	0	0.00%
Total Top-20 Finishes & Percentage	0	0.00%
Missed Cuts & Percentage	8	57.14%
Withdrawals & Percentage	1	7.14%

At age 16, Woods first participated in a PGA Tour event at the 1992 Nissan Los Angeles Open. Even though he missed the cut with rounds of 72 and 75, it was an impressive debut. From that event through the 1996 Open Championship, Woods competed in a total of six major championships and eight non-major tournaments. In the six majors, he finished as Low Amateur in the 1995 Masters and the 1996 Open Championship with a tie for 41st and a tie for 22nd, respectively. In the 1996 Open Championship, Woods shot a three-under par 281, which remains tied for the lowest aggregate score by an amateur. As with Nicklaus, Woods' best finishes were in major championships vs. regular PGA Tour events. His tie for 57th in the 1995 Motorola Western Open was the highlight for non-major tournament placements.

Overseas Tournament Placement Distribution – As Professionals (Excludes the Open)

For Nicklaus and Woods, the biggest prize in overseas golf would be the Open Championship. With that major championship excluded, the following provides a summary of each player's record in tournaments outside the United States and Canada during their years as professionals.

Jack Nicklaus Overseas Placements Minus the Open (1962 – 1986)		
Total Events Played	29	
Total Wins & Percentage	11	37.93%
Total Runner-up Finishes & Percentage	8	27.59%
Total Third Place Finishes & Percentage	2	6.90%
Total Fourth Place Finishes & Percentage	0	0.00%
Total Fifth Place Finishes & Percentage	3	10.34%
Total Top-10 Finishes & Percentage	24	82.76%
Total Top-20 Finishes & Percentage	26	89.66%
Missed Cuts & Percentage	0	0.00%
Withdrawals & Percentage	0	0.00%

The record above is another solid effort by Nicklaus with a win conversion rate just under 38.00%. The number of victories at 11 is occupied largely by six Australian Open Championships, but does include other prestigious wins such as the 1970 Piccadilly World Match Play Championship (most recently the Volvo World Match Play Championship). Nicklaus' consistency is in focus again with 24 of 29 (82.76%) finishes no worse than fifth.

Tiger Woods Overseas Placements Minus the Open (1996 – 2022)		
Total Events Played	43	
Total Wins & Percentage	13	30.23%
Total Runner-up Finishes & Percentage	8	18.60%
Total Third Place Finishes & Percentage	6	13.95%

Total Fourth Place Finishes & Percentage	2	4.65%
Total Fifth Place Finishes & Percentage	1	2.33%
Total Top-10 Finishes & Percentage	36	83.72%
Total Top-20 Finishes & Percentage	38	88.37%
Missed Cuts & Percentage	1	2.33%
Withdrawals & Percentage	1	2.33%

Here is another solid performance for Woods. A 30.23%-win rate in 43 events is remarkable, but what may be more significant is that he finished no worse than third in 62.79% of the events and in 30 (69.77%), no worse than fifth. Woods' 13 victories are also distributed in a fairly uniform manner with the most concentrated being three wins at the Deutsche Bank - SAP Open. This is a very impressive record with the continued global growth of the game.

Near-misses & Missed Opportunities

Both Nicklaus and Woods competed in events they didn't win even after numerous years of effort. In addition, they played in tournaments they did win, but likely thought they should have won more. This section describes two events apiece for each player – one under each of the two scenarios. Also, two events are discussed wherein Woods only played once in each, yet had he attempted more, could have likely been nice additions to his suite of titles. Since this chapter is on placements, we again see both players' consistency over the years even when victories were few and far between.

There is no more prominent record of near-misses for Nicklaus than his history at the Canadian Open. Even though this tournament has lost some luster over the years, it is still a national championship Nicklaus wanted to win.

Below are the Canadian Open champions and dates they won when Nicklaus finished runner-up:

1965: Gene Littler
1968: Bob Charles
1975: Tom Weiskopf

1976: Jerry Pate

1981: Peter Oosterhuis

1984: Greg Norman

1985: Curtis Strange

All seven champions won a combined 97 PGA victories including eight major championships.

Nicklaus finished in third place on two occasions one shot short of a playoff. These near-misses occurred during the following years.

1967: Billy Casper defeated Art Wall

1983: John Cook defeated Johnny Miller

Nicklaus also tied for fourth once and tied for fifth twice. This reflects 12 finishes in this tournament no worse than fifth place in 19 attempts, or 63.16% of the time. Oddly, Nicklaus did not play the Canadian Open from 1969 through 1973; the latter three years being some of the best in his career. The lone missed cut was in 1982 at age 42. Even without winning the event, such a record is incredible. The following is a summary of his top-10 performances from 1962 through 1986.

- **Events Played:** 19
- **Victories:** 0
- **2nd Place Finishes:** 7
- **Top-5 Finishes:** 12
- **Top-10 Finishes:** 12
- **Missed Cuts:** 1

Another tournament Nicklaus had great consistency in was the Doral Open (most recently the WGC Championship). Below is a summary of his top-10 performances from 1962 through 1986:

- **Events Played:** 24
- **Victories:** 2
- **2nd Place Finishes:** 5

- **Top-5 Finishes:**   12
- **Top-10 Finishes:**   15
- **Missed Cuts:**   1

While two wins is relatively small, the number of combined first and second place finishes occupies 29.16% of his efforts with top-five and top-10 placements reflecting 50.00% and 62.50%, respectively. Nicklaus' first top-five finish (solo third) occurred in 1962 and last for the 25-year range under review was in 1985 (tied for third). He also finished tied for fifth in 1991 and tied for 10th in 1993. Like the Canadian Open, the only missed cut came in 1981 at age 41 after Nicklaus began playing a further-reduced schedule.

These two examples display Nicklaus' ability to perform at a highly-consistent level over a lengthy number of years even if victories were not plentiful.

For Woods, it seemed during his first few years on the PGA Tour that he had won every different tournament he played. Yet, he never captured the Nissan Open (now the Genesis Invitational) after competing on 12 occasions.

Below are the Nissan Open/Genesis Invitational champions and dates they won when Woods competed:

1997:   Nick Faldo

1998:   Billy Mayfair

1999:   Ernie Els

2000:   Kirk Triplett

2001:   Robert Allenby

2003:   Mike Weir

2004:   Mike Weir

2005:   Adam Scott

2006:   Rory Sabbatini

2018:   Bubba Watson

2019:   J.B. Holmes

2020:   Adam Scott

The 10 different players above won a combined 85 PGA Tour events including 14 major championships. Woods accumulated four top-10 finishes in these 12 attempts. Below is a listing of his performance:

- **Events Played:** 12
- **Victories:** 0
- **2nd Place Finishes:** 2
- **Top-5 Finishes:** 3
- **Top-10 Finishes:** 4
- **Top-20 Finishes:** 8
- **Missed Cuts:** 1
- **Withdrawals:** 1

Woods had a sound record in the Nissan Open with one out of every four finishes in the top five but was unable to convert a victory. In 1998, Woods' only playoff loss on the PGA Tour occurred in this tournament.

The second tournament under review for Woods is the Byron Nelson Golf Classic (now the AT&T Byron Nelson). Below is a summary of his total top-10 performances:

- **Events Played:** 8
- **Victories:** 1
- **2nd Place Finishes:** 0
- **Top-5 Finishes:** 4
- **Top-10 Finishes:** 5
- **Missed Cuts:** 1

Although not as dominating as other tournaments, Woods still has a solid record in this event. After winning in his first year as a professional, Woods only competed seven more years with four more placements in the top 10. He achieved a 50.00% rate of top-five finishes and a 62.50% rate in the top 10. Woods ended his time at this venue in 2005 with a missed cut.

Two tournaments whose victories would burnish any touring professional's re'sume' are the Colonial National Invitation (currently the Charles Schwab

Challenge) and the Heritage Classic (currently the RBC Heritage). These events have been fixtures for over 50 years and the roster of champions is a "who's who" of golf. However, except for one attempt per tournament, Woods skipped them. Below are the results when he did compete:

- **1997 MasterCard Colonial ("Colonial")**
    - 67-65-64-72
        - T-4
- **1999 MCI Classic ("Heritage")**
    - 70-70-69-71
        - T-18

Woods played well in each tournament early in his career at 12-under par and four-under par, respectively. Neither course is a bomber's haven, instead relying on position off the tee and great iron play. Perhaps with the advent of the WGC events, it makes sense why Woods opted out of these two tournaments. But as his game matured, he likely could have added his name to the lists of champions.

Unfulfilled Promise

When considering the records of Nicklaus and Woods, implementing such a description as "unfulfilled promise" seems ludicrous. However, it applies in different ways when referring to the following five prestigious events.

- The Players (aka Tournament Players Championship et al.)
- Memorial Tournament
- World Series of Golf (aka WGC-Bridgestone Invitational et al.)
- Arnold Palmer Invitational (aka Florida Citrus Open Invitational et al.)
- FedEx Cup Playoffs

Jack Nicklaus (1962 – 1986) & Tiger Woods (1997 – 2022) The Players Summary							
Jack Nicklaus				Tiger Woods			
Year	Score (Aggregate)	Score (To Par)	Placement	Year	Score (Aggregate)	Score (To Par)	Placement
1962	No Tournament	N/A	N/A	1997	289	+1	T-31
1963	No Tournament	N/A	N/A	1998	290	+2	T-35
1964	No Tournament	N/A	N/A	1999	291	+3	T-10
1965	No Tournament	N/A	N/A	2000	279	-9	2
1966	No Tournament	N/A	N/A	2001	274	-14	1
1967	No Tournament	N/A	N/A	2002	287	-1	T-14
1968	No Tournament	N/A	N/A	2003	282	-6	T-11
1969	No Tournament	N/A	N/A	2004	285	-3	T-16
1970	No Tournament	N/A	N/A	2005	293	+5	T-53
1971	No Tournament	N/A	N/A	2006	289	+1	T-22
1972	No Tournament	N/A	N/A	2007	288	0	T-37
1973	No Tournament	N/A	N/A	2008	DNP	N/A	N/A
1974	272	-16	1	2009	283	-5	8
1975	287	+7	T-18	2010	212 (WD)	-4	N/A
1976	269	-19	1	2011	WD	N/A	N/A
1977	293	+5	T-5	2012	287	-1	T-40
1978	289	+1	1	2013	275	-13	1
1979	300	+12	T-33	2014	DNP	N/A	N/A
1980	284	-4	T-14	2015	291	+3	T-69
1981	293	+5	T-29	2016	DNP	N/A	N/A
1982	151	+7	MC	2017	DNP	N/A	N/A
1983	291	+3	T-19	2018	277	-11	T-11
1984	292	+4	T-33	2019	282	-6	T-30
1985	288	0	T-17	2020	No Tournament	N/A	N/A
1986	147	+3	MC	2021	DNP	N/A	N/A
				2022	DNP	N/A	N/A
AVG	72.00	0.17	15.55	AVG	71.18	-0.82	23.00

Upon review of the so-called "fifth major," a mixed bag emerges. Nicklaus won the event three times in thirteen attempts (23.08%) for the subject date range with his first title at age 34. Each of these victories was on a different course vs. the present location introduced in 1982. For Nicklaus, the flip side to the three wins was the two missed cuts after age 40. Woods was able to compete in 19 events at the same location and won the title twice (10.53%) with zero missed cuts. His first victory occurred at age 25 and his last at age 37.

Since Nicklaus outnumbers Woods by three to two in titles, a few items should be noted. For the first 12 years of his playing career, Nicklaus was unable to compete in this event as it did not exist. In at least eight of those 12 years, he had some of his best performances. It is therefore conceivable Nicklaus would have augmented his number of wins by a significant margin. Woods also missed out on seven complete playings due to injury, as well as the coronavirus cancellation in 2020. However, except for 2008, none were high-performing campaigns. With Nicklaus' three wins occurring at age 34 or later compared to Woods' lone win post-age 34, the probability of a higher win ratio in favor of Nicklaus is great.

Jack Nicklaus (1962 – 1986) & Tiger Woods (1997 – 2022) Memorial Tournament Summary							
Jack Nicklaus				Tiger Woods			
Year	Score (Aggregate)	Score (To Par)	Placement	Year	Score (Aggregate)	Score (To Par)	Placement
1962	No Tournament	N/A	N/A	1997	221	+5	T-67
1963	No Tournament	N/A	N/A	1998	288	0	T-51
1964	No Tournament	N/A	N/A	1999	273	-15	1
1965	No Tournament	N/A	N/A	2000	269	-19	1
1966	No Tournament	N/A	N/A	2001	271	-17	1
1967	No Tournament	N/A	N/A	2002	282	-6	T-22
1968	No Tournament	N/A	N/A	2003	279	-9	T-4
1969	No Tournament	N/A	N/A	2004	276	-12	3
1970	No Tournament	N/A	N/A	2005	276	-12	T-3
1971	No Tournament	N/A	N/A	2006	DNP	N/A	N/A
1972	No Tournament	N/A	N/A	2007	279	-9	T-15
1973	No Tournament	N/A	N/A	2008	DNP	N/A	N/A
1974	No Tournament	N/A	N/A	2009	276	-12	1
1975	No Tournament	N/A	N/A	2010	282	-6	T-19
1976	292	+4	T-8	2011	DNP	N/A	N/A
1977	281	-7	1	2012	279	-9	1
1978	288	0	T-4	2013	296	+8	T-65
1979	299	+11	T-27	2014	DNP	N/A	N/A

1980	288	0	T-20	2015	302	+14	71
1981	288	0	T-12	2016	DNP	N/A	N/A
1982	286	-2	T-11	2017	DNP	N/A	N/A
1983	291	+3	T-33	2018	279	-9	T-23
1984	280	-8	1	2019	279	-9	T-9
1985	299	+11	T-54	2020	294	+6	T-40
1986	277	-11	T-5	2021	DNP	N/A	N/A
				2022	DNP	N/A	N/A
AVG	72.02	0.02	16.00	AVG	70.44	-1.56	22.06

A similar scenario comes into focus with the Memorial Tournament as compared to the Players Championship. With the tournament's inception in 1976, Nicklaus missed his first fourteen years of professional competition to accrue a more complete record. Since that period encompassed perhaps 10 years of his peak, the likelihood of wins totaling more than the existing two is high. Yet, for the period under review, Nicklaus won two of 11 (18.18%) at ages 37 and 44. Woods also missed eight events and still won five times in 18 attempts (27.78%). Of these eight years, two (2006 and 2008) were comprised of great successes.

With a victory ratio of five to two in favor of Woods – along with a greater win percentage – the existing superiority is his. However, Woods only won once after age 36, while Nicklaus captured two titles. An unfulfilled promise impacts the records of both players with the greater adverse effect to Nicklaus. The data above show a probability the victory disparity between the players would be narrowed, if not erased.

Jack Nicklaus (1962 – 1986) & Tiger Woods (1997 – 2022) World Series of Golf Summary							
Jack Nicklaus				Tiger Woods			
Year	Score (Aggregate)	Score (To Par)	Placement	Year	Score (Aggregate)	Score (To Par)	Placement
1962	No Tournament	N/A	N/A	1997	278	-2	T-3
1963	No Tournament	N/A	N/A	1998	275	-5	T-5
1964	No Tournament	N/A	N/A	1999	270	-10	1
1965	No Tournament	N/A	N/A	2000	259	-21	1
1966	No Tournament	N/A	N/A	2001	268	-12	1
1967	No Tournament	N/A	N/A	2002	273*	-11	4

1968	No Tournament	N/A	N/A	2003	274	-6	T-4
1969	No Tournament	N/A	N/A	2004	273	-7	T-2
1970	No Tournament	N/A	N/A	2005	274	-6	1
1971	No Tournament	N/A	N/A	2006	270	-10	1
1972	No Tournament	N/A	N/A	2007	272	-8	1
1973	No Tournament	N/A	N/A	2008	DNP	N/A	N/A
1974	No Tournament	N/A	N/A	2009	268	-12	1
1975	No Tournament	N/A	N/A	2010	298	+18	T-78
1976	275	-5	1	2011	281	+1	T-37
1977	278	-2	T-5	2012	276	-4	T-8
1978	285	+7	7	2013	265	-15	1
1979	DNP	N/A	N/A	2014	211 (WD)	+1	N/A
1980	211 (WD)	+1	N/A	2015	DNP	N/A	N/A
1981	283	+3	T-10	2016	DNP	N/A	N/A
1982	285	+5	T-6	2017	DNP	N/A	N/A
1983	274	-6	2	2018	280	0	T-31
1984	280	0	10	2019	DNP	N/A	N/A
1985	DNP	N/A	N/A	2020	DNP	N/A	N/A
1986	282	+2	T-9	2021	DNP	N/A	N/A
				2022	No Tournament	N/A	N/A
AVG	70.09	0.56	6.25	AVG	68.52	-1.32	10.59

*Contested at the Sahalee Country Club in Sammamish, Washington.

The preceding records of Nicklaus and Woods reflect a similar scenario as in the Memorial Tournament, but there is more to the story. Originally, the World Series of Golf began in 1962 as an annual competition amongst the four major championship winners for the year and played at the South Course of the Firestone Country Club. Nicklaus competed in that event nine times with four victories, four runners-up, and one third-place finish. Concurrent with the tournament was the American Golf Classic in which Nicklaus played 10 times from 1962 through 1974 at the same location. He won that tournament once and accumulated eight additional top-10 finishes. Nicklaus then captured the 1975 PGA Championship at the same venue. Therefore, between the American Golf Classic, PGA Championship, and expanded World Series of Golf, Nicklaus was victorious on the South Course three times out of 20, or 15.00%.

For Woods, this tournament's transition to a World Golf Championship in 1999 coincided with a sterling record of dominance. Albeit a limited-field event, he was able to collect eight titles in 18 attempts, or a win rate of 44.44%. Woods' eight wins equal the record set by Sam Snead in the Greater Greensboro Open and cements his place as the most successful golfer to play the South Course of the Firestone Country Club.

Woods achieved his first seven victories beginning at age 23 and concluding at age 33. This left his eighth win at age 37. With the first expanded version of the World Series of Golf commencing when Nicklaus was 36 and having won the inaugural, both he and Woods were victorious only once after turning 36 years of age. Nicklaus' other two wins at ages 29 and 35 were against full fields and he had six additional placements from second to fifth. It is conceivable by extrapolation of this data that Nicklaus could have won several times at the South Course had a prestigious limited-field event been played there earlier and consistently throughout his career.

Jack Nicklaus (1962 – 1986) & Tiger Woods (1997 – 2022) Arnold Palmer Invitational Summary							
Jack Nicklaus				Tiger Woods			
Year	Score (Aggregate)	Score (To Par)	Placement	Year	Score (Aggregate)	Score (To Par)	Placement
1962	No Tournament	N/A	N/A	1997	278	-10	T-9
1963	No Tournament	N/A	N/A	1998	284	-4	T-13
1964	No Tournament	N/A	N/A	1999	290	+2	T-56
1965	No Tournament	N/A	N/A	2000	270	-18	1
1966	281	-3	T-2	2001	273	-15	1
1967	278	-6	T-7	2002	275	-13	1
1968	276	-12	3	2003	269	-19	1
1969	283	-5	T-10	2004	288	0	T-46
1970	280	-8	T-19	2005	287	-1	T-23
1971	DNP	N/A	N/A	2006	284	-4	T-20
1972	281	-7	T-10	2007	283	+3	T-22
1973	DNP	N/A	N/A	2008	270	-10	1
1974	DNP	N/A	N/A	2009	275	-5	1
1975	DNP	N/A	N/A	2010	DNP	N/A	N/A
1976	DNP	N/A	N/A	2011	287	-1	T-24
1977	DNP	N/A	N/A	2012	275	-13	1

1978	DNP	N/A	N/A	2013	275	-13	1
1979	288	0	T-30	2014	DNP	N/A	N/A
1980	DNP	N/A	N/A	2015	DNP	N/A	N/A
1981	DNP	N/A	N/A	2016	DNP	N/A	N/A
1982	278	-10	T-2	2017	DNP	N/A	N/A
1983	287	-1	T-5	2018	278	-10	T-5
1984	280	-8	T-9	2019	DNP	N/A	N/A
1985	DNP	N/A	N/A	2020	DNP	N/A	N/A
1986	DNP	N/A	N/A	2021	DNP	N/A	N/A
				2022	DNP	N/A	N/A
AVG	70.30	-1.50	9.70	AVG	69.72	-1.93	13.29

Across the 25-year span for Nicklaus, he only played in the Arnold Palmer Invitational on 10 occasions. Not only did he miss his first four years as a playing professional due to the event not underway, he also elected not to compete during a handful of his best performing years. Even though Nicklaus never won the tournament, he did achieve four top-five finishes (40.00%) and eight no worse than 10th (80.00%).

For Woods, this is arguably his most remarkable performance in any tournament. Of the 17 times he competed, Woods won eight, or 47.06%. Furthermore, in two other playings, he attained one top-five and one top-10 placement.

Prior to 1979, the site for this tournament was the Rio Pinar Country Club. As has been documented, 1979 was Nicklaus' worst year as a professional during the years under review and he had a substandard finish. This was also the first year the tournament was contested at the Bay Hill Club and Lodge, where it remains.

Nicklaus never won the event in 10 attempts, but his record is respectable at both venues. For Woods, all eight wins occurred at the Bay Hill Club and Lodge and none from age 39 going forward. It is conceivable had this tournament been played at the most recent site throughout Nicklaus' career, he would have been victorious.

FedEx Cup Playoffs

Let's acknowledge the FedEx Cup Playoffs. For Nicklaus and Woods, the unfulfilled promise concept applies to both.

With its debut in 2007, the FedEx Cup Playoffs consisted of four limited-field tournaments – two with a 36-hole cut and two without. This format continued through 2018, before being curtailed to three limited-field events with one having a 36-hole cut and two without. Each year, a qualifying basis was accumulated throughout so a final roster of players was set for the first tournament and pared to 70 and 30 players, respectively, for the last two events.

Nicklaus was unable to compete in the FedEx Cup Playoffs as he was 67 years of age by the time the first version commenced. It is easy to extrapolate within reason for him if the playoffs had been established during his career.

Based on his win rate of 27.27% in limited-field events, major championship prowess, consistency with which he ranked at or near the top of the annual money lists, consistency with which he ranked at or near the top of annual scoring, and that he won a minimum of two tournaments every year from 1962 through 1978, he would have qualified, factored heavily in many outcomes, and won multiple.

While Woods won the inaugural FedEx Cup Playoffs in 2007 and again in 2009, he was shorted many opportunities to supplement the two victories. During at least eight years (1997, 1999, 2000, 2001, 2002, 2005, 2006, and 2008), Woods' electrifying performances in total victories/win percentages, major championship effectiveness, money rankings, and scoring rankings prove he would have won more titles. This does not exclude the other years Woods competed up to that point.

THE TOP FIVE

"Professional golf is the only sport where, if you win 20% of the time, you're the best." – Jack Nicklaus

"I want to be what I've always wanted to be: dominant." – Tiger Woods

When examining the top calendar-year performances in competitive golf, most would agree there are four years that stand out. They are below in chronological order with the respective subjects.

1930: Bobby Jones
1945: Byron Nelson
1953: Ben Hogan
2000: Tiger Woods

Let's review each year in greater detail followed by the performances of Jack Nicklaus and Tiger Woods during their five most successful calendar years.

The Impregnable Quadrilateral

By capturing the Impregnable Quadrilateral, Bobby Jones accomplished a feat that many at the time believed would never have occurred and has not occurred since. Although the composition of what is now referred to as the Grand Slam differed in 1930, Jones won the four most sought-after titles of the day and in the same calendar year.

- **(British) Amateur Championship**
  - ○ Won the final 7 & 6

- **Open Championship**
  - Shot 291 to win by two shots
- **U.S. Open Championship**
  - Shot 287 to win by two shots
- **U.S. Amateur Championship**
  - Won the final 8 & 7

Jones competed in six events during the year and won five for a victory percentage of 83.33%. Of the non-major championships, he finished second by one shot to Horton Smith in the Savannah Open and won the Southeastern Open by 13 shots. Excluding the match play events, Jones' stroke average was 71.31.

A Streak Unequaled

It is safe to say Byron Nelson's total of 18 victories in 1945 including 11 in succession will never be equaled. Regardless of the size and strength of the fields Nelson played against (i.e. Sam Snead competed the entire season and Ben Hogan for half), the following should be highlighted.

- **Official Tournaments Played**
  - 30
- **Official Tournament Victories**
  - 18 (60.00%)
    - 11 consecutively, including the PGA Championship
- **Official Runner-up Finishes**
  - 7
- **Official Third-place Finishes**
  - 1
- **Official Fourth-place Finishes**
  - 2
- **Official Sixth-place Finishes**
  - 1
- **Official Ninth-place Finishes**
  - 1
- **Stroke Average**
  - 68.33
- **Final-round Stroke Average**
  - 67.68

- **Missed Cuts**
  - o 0

From the 30 tournaments entered, Nelson's victory percentage was 60.00%. When combining first- and second-place finishes, he achieved an 83.33% success rate and never finished outside the top-10. Due to World War II, the only major championship played was the PGA Championship. Nelson won that in match play by a final margin of 4 & 3. Lastly, his non-adjusted stroke average of 68.33 was the lowest until the year 2000.

The Triple Crown

Ben Hogan at age 40 was perfect in *official* events during his brief campaign of 1953. The titles and victory margins were comprised of:

- **Masters**
  - o Shot a then-record 274 to win by five shots
- **Pan American Open**
  - o Shot 286 to win by three shots
- **Colonial National Invitation**
  - o Shot 282 to win by five shots
- **U.S. Open Championship**
  - o Shot 283 to win by six shots
- **Open Championship**
  - o Shot 282 to win by four shots

With this performance, Hogan became the first and thus far only player to win the Masters, U.S. Open, and Open Championship in succession during one season. Unfortunately, the Open Championship and PGA Championship had overlapping schedules and he was unable to compete in the latter. This prevented an attempt to win the modern version of the Grand Slam.

Hogan did compete in one other tournament in 1953. The Greenbrier Pro-Am was an unofficial event and he shot rounds of 67-68-68-69 for an aggregate of 272, which placed him in a tie for third behind winner Sam Snead. Even if this were an official tournament, Hogan's win percentage would have equaled Jones in 1930 – 83.33%.

For the five wins, Hogan averaged 70.35 strokes per round with an average victory margin of 4.60 shots.

The Modern Standard

During the year 2000, Tiger Woods ushered in a new standard for calendar-year performance in professional golf. The season's highlights are below.

- **Official Tournaments Played**
  - 20
- **Official Tournament Victories**
  - 9 (45.00%)
    - Three majors and three regular tournaments consecutively, both including the PGA Championship
- **Official Runner-up Finishes**
  - 4 (20.00%)
- **Official Top-5 Finishes**
  - 17 (85.00%)
- **Official Top-10 Finishes**
  - 17 (85.00%)
- **Major Championship Victories**
  - 3 (75.00%)
- **Major Championship Top-5 Finishes**
  - 4 (100.00%)
- **Major Championship Top-10 Finishes**
  - 4 (100.00%)
- **Stroke Average**
  - 67.79 (adjusted) – all
  - 68.17 (non-adjusted) – all
  - 68.44 (non-adjusted) – major championships
- **Missed Cuts**
  - 0

Woods won 45.00% of the official events he played and placed in the top five at a staggering rate of 85.00%. This is the best single-season win percentage in the modern era. During that year, he finished fifth in the Masters and won the remaining three major championships in succession including the U.S. Open by a record 15 shots and the Open Championship by eight shots.

Woods completed the year with the lowest stroke average in history earning the Vardon Trophy, Player of the Year, and Leading Money Winner honors. Woods won nearly twice as much money as runner-up Phil Mickelson and played in three fewer events. In addition, Woods captured the U.S. and Open Championships along with the Canadian Open, which had only been accomplished once by Lee Trevino in 1971.

Woods also played in the Deutsche Bank-SAP Open TPC of Europe and the Johnnie Walker Classic. He finished in a tie for third place and in first place, respectively. With these two tournaments included, Woods completed the year with 10 wins out of 22 events, or 45.45% and a total non-adjusted stroke average of 68.11.

The Greatest 12 Months

Yet, with the wonderful single-season records of great play described above, all things considered, the greatest golf played over 12 months in succession must be Woods' *worldwide* performance from 06/18/00 through 06/03/01. A summary is as follows:

- **Tournaments Played**
    - 23
- **Victories**
    - 11 (47.83%)
        - 3 consecutively (twice)
- **Runner-up Finishes**
    - 2 (8.69%)
- **Top-5 Finishes**
    - 18 (78.26%)
- **Top-10 Finishes**
    - 19 (82.61%)
- **Major Championship Victories**
    - 4 (100.00%)
- **Stroke Average**
    - 67.84 (non-adjusted) – all

      ○   67.69 (non-adjusted) – major championships
           ■ Aggregate score of 53-under par
- **Missed Cuts**
      ○   0

While Woods' victory sum is less than Nelson's total in 1945 as is the number in succession, what makes Woods' performance so monumental is the titles he held concurrently in the modern era. Woods was the champion of:

- **Masters**
- **U.S. Open Championship**
- **Open Championship**
- **PGA Championship**
- **The Players**
- **WGC NEC Invitational**
- **Memorial Tournament**
- **Arnold Palmer Invitational**
- **Canadian Open**
- **Deutsche Bank – SAP Open TPC of Europe**
- **Johnnie Walker Classic**

Inclusive of all four major championships, Woods held arguably the seven most prestigious titles in the professional game: The Players, WGC NEC Invitational, and the Memorial Tournament round out the last three. Even though Woods' top-5 and top-10 placement percentages dipped slightly from the calendar year 2000, his non-adjusted stroke averages improved overall and in major championship play by .33 and .75, respectively.

Where does Nicklaus fit in the discussion of great play during a year, calendar or otherwise?

A Golden Year for the Golden Bear

Similar to Woods above and his best record over 12 months in succession, the following provides highlights of Nicklaus' *worldwide* performance from 07/25/71 through 07/15/72.

- **Tournaments Played**
  - 25
- **Victories**
  - 9 (36.00%)
    - 4 consecutively
    - 5 consecutively (stroke-play)
- **Runner-up Finishes**
  - 5 (20.00%)
- **Top-5 Finishes**
  - 17 (68.00%)
- **Top-10 Finishes**
  - 20 (80.00%)
- **Major Championship Victories**
  - 2 (66.67%)
    - 1971 PGA Championship played in February
- **Major Championship Runner-up Finishes**
  - 1 (33.33%)
    - 1972 Open Championship
- **Major Championship Top-5 Finishes**
  - 3 (100.00%)
- **Stroke Average**
  - 69.99 (non-adjusted) – all
  - 71.25 (non-adjusted) – major championships
- **Missed Cuts**
  - 0

Nicklaus' performance does not have the luster of Woods' respective period, but it is still very impressive. Unfortunately, the 1971 PGA Championship, which he won, was contested in February and not factored into this particular study. So, while Nicklaus was the PGA Championship titleholder, he didn't win the event during this period. Otherwise, his major championship victory percentage would be raised to 75.00%. The difficult weather and course conditions of the 1972 Masters and U.S. Open helped elevate his major championship scoring average. However, Nicklaus was still able to win five consecutive stroke-play events during one stretch and amass a wonderful year.

When Nicklaus' year of worldwide play is juxtaposed against that of Woods, it places in greater perspective the latter player's unequaled performance.

Jack Nicklaus Official Worldwide Tournaments (07/25/71 – 07/15/72)		
Total Events Played	25	
Victories & Percentage	9	36.00%
Runner-up Placements & Percentage	5	20.00%
Top-5 Placements & Percentage	17	68.00%
Top-10 Placements & Percentage	20	80.00%
Missed Cuts & Percentage	0	0.00%
Total Stroke Average	69.99	
Major Championships Played	3	
Victories & Percentage	2	66.67%
Runner-up Placements & Percentage	1	33.33%
Top-5 Placements & Percentage	3	100.00%
Top-10 Placements & Percentage	3	100.00%
Missed Cuts & Percentage	0	0.00%
Major Championship Stroke Average	71.25	

Tiger Woods Official Worldwide Tournaments (06/18/00 – 06/03/01)		
Total Events Played	23	
Victories & Percentage	11	47.83%
Runner-up Placements & Percentage	2	8.70%
Top-5 Placements & Percentage	18	78.26%
Top-10 Placements & Percentage	19	82.61%
Missed Cuts & Percentage	0	0.00%
Total Stroke Average	67.84	
Major Championships Played	4	
Victories & Percentage	4	100.00%
Runner-up Placements & Percentage	0	0.00%
Top-5 Placements & Percentage	4	100.00%
Top-10 Placements & Percentage	4	100.00%
Missed Cuts & Percentage	0	0.00%
Major Championship Stroke Average	67.69	

The Top Five – Random Aggregate

Originally, the concept for this chapter was to take a handful of top annual, worldwide performances by Jack Nicklaus and Tiger Woods and compare them individually and collectively. The previous pages in this chapter provide a backdrop for the next two sections. Below are five years selected for a comparative *aggregate* analysis:

Jack Nicklaus	Tiger Woods
1965	2000
1971	2002
1972	2005
1973	2006
1975	2007

While major championship play will generally supersede all other factors in determining successful annual performances by Nicklaus and Woods, the years above have other criteria to encompass a better blend of total achievement. My goal was to select years where each player had the most impact. The below schematics depict 15 items in each to illustrate a well-rounded view of the prescribed periods.

Jack Nicklaus Top Five Individual Years Official Worldwide Tournaments (1965, 1971, 1972, 1973, 1975)		
Total Events Played	108	
Victories & Percentage	33	30.56%
Runner-up Placements & Percentage	17	15.74%
Top-5 Placements & Percentage	74	68.52%
Top-10 Placements & Percentage	91	84.26%
Missed Cuts & Percentage	0	0.00%
Average Money Rank	1	
Average Scoring Rank & Total Stroke Average	1	70.03
Major Championships Played	20	
Victories & Percentage	7	35.00%
Runner-up Placements & Percentage	4	20.00%
Top-5 Placements & Percentage	16	80.00%
Top-10 Placements & Percentage	17	85.00%
Missed Cuts & Percentage	0	0.00%
Stroke Average	70.73	

Tiger Woods Top Five Individual Years Official Worldwide Tournaments (2000, 2002, 2005, 2006, 2007)		
Total Events Played	102	
Victories & Percentage	39	38.24%
Runner-up Placements & Percentage	17	16.67%
Top-5 Placements & Percentage	70	68.63%
Top-10 Placements & Percentage	78	76.47%
Missed Cuts & Percentage	3	2.94%
Average Money Rank	1	
Average Scoring Rank & Total Stroke Average	1	68.71
Major Championships Played	20	
Victories & Percentage	10	50.00%
Runner-up Placements & Percentage	4	20.00%
Top-5 Placements & Percentage	17	85.00%
Top-10 Placements & Percentage	17	85.00%
Missed Cuts & Percentage	1	5.00%
Stroke Average	69.59	

Thanks in large part to Woods' stellar performance in 2000, he emerges more dominant over his five years than Nicklaus in his. Woods won six more times (including three major championships) and by greater overall margins while playing six fewer events.

However, Nicklaus outshines Woods with his consistency. In six additional events, he missed zero cuts (0/108) whereas Woods missed three (3/102). And when the total number of tournaments without a cut are deducted, the ratios of cuts missed are 0/95 and 3/76, respectively.

Both players led the money lists and scoring averages. Woods distanced himself slightly further in each over his next challengers than Nicklaus did relative to his rivals.

The Top Five – Random Successive

As in the preceding review of hand-selected annual performances by Jack Nicklaus and Tiger Woods, the following examines their top five years *in succession*. There is variation in the years and criteria measured, but the results are similar. Here are the players' respective consecutive five years for a comparative analysis.

Jack Nicklaus	**Tiger Woods**
1971	1999
1972	2000
1973	2001
1974	2002
1975	2003

Jack Nicklaus Five-year Summary from 1971 – 1975 Official Worldwide Tournaments (Age 31 – 35)		
Total Events Played	100	
Total Wins & Percentage	30	30.00%
Full-field Events Played & Percentage of Total	88	88.00%
Full-field Wins & Percentage	25	28.41%
Limited-field Events Played & Percentage of Total	12	12.00%

Limited-field Wins & Percentage	5	41.67%
Total Runner-up Finishes & Percentage	12	12.00%
Total Top-five Finishes & Percentage	64	64.00%
Total Top-10 Finishes & Percentage	82	82.00%
Missed Cuts & Percentage	0	0.00%
Major Championships Played	20	
Major Championship Wins & Percentage	6	30.00%
Major Championship Runner-up Finishes & Percentage	4	20.00%
Major Championship Top-five Finishes & Percentage	17	85.00%
Major Championship Top-10 Finishes & Percentage	19	95.00%
Ryder Cup Record & Win Percentage	11-4-2	70.59%

With the level of consistency and longevity Nicklaus achieved throughout his career, the above represents his greatest level of play over a successive, medium-length term.

Like the prior analysis, the most striking feature besides winning at a rate of 30.00% is that Nicklaus did not miss a single cut. While he competed in a total of 100 events, 88 were against full-fields and necessitated playing well enough to advance beyond a prescribed cut. And with a 64.00% finish rate in the top five, along with an 82.00% completion rate in the top 10, Nicklaus' sustained ability to contend shows an amazing capacity for great play.

Equal to his total win percentage, Nicklaus won six of 20 major championships for another 30.00% success rate. What is also impressive is that he finished either first or second 50.00% of the time in major championships. Moreover, top-five and top-10 finish rates in major championships of 85.00% and 95.00%, respectively, are astounding. The only championship he missed completing in the top 10 was the 1972 PGA Championship, where he tied for 13th largely due to an injured finger which prevented adequate preparation.

Tiger Woods Five-year Summary from 1999 – 2003 Official Worldwide Tournaments (Age 23 – 27)		
Total Events Played	107	
Total Wins & Percentage	37	34.58%
Full-field Events Played & Percentage of Total	84	78.50%
Full-field Wins & Percentage	27	32.14%

Limited-field Events Played & Percentage of Total	23	21.50%
Limited-field Wins & Percentage	10	43.48%
Total Runner-up Finishes & Percentage	10	9.35%
Total Top-five Finishes & Percentage	67	62.62%
Total Top-10 Finishes & Percentage	77	71.96%
Missed Cuts & Percentage	0	0.00%
Major Championships Played	20	
Major Championship Wins & Percentage	7	35.00%
Major Championship Runner-up Finishes & Percentage	1	5.00%
Major Championship Top-five Finishes & Percentage	11	55.00%
Major Championship Top-10 Finishes & Percentage	12	60.00%
Ryder Cup Record & Win Percentage	4-5-1	45.00%

There is no way to review a five-year span of Woods' best play without including the year 2000. Since Woods' performance in 2003 exceeded that of 1998, the above range of years made sense.

The year 2000 helped Woods register an incredible 34.58% victory percentage for the five-year period. As with Nicklaus, Woods did not miss a single cut, which equates to 84 eligible tournaments. While Woods' win rate is superb, his finishes as runner-up, in the top-five, and top-10 are 9.35%, 62.62%, and 71.96%, respectively.

Woods won an impressive 35.00% of the major championships he played. This points to the impact of the year 2000, where he won three. Woods' lone runner-up placement in majors during the five-year period came at the 2002 PGA Championship where he finished with four straight birdies to lose to Rich Beem by one shot. Furthermore, Woods' top-five and top-10 placements were relatively flat at 55.00% and 60.00%, respectively.

When reviewing the two records as a comparative analysis, both Nicklaus and Woods came up short in 70 events. This is not a derogatory comment as both win percentages are remarkable. What should be noted is Woods played in seven additional tournaments than did Nicklaus and won them all, thus the victory percentage of 34.58% vs. 30.00%.

Both players' records in major championships are superb. Nicklaus is behind in winning by one victory or 5.00% (six wins at 30.00% vs. Woods at seven wins at 35.00%), but his level of being in contention is unmatched. Nicklaus' numbers when factoring in runner-up, top-five, and top-10 placements dwarf Woods' corresponding numbers by three (15.00%), six (30.00%), and seven (35.00%).

One other aspect is the great play for Nicklaus occurred when he was aged 31 through 35, while Woods' ages were 23 through 27.

Lastly, the themes of consistency/longevity (Nicklaus) and dominance (Woods) arise again. Woods won more, generally by larger margins, while Nicklaus contended on a more frequent basis with an overall placement level that will likely never be equaled.

YEAR-TO-YEAR SUMMARY

"Jack seemed to go for broke only when he was behind at the end of a tournament and it was so impressive. We were probably lucky he didn't try to do it more often." – Gary Player **Golf Digest** – *December 2002*

"Since 2000, I probably haven't improved that much physically, but my management is much better." – Tiger Woods **Golf Digest** – *December 2002*

With this book focusing on specific items and achievements within the careers of Jack Nicklaus and Tiger Woods, the final chapter will attempt to wrap much of it all together. By reviewing each player on a year-to-year basis, significant measurements will be touched on.

Annual Top-10 Placement Distribution

Pertaining to the aforementioned timeframes of Nicklaus and Woods, the following lists each player's annual distribution of placements from first to 10th with corresponding totals. Both tables are comprised of PGA-sanctioned events and include the four major championships.

Jack Nicklaus Top-10 PGA Placement Distribution by Year (1962 – 1986)											
Year	Win	2nd	3rd	4th	5th	6th	7th	8th	9th	10th	Total
1962	3	3	4	1	2	0	1	1	1	0	16
1963	5	2	3	1	3	0	1	1	1	1	18
1964	4	7	3	3	1	0	0	0	0	0	18

1965	5	4	2	3	2	1	0	1	1	0	19
1966	3	3	3	1	1	1	0	1	0	0	13
1967	5	3	3	3	0	0	1	1	0	0	16
1968	2	4	1	2	3	0	0	1	0	1	14
1969	3	1	0	2	0	4	1	0	0	1	12
1970	3	3	2	0	1	1	2	1	0	0	13
1971	5	3	3	1	1	0	0	0	3	0	16
1972	7	4	0	0	1	0	0	0	1	2	15
1973	7	1	1	2	2	2	0	0	2	0	17
1974	2	3	1	2	1	1	1	0	1	1	13
1975	5	1	4	1	0	2	1	0	1	0	15
1976	2	3	1	2	0	1	1	2	0	0	12
1977	3	3	1	1	3	1	1	1	0	1	15
1978	4	2	0	1	0	1	2	0	0	1	11
1979	0	1	1	1	0	0	0	0	1	0	4
1980	2	1	0	1	0	0	0	0	0	0	4
1981	0	3	0	1	0	1	1	0	1	1	8
1982	1	3	2	0	0	1	0	0	0	1	8
1983	0	3	1	0	1	1	0	1	0	1	8
1984	1	2	1	0	0	0	0	0	1	1	6
1985	0	2	1	0	0	1	0	0	0	0	4
1986	1	0	0	0	1	0	0	1	1	0	4
Total	73	65	38	29	23	19	13	12	15	12	299

Below provides perspective on the numbers:

- **Victories:** 73
  - o Nicklaus' wins comprise 24.41% of the total.
- **Top-two:** 138
  - o Nicklaus finished no worse than second (or tied for second) 46.15% of the total.
- **Top-three:** 176
  - o Nicklaus finished no worse than third (or tied for third) 58.86% of the total.
- **Top-five:** 228
  - o Nicklaus finished in the upper half 76.25% of the total.

- **Tournaments Played:** 480
  - o Of the total events played, Nicklaus finished in the top 10 62.29% of the time.

					Tiger Woods Top-10 PGA Placement Distribution by Year (1996 – 2022)						
Year	Win	2nd	3rd	4th	5th	6th	7th	8th	9th	10th	Total
1996	2	0	2	0	1	0	0	0	0	0	5
1997	4	1	1	1	0	0	0	1	1	0	9
1998	1	2	2	2	1	0	1	1	2	1	13
1999	8	1	2	0	2	0	2	0	0	1	16
2000	9	4	1	1	2	0	0	0	0	0	17
2001	5	0	1	1	1	0	0	1	0	0	9
2002	5	2	2	1	1	0	1	0	0	1	13
2003	5	2	0	3	1	0	1	0	0	0	12
2004	1	3	3	2	0	0	2	0	2	1	14
2005	6	4	2	1	0	0	0	0	0	0	13
2006	8	1	1	0	0	0	0	0	1	0	11
2007	7	3	0	0	0	1	0	0	1	0	12
2008	4	1	0	0	1	0	0	0	0	0	6
2009	6	3	0	1	0	2	0	1	1	0	14
2010	0	0	0	2	0	0	0	0	0	0	2
2011	0	0	0	1	0	0	0	0	0	1	2
2012	3	1	2	1	0	0	0	2	0	0	9
2013	5	1	0	1	0	1	0	0	0	0	8
2014	0	0	0	0	0	0	0	0	0	0	0
2015	0	0	0	0	0	0	0	0	0	1	1
2016	X	X	X	X	X	X	X	X	X	X	0
2017	0	0	0	0	0	0	0	0	0	0	0
2018	1	2	0	1	1	2	0	0	0	0	7
2019	1	0	0	0	1	0	0	0	1	1	4
2020	1	0	0	0	0	0	0	0	1	0	2
2021	X	X	X	X	X	X	X	X	X	X	0
2022	0	0	0	0	0	0	0	0	0	0	0
Total	82	31	19	19	12	6	7	6	10	7	199

Below provides perspective on the numbers:

- **Victories:** 82
  - Woods' wins comprise 41.21% of the total.
- **Top-two:** 113
  - Woods finished no worse than second (or tied for second) 56.78% of the total.
- **Top-three:** 132
  - Woods finished no worse than third (or tied for third) 66.33% of the total.
- **Top-five:** 163
  - Woods finished in the upper half 81.91% of the total.
- **Tournaments Played:** 357
  - Of the total events played, Woods finished in the top 10 55.74% of the time.

Nicklaus completed a remarkable record of 17 consecutive years with at least **two** victories. From 1962 through 1978, he won 68 events, an average of four per year. Woods' closest consecutive multi-win seasons is five, twice. This occurred from 1999 through 2003 and 2005 through 2009. Woods did win at least once per year from 1996 through 2009 for a total of 71 victories or an average of 5.07 per year.

Although Nicklaus twice won seven events (1972 and 1973), Woods equaled or bettered this number on four occasions. For the years 1999, 2000, 2006, and 2007, Woods displayed incredible play with an average of eight.

Composite Summary as Professionals

With the above placement detail, the following chart conveys additional composite data on the records of Nicklaus and Woods by bringing major championship performances into focus.

Jack Nicklaus & Tiger Woods Composite Summary as Professionals			
	Nicklaus	**Woods**	**Variance**
Total PGA Events Played	480	357	123
Total PGA Event Victories	73	82	(9)
PGA Event Victory Percentage	15.21%	22.97%	(7.76%)
Total Major Championships Played	100	84	16
Total Major Championship Victories	18	15	3
Major Championship Victory Percentage	18.00%	17.86%	.14%
Total Top-5 Placements	228	163	65
Top-5 Placement Percentage	47.50%	45.66%	1.84%
Major Championship Top-5 Placements	54	33	21
Major Championship Top-5 Percentage	54.00%	39.29%	14.71%
Total Top-10 Placements	299	199	100
Top-10 Placement Percentage	62.24%	55.74%	6.50%
Major Championship Top-10 Placements	67	41	26
Major Championship Top-10 Percentage	67.00%	48.81%	18.19%

At the highest level of professional golf, especially in major championships, there has not been a player as consistent over such a long period of time as Nicklaus. Nicklaus was able to achieve such a record against the greatest collection of marquee players from the waning days of Hogan/Snead, the primes of Casper/Palmer/Player, the emergence and primes of Floyd/Irwin/Miller/Trevino/Watson, and through the beginnings of Ballesteros/Norman, to mention just a few.

Woods shows his victory conversion rate to be the greatest the modern professional game has seen. In an era of more global influence, Woods' ability is amazing. The Woods era was punctuated not only by top-level Americans as Duval/Furyk/Mickelson, but talent outside the U.S. such as Els/Goosen/Singh and Harrington/McIlroy/Scott. Woods' dominance truly set him apart across all eras to date.

Accomplishments Per Age Decade

The following provides comparative detail on Nicklaus and Woods during their 20s and 30s. The two players' records are the greatest in the game, yet each exhibits a different texture.

With Woods' start to his professional career being the hottest in history, it laid the groundwork for his dominant play. Nicklaus also had an exceptional start, but was short of Woods. Yet, Nicklaus was able to build and sustain a high level of play over a longer period, which exemplifies his adaptability, consistency, and longevity. The segregation of accomplishments for both players within the age buckets allows these themes to stand out.

Jack Nicklaus & Tiger Woods as Professionals (20s)			
	Nicklaus	Woods	Variance
Years on Tour	8.00	9.25	(1.25)
Total PGA Events Played	192	185	7
Major Championships Played	32	36	(4)
Full-field Events Played	186	146	40
Limited-field Events Played	6	39	(33)
Total PGA Victories	30	46	(16)
Major Championship Victories	7	10	(3)
Full-field Victories	28	33	(5)
Limited-field Victories	2	13	(11)
Top-5 Placements	104	100	4
Top-10 Placements	126	119	7
Major Championship Top-5 Placements	19	17	2
Major Championship Top-10 Placements	20	21	(1)
Total Missed Cuts	9	3	6
Major Championship Missed Cuts	3	0	3
Total PGA Victory Percentage	15.63%	24.86%	(9.23%)
Major Championship Victory Percentage	21.88%	27.78%	(5.90%)
Full-field Victory Percentage	15.05%	22.60%	(7.55%)
Limited-field Victory Percentage	33.33%	33.33%	0.00%
Top-5 Percentage	54.17%	54.05%	0.12%

Top-10 Percentage	65.63%	64.32%	1.31%
Major Championship Top-5 Percentage	59.38%	47.22%	12.16%
Major Championship Top-10 Percentage	62.50%	58.33%	4.17%
Total Missed Cut Percentage	4.84%	2.05%	2.79%
Major Championship Missed Cut Percentage	9.38%	0.00%	9.38%
Average Scoring Rank	1.50	1.44	0.06
Average Money Rank	1.88	1.78	0.10

When reviewing Nicklaus' and Woods' records during their 20s, it is easy to forget how good Nicklaus was and how good his above record is. That may be the ultimate compliment to Woods because he exceeds Nicklaus in nearly every category.

Woods had a 1.25-year head start, but it has little bearing. Perhaps the most significant achievement listed is that Woods won 10 major championships out of his first 36 without missing a single cut. Even though Nicklaus played in four fewer major championships, it is unlikely he would have won three of an additional four. And the missed cut differential in major championships between the two players is also noteworthy in favor of Woods. Finally, Woods only missed three total cuts out of 146 full-field events, which is extraordinary.

Jack Nicklaus & Tiger Woods as Professionals (30s)			
	Nicklaus	Woods	Variance
Years on Tour	10	10	0
Total PGA Events Played	180	128	52
Major Championships Played	40	34	6
Full-field Events Played	162	87	75
Limited-field Events Played	18	41	(23)
Total PGA Victories	38	33	5
Major Championship Victories	8	4	4
Full-field Victories	31	22	9
Limited-field Victories	7	11	(4)
Top-5 Placements	96	55	41
Top-10 Placements	131	67	64
Major Championship Top-5 Placements	27	14	13

Major Championship Top-10 Placements	35	17	18
Total Missed Cuts	7	12	(5)
Major Championship Missed Cuts	1	7	(6)
Total PGA Victory Percentage	21.11%	25.78%	(4.67%)
Major Championship Victory Percentage	20.00%	11.76%	8.24%
Full-field Victory Percentage	19.14%	25.29%	(6.15%)
Limited-field Victory Percentage	38.89%	26.83%	12.06%
Top-5 Percentage	53.33%	42.97%	10.36%
Top-10 Percentage	72.78%	52.34%	20.44%
Major Championship Top-5 Percentage	67.50%	41.18%	26.32%
Major Championship Top-10 Percentage	87.50%	50.00%	37.50%
Total Missed Cut Percentage	4.32%	13.79%	(9.47%)
Major Championship Missed Cut Percentage	2.50%	20.59%	(18.09%)
Average Scoring Rank	10.70	59.20	(48.50)
Average Money Rank	5.80	56.70	(50.90)

Opposite the previous chart, Nicklaus emerges with a superior record nearly across the board over Woods. While Woods encountered issues in his personal life during this time, it should in no way detract from Nicklaus' accomplishments.

Ironically, Nicklaus' win percentage in major championships is lower at 20.00% than his earlier performance winning seven of 32 (21.88%), yet he was able to compete in all 40, winning eight. Both percentages are below Woods' earlier exceptional mark of 27.78%, however, Woods' major championship win rate dropped dramatically in the latter decade.

While Nicklaus "only" won eight of 40 major championships, his top-five and top-10 performances supplement the victory percentage. Nicklaus dwarfs Woods with his level of consistency and with just one missed cut in the 40 major championships, there is no contest. Also, the juxtaposition of Woods' win percentages to his average scoring and money rankings is striking when compared to that of Nicklaus. However, Woods' overall win percentages are still the greatest the professional game has seen for a sustained duration. The consistency of Nicklaus fully resonates in the chart as does the dominance of Woods.

EPILOGUE

*"Still (Jack) charitably declares that somebody will beat his records. 'People are jumping higher and running faster all the time,' he says." – Charles Price **Golf Magazine** – "Who is the Greatest Player in History?" January 1979*

*"People make too big a deal out of me catching Jack. It's something I'd like to have happen in my career, but I'm not going to lose any sleep if it doesn't happen." – Tiger Woods **Golf Digest** – December 2002*

The goal of this book was not to present a 1,000-page meandering analysis with my opinion throughout on who has been the better player. Instead, I wanted to furnish an array of verifiable data in multiple forms for ease of comprehension, reference, and as free from subjectivity as possible. Another goal was to bring records into their proper context and with as consistent treatment as possible over time. That said, I purposely avoided three topics to a large extent.

Caddy Influence

How big of an influence was Steve Williams on the prime of Tiger Woods' career? There is no way to know with certainty, due to the wealth of innate talent Woods displayed. Conversely, Jack Nicklaus was assigned random caddies throughout part of his career. Would his record be improved if Angelo Argea had been with him exclusively?

Equipment Technology

I did not research this area thoroughly. The section on driving distance provided enough allusions to the impact of equipment technology, at least from one perspective. Golf balls are more advanced and uniform to fly longer, straighter, and bore better through the wind. Clubs have extended shafts and larger sweet spots with stronger lofts. Improvements in equipment have made the game easier to learn and more enjoyable to play for greater numbers of people. Which player does this help?

Scoring will continually improve as records are meant to be broken. But for this study, do equipment advancements work in Woods' favor or against it? The fields Woods faced have been more global, yet is this because players as a collective are more talented? Or has more forgiving equipment helped elevate larger numbers?

For Nicklaus, was he able to achieve more against the fields he faced over 25 years due to less-forgiving equipment if fewer players in his era could master its use?

Golf Swing

During Woods' prime, many analysts considered his swing the most fundamentally-sound. Nicklaus and the top players in his era had more unique, but efficient golf swings. Suffice to say, both players were effective.

When compiling data for this book, the following thoughts surfaced.

- **Re-examined Topics**
  - The totality of Nicklaus' record is greater than I initially remembered.
  - The win conversion rate for Woods is greater than I initially remembered.
- **Questions**
  - What if the standards to qualify for Player of the Year, Ryder Cup, and the Vardon Trophy were the same in Nicklaus' era as in Woods' era?

- What if Woods had played a greater variety of tournaments to test his versatility?
- How would Nicklaus' record be different if he had the opportunity to compete in as many limited-field, no-cut events such as the WGC Championships?
- How would the careers of players such as Lee Trevino and Tom Watson been different if Nicklaus had not been around as a motivator? Would Arnold Palmer and Gary Player have achieved more? What about Tom Weiskopf?
- How would the careers of players such as Ernie Els and Phil Mickelson been different if Woods had not been their contemporary? Would David Duval have achieved more?
- How would Ben Hogan have factored into the record books if he had not been severely injured in the 1949 bus/car wreck? Would he be the player with the record(s) Nicklaus and Woods sought to eclipse?

Pursuant to the above items, one intangible for both players is motivation. If we accept Nicklaus' prime motivating factor in the game of golf was winning major championships (i.e. surpassing Bobby Jones' record), then by age 33 he succeeded. Whether referring to Jones' 13 major championships (amateur/professional) or Walter Hagen's 11 (all professional), Nicklaus attained 14 and 12, respectively, at the conclusion of the PGA Championship in 1973. From this point on in his career, how consistently motivated did he remain with a growing family and burgeoning golf course design firm?

For Woods, with all the records he set as an amateur and professional, is he still motivated after more than 35 years of competitive golf? Is the cornerstone of Nicklaus' career – the 18 major championship wins – still a target?

Many people consider comparisons of eras a pointless exercise. Whether the subject is sports teams, NFL quarterbacks, or professional golfers, there is no set formula or scientific evidence to prove one's position. In <u>The Greatest Game of All</u>, Bobby Jones wrote, *"Comparisons and superlatives have been liberally used on our sports pages. I do not like to compare players of one era with those of another, nor do I feel the necessity for proclaiming that anyone is the greatest, even in his own time. Insofar as contemporaries are concerned, the* record book speaks for itself; comparisons from era to era involve too much of the unmeasurable effect of differences in golf courses and equipment."*

Consider Presidents of the United States. Most historians agree Abraham Lincoln and George Washington are the two greatest. Although they were exceptional leaders and motivators, if either were transported during their presidencies to present-day America, they would scarcely know which end was up with all the changes and advancements. The point is that individuals deemed great in their era are a product of the time in its entirety. Woods has been building on what Nicklaus established, therefore an inherent flaw comparing the two players is present.

With respect to professional golf and the eras of Nicklaus and Woods, the game has changed considerably due largely to technological advancements in equipment coupled with improved course conditioning. As Craig Stadler noted when asked at age 51 how he would compare to himself at age 28, *"The equipment and my game tee-to-green have improved light years. I drive it 25 yards farther and a lot straighter. I am a better iron player, but not as good a putter. The 51-year-old me would win 1-up."*

In an era where a premium was placed on ball-striking accuracy, Nicklaus was the first great player to successfully incorporate three elements not seen before to a significant degree, which influenced the future of the game.

Power

Power entails more than just long driving. Nicklaus was able to play towering long-iron shots over obstacles and second shots into the greens of par-five holes for routine eagle and birdie conversions. Tom Watson referred to Nicklaus as the "greatest player from the rough," which is another testament to his ability to propel shots from heavy lies out and onto the green to hold.

Course Management

Nicklaus was the first player to thoroughly dissect tournament sites and map out a strategy with copious notes and yardages. Nicklaus also had the discipline to stay with his strategy. Hogan was an exceptional course manager, but Nicklaus took the concept further.

Clutch Putting

While there have been purer putters in Nicklaus' era (i.e. Bobby Locke, Billy Casper, and Ben Crenshaw), none were able to make more critical putts over a longer period. Not only did Nicklaus make numerous momentum-sustaining putts and key putts for victory, he was arguably the greatest lag-putter ever.

In the Woods era, power and the ability to recover reigned supreme. In his prime, other than perhaps John Daly, no player was more powerful. Some commentators have referred to Woods as "Jack Nicklaus with a short game." Below are the key combination of elements Woods brought to the game:

Short Game Wizardry

In Woods' prime, there was no weakness in his short game. Such an advantage allowed Woods to play aggressively into greens because his ability to hole out in two shots – if not one – was second to none. And that ability seemed to improve as championship pressure mounted.

Power

Like Nicklaus, Woods' power allowed him to play shots others could not. Woods took full advantage on par fives which in many cases won him championships almost before they began.

Clutch Putting

In his prime, Woods may have been the greatest putter under pressure ever to play the game. During an era of more pristine, overall consistent and faster putting surfaces, Woods was able to make an inordinate number of long putts. In many cases, he made such putts for victories. Although his putting touch did not last as long as Nicklaus' did, some observers believe at his peak, Woods converted more.

To further expand on the games of Nicklaus and Woods, below are 15 facets and my ratings for each player.

Jack Nicklaus & Tiger Woods Game Comparison			
	Nicklaus	**Woods**	**Draw**
Driving	X		
Fairway Woods			X
Long Irons	X		
Middle Irons	X		
Short Irons		X	
Pitching		X	
Chipping		X	
Bunker Play		X	
Putting			X
Swing Mechanics			X
Swing Tempo	X		
Course Management	X		
Creativity		X	
Power	X		
Scrambling		X	

Realizing I would try to minimize subjectivity, the above topics are relevant. My ratings were not pre-disposed to balancing out per player. While the above list is certainly debatable, below are some related thoughts.

Most observers consider Nicklaus the better driver and long iron player. Even at age 40, he led in the PGA Tour's "Total Driving" statistic with a score of 23 – 10th in distance and 13th in accuracy. To date, this is easily the lowest composite. During Woods' pinnacle of 2000, he led at 56, but was still noticeably higher than Nicklaus in 1980.

Virtually all observers would rate Woods better with shots around the green. At his peak, arguably only Seve Ballesteros and Phil Mickelson rivaled Woods.

Although Woods may have holed more long putts, Nicklaus was a more consistent putter over a longer period on less uniform and pristine greens, thus a draw.

Both players' swings held up on more occasions under the greatest championship pressure. As many believe Woods' swing in 2000 was superior, Nicklaus' swing resulted in a consistency and longevity in major championship play unlike any other, thus a draw on mechanics.

One final segment regarding the growth and advancement of the game of golf:

Does growth in the game of golf automatically translate to overall better players and deeper fields? While it is a safe bet to predict the player at number 50 on the money list in Woods' era was better than number 50 on the money list in Nicklaus' era, we can never be 100% certain, all things being equal. If the latter player was brought to the future with all the advancements, his skills would improve just as the former player's skills would diminish if transported back to less-forgiving equipment and less-pristinely manicured courses. Both players would eventually adjust, but would they excel? If this concept is applied to Nicklaus and Woods, how would that affect each player?

Modern technology has made golf an easier, more enjoyable game. Thus, skills required in the Nicklaus era (and before), such as the ability to hit a one-iron when needed as a second shot on a long par four into the wind or a risk/reward second shot to a reachable par five are no longer necessary, therefore no longer developed and honed. The hybrid clubs have made these shots easier to execute, thus more people can play them.

The questions then become –

1. Has the technology progression in equipment lifted more competitors to a higher level of play in Woods' era than in Nicklaus' era?
2. If the answer above is "yes," are the players truly better at an innate level?
3. Have these advancements made Woods' dominance that much more impressive?
4. Or do they show how good Nicklaus and his top cadre of challengers really were?
5. Do the last two questions apply concurrently?

An article from "USA Today" dated 07/14/07 reported Brandt Snedeker's experience playing a round of golf with equipment from the 1980s. Below are some excerpts:

"I don't know how to explain the sound" at impact with the old clubs and ball, he says. "It feels like the ball is getting stuck on the clubface. The old ball feels so soft, like a marshmallow."

His oversized metal woods, perimeter-weighted irons and state-of-the-art shafts and golf balls were pitted against woods actually made of wood; heavy, steel shafts and diminutive irons that were far less forgiving than today's advanced sets and balls last seen 20-25 years ago.

Only a red-hot 1988 putter kept matters so close. With the old flat stick, Snedeker made birdies from 3, 4, 25 and 30 feet and holed many par-saving putts of 4-8 feet. With his up-to-date putter he made three birdies but had two three-putts and just missed on five other putts for birdie.

The rest of the round, however, was marked by a one-club difference in length between the old and new irons. There was a 25-30-yard difference between drivers, 40-50 yards when he mishit the old driver. Mishits with his current equipment meant off-line landings of 5-10 yards; with the old clubs, as much as 50 yards off-line.

"I truly appreciate growing up in the generation that I did," Snedeker says, "because I don't think I would have grown up to be a pro golfer if I had to have played with the old stuff. It is so much different, so much tougher."

"It makes me really appreciate the guys that came before me," Snedeker says of hitting the old clubs. "The way Bobby Jones played golf, Jack Nicklaus, Arnold Palmer, Ben Hogan, Lee Trevino, Johnny Miller. Those guys were phenomenal."

"They had to be unbelievable ball strikers to hit the ball straight and as solid as they did."

The inference above is that the overall precision once demanded has to a large degree been diminished. The same can be said of the skill once required to drive the golf ball. In past eras, the dominant players were also the best drivers.

Regardless of opinion as to who the greatest player between Nicklaus and Woods is, the data in this book has proven two things.

- For over 30 years, Jack Nicklaus was on the first page of more leaderboards under the greatest championship pressure, against the most varied fields, and on a wider number of sites than any player in history.
- For approximately 15 years, Tiger Woods dominated a more global roster of challengers, under the greatest championship pressure, than any player in history.

Ultimately, it is up to the reader to decide what defines greatness. Truly great players from one era would prove formidable in any era.

APPENDICES

The below list outlines the subsequent spreadsheets and trends pertaining to the careers of Jack Nicklaus and Tiger Woods. Various aspects of the data have been previously illustrated.

- Amateur Performances in PGA Events
- Major Championship Scoring – Sub-70 Scores (25 Years)
- PGA Tournament Placement Comparison Rollup
- PGA Tournament Full-field Placement Comparison Rollup
- PGA Tournament Limited-field Placement Comparison Rollup
- PGA Tournament Amateur Placement Comparison Rollup
- Overseas Placement Comparison Rollup (Excludes Open Championship)
- Major Championship Placement Comparison Rollup
- Masters Tournament Placement Comparison Rollup
- U.S. Open Championship Placement Comparison Rollup
- Open Championship Placement Comparison Rollup
- PGA Championship Placement Comparison Rollup

Amateur Performances in PGA Events

Jack Nicklaus							
Year	Tournament	Scores Per Round				Placement	Age
1957	**U. S. Open**	**80**	**80**			**MC**	**17**
1958	Rubber City Open	67	66	76	68	12	18
1958	**U. S. Open**	**79**	**75**	**73**	**77**	**T-41**	**18**
1959	**Masters**	**76**	**74**			**MC**	**19**
1959	**U. S. Open**	**77**	**77**			**MC**	**19**
1959	Gleneagles Chicago Open	67	69	76	73	T-26	19
1959	Motor City Open	75	74	72	71	T-45	19
1959	Buick Open	76	70	70	72	T-12	19
1960	**Masters**	**75**	**71**	**72**	**75**	**T-13**	**20**
1960	**U. S. Open**	**71**	**71**	**69**	**71**	**2**	**20**
1961	**Masters**	**70**	**75**	**70**	**72**	**T-7**	**21**
1961	Colonial National Invitation	75	74	76	72	T-38	21
1961	**U. S. Open**	**75**	**69**	**70**	**70**	**T-4**	**21**
1961	Buick Open	74	72	72	74	T-24	21
1961	American Golf Classic	76	73	74	76	T-55	21

Tiger Woods							
Year	Tournament	Scores Per Round				Placement	Age
1992	Nissan Los Angeles Open	72	75			MC	16
1993	Nissan Los Angeles Open	74	78			MC	17
1993	Honda Classic	72	78			MC	17
1993	GTE Byron Nelson Classic	77	72			MC	17
1994	Nestle Invitational	80	77			MC	18
1994	Buick Classic	75	70			MC	18
1994	Motorola Western Open	74	75			MC	18
1995	**Masters**	**72**	**72**	**77**	**72**	**T-41**	**19**
1995	**U. S. Open**	**74**				**WD**	**19**
1995	Motorola Western Open	74	71	77	69	T-57	19
1995	**Open Championship**	**74**	**71**	**72**	**78**	**T-68**	**19**
1996	**Masters**	**75**	**75**			**MC**	**20**
1996	**U. S. Open**	**76**	**69**	**77**	**72**	**T-82**	**20**
1996	**Open Championship**	**75**	**66**	**70**	**70**	**T-22**	**20**

Major Championship Scoring – Sub-70 Scores (25 Years)

18-Hole Scores in the 60s as Professionals - Masters Tournament											
	60	61	62	63	64	65	66	67	68	69	Total	Average
Nicklaus	0	0	0	0	1	2	3	6	6	14	32	67.75
Woods	0	0	0	0	0	2	6	2	9	7	26	67.50
Variance	0	0	0	0	1	0	(3)	4	(3)	7	6	0.25

18-Hole Scores in the 60s as Professionals - U.S. Open Championship											
	60	61	62	63	64	65	66	67	68	69	Total	Average
Nicklaus	0	0	0	1	0	1	0	4	8	8	22	67.82
Woods	0	0	0	0	0	1	2	3	4	10	20	68.00
Variance	0	0	0	1	0	0	(2)	1	4	(2)	2	(0.18)

18-Hole Scores in the 60s as Professionals - Open Championship											
	60	61	62	63	64	65	66	67	68	69	Total	Average
Nicklaus	0	0	0	0	0	2	4	3	6	13	28	67.86
Woods	0	0	0	0	1	3	4	8	3	6	25	67.08
Variance	0	0	0	0	(1)	(1)	0	(5)	3	7	3	0.78

18-Hole Scores in the 60s as Professionals - PGA Championship											
	60	61	62	63	64	65	66	67	68	69	Total	Average
Nicklaus	0	0	0	0	1	1	4	5	9	18	38	67.95
Woods	0	0	0	1	1	1	5	7	5	10	30	67.37
Variance	0	0	0	(1)	0	0	(1)	(2)	4	8	8	0.58
											120	67.85
											101	67.46
											19	0.39

PGA Tournament Placement Comparison Rollup

Jack Nicklaus (1962 - 1986)				Tiger Woods (1996 - 2022)		
Placement	Frequency	Percentage		Placement	Frequency	Percentage
1	73	15.21%		1	82	22.97%
2	65	13.54%		2	31	8.68%
3	38	7.92%		3	19	5.32%
4	29	6.04%		4	19	5.32%
5	23	4.79%		5	12	3.36%
6	19	3.96%		6	6	1.68%
7	13	2.71%		7	7	1.96%
8	12	2.50%		8	6	1.68%
9	15	3.13%		9	10	2.80%
10	12	2.50%		10	7	1.96%
11	17	3.54%		11	9	2.52%
12	6	1.25%		12	7	1.96%
13	6	1.25%		13	6	1.68%
14	7	1.46%		14	1	0.28%
15	9	1.88%		15	5	1.40%
16	8	1.67%		16	3	0.84%
17	8	1.67%		17	5	1.40%
18	6	1.25%		18	6	1.68%
19	4	0.83%		19	2	0.56%
20	3	0.63%		20	6	1.68%
21 - 25	21	4.38%		21 - 25	20	5.60%
26 - 30	14	2.92%		26 - 30	8	2.24%
31 - 35	14	2.92%		31 - 35	9	2.52%
36 - 40	4	0.83%		36 - 40	16	4.48%
41 - 45	5	1.04%		41 - 45	2	0.56%
46 - 50	6	1.25%		46 - 50	3	0.84%
51 - 55	8	1.67%		51 - 55	5	1.40%
56 - 60	1	0.21%		56 - 60	3	0.84%
61 - 65	2	0.42%		61 - 65	2	0.56%
66 - 70	2	0.42%		66 - 70	4	1.12%
71 - 75	0	0.00%		71 - 75	2	0.56%
76 - 80	0	0.00%		76 - 80	2	0.56%
MC	26	5.42%		MC	22	6.16%
WD	4	0.83%		WD	10	2.80%
Total	480	100.00%		Total	357	100.00%

Comparative Summary		
Player	Wins	Win Percentage
Nicklaus	73	15.21%
Woods	82	22.97%
Variance	(9)	-7.76%
Player	Top-5s	Top-5 Percentage
Nicklaus	228	47.50%
Woods	163	45.66%
Variance	65	1.84%
Player	Top-10s	Top-10 Percentage
Nicklaus	299	62.29%
Woods	199	55.74%
Variance	100	6.55%
Player	Missed Cuts	Missed Cut Percentage
Nicklaus	26	5.42%
Woods	22	6.16%
Variance	4	-0.74%
Player	Withdrawals	Withdrawal Percentage
Nicklaus	4	0.83%
Woods	10	2.80%
Variance	(6)	-1.97%

PGA Tournament Full-field Placement Comparison Rollup

Jack Nicklaus (1962 - 1986)			Tiger Woods (1996 - 2022)		
Placement	Frequency	Percentage	Placement	Frequency	Percentage
1	64	14.32%	1	56	21.21%
2	63	14.09%	2	22	8.33%
3	38	8.50%	3	16	6.06%
4	27	6.04%	4	14	5.30%
5	20	4.47%	5	6	2.27%
6	18	4.03%	6	5	1.89%
7	12	2.68%	7	6	2.27%
8	12	2.68%	8	3	1.14%
9	12	2.68%	9	6	2.27%
10	9	2.01%	10	4	1.52%
11	15	3.36%	11	6	2.27%
12	6	1.34%	12	5	1.89%
13	6	1.34%	13	5	1.89%
14	6	1.34%	14	1	0.38%
15	7	1.57%	15	4	1.52%
16	7	1.57%	16	3	1.14%
17	8	1.79%	17	2	0.76%
18	6	1.34%	18	6	2.27%
19	4	0.89%	19	2	0.76%
20	3	0.67%	20	5	1.89%
21 - 25	20	4.47%	21 - 25	16	6.06%
26 - 30	14	3.13%	26 - 30	7	2.65%
31 - 35	13	2.91%	31 - 35	5	1.89%
36 - 40	4	0.89%	36 - 40	12	4.55%
41 - 45	5	1.12%	41 - 45	2	0.76%
46 - 50	6	1.34%	46 - 50	3	1.14%
51 - 55	8	1.79%	51 - 55	4	1.52%
56 - 60	1	0.22%	56 - 60	2	0.76%
61 - 65	2	0.45%	61 - 65	1	0.38%
66 - 70	2	0.45%	66 - 70	4	1.52%
71 - 75	0	0.00%	71 - 75	1	0.38%
76 - 80	0	0.00%	76 - 80	1	0.38%
MC	26	5.82%	MC	22	8.33%
WD	3	0.67%	WD	7	2.65%
Total	**447**	**100.00%**	**Total**	**264**	**100.00%**

Comparative Summary		
Player	**Wins**	**Win Percentage**
Nicklaus	64	14.32%
Woods	56	21.21%
Variance	**8**	**-6.89%**
Player	**Top-5s**	**Top-5 Percentage**
Nicklaus	212	47.43%
Woods	114	43.18%
Variance	**98**	**4.25%**
Player	**Top-10s**	**Top-10 Percentage**
Nicklaus	275	61.52%
Woods	138	52.27%
Variance	**137**	**9.25%**
Player	**Missed Cuts**	**Missed Cut Percentage**
Nicklaus	26	5.82%
Woods	22	8.33%
Variance	**4**	**-2.51%**
Player	**Withdrawals**	**Withdrawal Percentage**
Nicklaus	3	0.67%
Woods	7	2.65%
Variance	**(4)**	**-1.98%**

PGA Tournament Limited-field Placement Comparison Rollup

Jack Nicklaus (1962 - 1986)			Tiger Woods (1996 - 2022)		
Placement	Frequency	Percentage	Placement	Frequency	Percentage
1	9	27.27%	1	26	27.96%
2	2	6.06%	2	9	9.68%
3	0	0.00%	3	3	3.23%
4	2	6.06%	4	5	5.38%
5	3	9.09%	5	6	6.45%
6	1	3.03%	6	1	1.08%
7	1	3.03%	7	1	1.08%
8	0	0.00%	8	3	3.23%
9	3	9.09%	9	4	4.30%
10	3	9.09%	10	3	3.23%
11	2	6.06%	11	3	3.23%
12	0	0.00%	12	2	2.15%
13	0	0.00%	13	1	1.08%
14	1	3.03%	14	0	0.00%
15	2	6.06%	15	1	1.08%
16	1	3.03%	16	0	0.00%
17	0	0.00%	17	3	3.23%
18	0	0.00%	18	0	0.00%
19	0	0.00%	19	0	0.00%
20	0	0.00%	20	1	1.08%
21 - 25	1	3.03%	21 - 25	4	4.30%
26 - 30	0	0.00%	26 - 30	1	1.08%
31 - 35	1	3.03%	31 - 35	4	4.30%
36 - 40	0	0.00%	36 - 40	4	4.30%
41 - 45	0	0.00%	41 - 45	0	0.00%
46 - 50	0	0.00%	46 - 50	0	0.00%
51 - 55	0	0.00%	51 - 55	1	1.08%
56 - 60	0	0.00%	56 - 60	1	1.08%
61 - 65	0	0.00%	61 - 65	1	1.08%
66 - 70	0	0.00%	66 - 70	0	0.00%
71 - 75	0	0.00%	71 - 75	1	1.08%
76 - 80	0	0.00%	76 - 80	1	1.08%
MC	0	0.00%	MC	0	0.00%
WD	1	3.03%	WD	3	3.23%
Total	33	100.00%	Total	93	100.00%

Comparative Summary		
Player	Wins	Win Percentage
Nicklaus	9	27.27%
Woods	26	27.96%
Variance	(17)	-0.69%
Player	Top-5s	Top-5 Percentage
Nicklaus	16	48.48%
Woods	49	52.69%
Variance	(33)	-4.21%
Player	Top-10s	Top-10 Percentage
Nicklaus	24	72.73%
Woods	61	65.59%
Variance	(37)	7.14%
Player	Missed Cuts	Missed Cut Percentage
Nicklaus	0	0.00%
Woods	0	0.00%
Variance	0	0.00%
Player	Withdrawals	Withdrawal Percentage
Nicklaus	1	3.03%
Woods	3	3.23%
Variance	(2)	-0.20%

PGA Tournament Amateur Placement Comparison Rollup

Jack Nicklaus (1957 - 1961)			Tiger Woods (1992 - 1996)		
Placement	Frequency	Percentage	Placement	Frequency	Percentage
1	0	0.00%	1	0	0.00%
2	1	6.67%	2	0	0.00%
3	0	0.00%	3	0	0.00%
4	1	6.67%	4	0	0.00%
5	0	0.00%	5	0	0.00%
6	0	0.00%	6	0	0.00%
7	1	6.67%	7	0	0.00%
8	0	0.00%	8	0	0.00%
9	0	0.00%	9	0	0.00%
10	0	0.00%	10	0	0.00%
11	0	0.00%	11	0	0.00%
12	2	13.33%	12	0	0.00%
13	1	6.67%	13	0	0.00%
14	0	0.00%	14	0	0.00%
15	0	0.00%	15	0	0.00%
16	0	0.00%	16	0	0.00%
17	0	0.00%	17	0	0.00%
18	0	0.00%	18	0	0.00%
19	0	0.00%	19	0	0.00%
20	0	0.00%	20	0	0.00%
21 - 25	1	6.67%	21 - 25	1	7.14%
26 - 30	1	6.67%	26 - 30	0	0.00%
31 - 35	0	0.00%	31 - 35	0	0.00%
36 - 40	1	6.67%	36 - 40	0	0.00%
41 - 45	2	13.33%	41 - 45	1	7.14%
46 - 50	0	0.00%	46 - 50	0	0.00%
51 - 55	1	6.67%	51 - 55	0	0.00%
56 - 60	0	0.00%	56 - 60	1	7.14%
61 - 65	0	0.00%	61 - 65	0	0.00%
66 - 70	0	0.00%	66 - 70	1	7.14%
71 - 75	0	0.00%	71 - 75	0	0.00%
76 - 80	0	0.00%	76 - 80	0	0.00%
81 - 85	0	0.00%	81 - 85	1	7.14%
MC	3	20.00%	MC	8	57.14%
WD	0	0.00%	WD	1	7.14%
Total	15	100.00%	Total	14	100.00%

Comparative Summary		
Player	Wins	Win Percentage
Nicklaus	0	0.00%
Woods	0	0.00%
Variance	**0**	**0.00%**
Player	Top-5s	Top-5 Percentage
Nicklaus	2	13.33%
Woods	0	0.00%
Variance	**2**	**13.33%**
Player	Top-10s	Top-10 Percentage
Nicklaus	3	20.00%
Woods	0	0.00%
Variance	**3**	**20.00%**
Player	Missed Cuts	Missed Cut Percentage
Nicklaus	3	20.00%
Woods	8	57.14%
Variance	**(5)**	**-37.14%**
Player	Withdrawals	Withdrawal Percentage
Nicklaus	0	0.00%
Woods	1	7.14%
Variance	**(1)**	**-7.14%**

Overseas Placement Comparison Rollup (Excludes Open Championship)

Jack Nicklaus (1962 - 1986)		
Placement	Frequency	Percentage
1	11	37.93%
2	8	27.59%
3	2	6.90%
4	0	0.00%
5	3	10.34%
6	0	0.00%
7	0	0.00%
8	0	0.00%
9	0	0.00%
10	0	0.00%
11	0	0.00%
12	0	0.00%
13	1	3.45%
14	1	3.45%
15	0	0.00%
16	0	0.00%
17	0	0.00%
18	0	0.00%
19	0	0.00%
20	0	0.00%
21 - 25	1	3.45%
26 - 30	0	0.00%
31 - 35	0	0.00%
36 - 40	1	3.45%
41 - 45	1	3.45%
46 - 50	0	0.00%
51 - 55	0	0.00%
56 - 60	0	0.00%
61 - 65	0	0.00%
66 - 70	0	0.00%
71 - 75	0	0.00%
76 - 80	0	0.00%
MC	0	0.00%
WD	0	0.00%
Total	29	100.00%

Tiger Woods (1996 - 2022)		
Placement	Frequency	Percentage
1	13	30.23%
2	8	18.60%
3	6	13.95%
4	2	4.65%
5	1	2.33%
6	3	6.98%
7	0	0.00%
8	2	4.65%
9	1	2.33%
10	0	0.00%
11	0	0.00%
12	0	0.00%
13	0	0.00%
14	0	0.00%
15	1	2.33%
16	0	0.00%
17	0	0.00%
18	0	0.00%
19	0	0.00%
20	1	2.33%
21 - 25	1	2.33%
26 - 30	1	2.33%
31 - 35	0	0.00%
36 - 40	0	0.00%
41 - 45	1	2.33%
46 - 50	0	0.00%
51 - 55	0	0.00%
56 - 60	0	0.00%
61 - 65	0	0.00%
66 - 70	0	0.00%
71 - 75	0	0.00%
76 - 80	0	0.00%
MC	1	2.33%
WD	1	2.33%
Total	43	100.00%

Comparative Summary		
Player	Wins	Win Percentage
Nicklaus	11	37.93%
Woods	13	30.23%
Variance	(2)	**7.70%**
Player	Top-5s	Top-5 Percentage
Nicklaus	24	82.76%
Woods	30	69.77%
Variance	(6)	**12.99%**
Player	Top-10s	Top-10 Percentage
Nicklaus	24	82.76%
Woods	36	83.72%
Variance	(12)	**-0.96%**
Player	Missed Cuts	Missed Cut Percentage
Nicklaus	0	0.00%
Woods	1	2.33%
Variance	(1)	**-2.33%**
Player	Withdrawals	Withdrawal Percentage
Nicklaus	0	0.00%
Woods	1	2.33%
Variance	(1)	**-2.33%**

Major Championship Placement Comparison Rollup

Jack Nicklaus (1962 - 1986)			Tiger Woods (1997 - 2022)		
Placement	Frequency	Percentage	Placement	Frequency	Percentage
1	18	18.00%	1	15	17.86%
2	18	18.00%	2	7	8.33%
3	9	9.00%	3	4	4.76%
4	7	7.00%	4	6	7.14%
5	2	2.00%	5	1	1.19%
6	5	5.00%	6	4	4.76%
7	2	2.00%	7	1	1.19%
8	2	2.00%	8	1	1.19%
9	1	1.00%	9	1	1.19%
10	3	3.00%	10	1	1.19%
11	2	2.00%	11	1	1.19%
12	1	1.00%	12	2	2.38%
13	1	1.00%	13	0	0.00%
14	0	0.00%	14	0	0.00%
15	2	2.00%	15	1	1.19%
16	2	2.00%	16	0	0.00%
17	0	0.00%	17	2	2.38%
18	1	1.00%	18	2	2.38%
19	0	0.00%	19	1	1.19%
20	0	0.00%	20	1	1.19%
21 - 25	7	7.00%	21 - 25	7	8.33%
26 - 30	1	1.00%	26 - 30	4	4.76%
31 - 35	5	5.00%	31 - 35	2	2.38%
36 - 40	0	0.00%	36 - 40	5	5.95%
41 - 45	1	1.00%	41 - 45	0	0.00%
46 - 50	1	1.00%	46 - 50	1	1.19%
51 - 55	1	1.00%	51 - 55	0	0.00%
56 - 60	0	0.00%	56 - 60	0	0.00%
61 - 65	1	1.00%	61 - 65	0	0.00%
66 - 70	0	0.00%	66 - 70	1	1.19%
71 - 75	0	0.00%	71 - 75	0	0.00%
76 - 80	0	0.00%	76 - 80	0	0.00%
MC	6	6.00%	MC	12	14.29%
WD	1	1.00%	WD	1	1.19%
Total	100	100.00%	Total	84	100.00%

Comparative Summary		
Player	**Wins**	**Win Percentage**
Nicklaus	18	18.00%
Woods	15	17.86%
Variance	**3**	**0.14%**
Player	**Top-5s**	**Top-5 Percentage**
Nicklaus	54	54.00%
Woods	33	39.29%
Variance	**21**	**14.71%**
Player	**Top-10s**	**Top-10 Percentage**
Nicklaus	67	67.00%
Woods	41	48.81%
Variance	**26**	**18.19%**
Player	**Missed Cuts**	**Missed Cut Percentage**
Nicklaus	6	6.00%
Woods	12	14.29%
Variance	**(6)**	**-8.29%**
Player	**Withdrawals**	**Withdrawal Percentage**
Nicklaus	1	1.00%
Woods	1	1.19%
Variance	**0**	**-0.19%**

Masters Tournament Placement Comparison Rollup

Jack Nicklaus (1962 - 1986)		
Placement	Frequency	Percentage
1	6	24.00%
2	4	16.00%
3	2	8.00%
4	2	8.00%
5	1	4.00%
6	1	4.00%
7	1	4.00%
8	1	4.00%
9	0	0.00%
10	0	0.00%
11	0	0.00%
12	0	0.00%
13	0	0.00%
14	0	0.00%
15	2	8.00%
16	0	0.00%
17	0	0.00%
18	1	4.00%
19	0	0.00%
20	0	0.00%
21 - 25	1	4.00%
26 - 30	0	0.00%
31 - 35	1	4.00%
36 - 40	0	0.00%
41 - 45	0	0.00%
46 - 50	0	0.00%
51 - 55	0	0.00%
56 - 60	0	0.00%
61 - 65	0	0.00%
66 - 70	0	0.00%
71 - 75	0	0.00%
76 - 80	0	0.00%
MC	1	4.00%
WD	1	4.00%
Total	**25**	**100.00%**

Tiger Woods (1997 - 2022)		
Placement	Frequency	Percentage
1	5	22.73%
2	2	9.09%
3	1	4.55%
4	3	13.64%
5	1	4.55%
6	1	4.55%
7	0	0.00%
8	1	4.55%
9	0	0.00%
10	0	0.00%
11	0	0.00%
12	0	0.00%
13	0	0.00%
14	0	0.00%
15	1	4.55%
16	0	0.00%
17	1	4.55%
18	1	4.55%
19	0	0.00%
20	0	0.00%
21 - 25	1	4.55%
26 - 30	0	0.00%
31 - 35	1	4.55%
36 - 40	2	9.09%
41 - 45	0	0.00%
46 - 50	1	4.55%
51 - 55	0	0.00%
56 - 60	0	0.00%
61 - 65	0	0.00%
66 - 70	0	0.00%
71 - 75	0	0.00%
76 - 80	0	0.00%
MC	0	0.00%
WD	0	0.00%
Total	**22**	**100.00%**

Comparative Summary		
Player	Wins	Win Percentage
Nicklaus	6	24.00%
Woods	5	22.73%
Variance	1	1.27%
Player	Top-5s	Top-5 Percentage
Nicklaus	15	60.00%
Woods	12	54.55%
Variance	3	5.45%
Player	Top-10s	Top-10 Percentage
Nicklaus	18	72.00%
Woods	14	63.64%
Variance	4	8.36%
Player	Missed Cuts	Missed Cut Percentage
Nicklaus	1	4.00%
Woods	0	0.00%
Variance	1	4.00%
Player	Withdrawals	Withdrawal Percentage
Nicklaus	1	4.00%
Woods	0	0.00%
Variance	1	4.00%

U.S. Open Championship Placement Comparison Rollup

Jack Nicklaus (1962 - 1986)		
Placement	Frequency	Percentage
1	4	16.00%
2	3	12.00%
3	1	4.00%
4	1	4.00%
5	0	0.00%
6	2	8.00%
7	1	4.00%
8	1	4.00%
9	1	4.00%
10	2	8.00%
11	1	4.00%
12	0	0.00%
13	0	0.00%
14	0	0.00%
15	0	0.00%
16	0	0.00%
17	0	0.00%
18	0	0.00%
19	0	0.00%
20	0	0.00%
21 - 25	3	12.00%
26 - 30	0	0.00%
31 - 35	1	4.00%
36 - 40	0	0.00%
41 - 45	1	4.00%
46 - 50	0	0.00%
51 - 55	1	4.00%
56 - 60	0	0.00%
61 - 65	0	0.00%
66 - 70	0	0.00%
71 - 75	0	0.00%
76 - 80	0	0.00%
MC	2	8.00%
WD	0	0.00%
Total	**25**	**100.00%**

Tiger Woods (1997 - 2022)		
Placement	Frequency	Percentage
1	3	15.00%
2	2	10.00%
3	1	5.00%
4	1	5.00%
5	0	0.00%
6	1	5.00%
7	0	0.00%
8	0	0.00%
9	0	0.00%
10	0	0.00%
11	0	0.00%
12	1	5.00%
13	0	0.00%
14	0	0.00%
15	0	0.00%
16	0	0.00%
17	1	5.00%
18	1	5.00%
19	1	5.00%
20	1	5.00%
21 - 25	2	10.00%
26 - 30	0	0.00%
31 - 35	1	5.00%
36 - 40	0	0.00%
41 - 45	0	0.00%
46 - 50	0	0.00%
51 - 55	0	0.00%
56 - 60	0	0.00%
61 - 65	0	0.00%
66 - 70	0	0.00%
71 - 75	0	0.00%
76 - 80	0	0.00%
MC	4	20.00%
WD	0	0.00%
Total	**20**	**100.00%**

Comparative Summary		
Player	**Wins**	**Win Percentage**
Nicklaus	4	16.00%
Woods	3	15.00%
Variance	**1**	**1.00%**
Player	**Top-5s**	**Top-5 Percentage**
Nicklaus	9	36.00%
Woods	7	35.00%
Variance	**2**	**1.00%**
Player	**Top-10s**	**Top-10 Percentage**
Nicklaus	16	64.00%
Woods	8	40.00%
Variance	**8**	**24.00%**
Player	**Missed Cuts**	**Missed Cut Percentage**
Nicklaus	2	8.00%
Woods	4	20.00%
Variance	**(2)**	**-12.00%**
Player	**Withdrawals**	**Withdrawal Percentage**
Nicklaus	0	0.00%
Woods	0	0.00%
Variance	**0**	**0.00%**

Open Championship Placement Comparison Rollup

Jack Nicklaus (1962 - 1986)		
Placement	Frequency	Percentage
1	3	12.00%
2	7	28.00%
3	3	12.00%
4	2	8.00%
5	1	4.00%
6	1	4.00%
7	0	0.00%
8	0	0.00%
9	0	0.00%
10	1	4.00%
11	0	0.00%
12	1	4.00%
13	0	0.00%
14	0	0.00%
15	0	0.00%
16	0	0.00%
17	0	0.00%
18	0	0.00%
19	0	0.00%
20	0	0.00%
21 - 25	1	4.00%
26 - 30	1	4.00%
31 - 35	2	8.00%
36 - 40	0	0.00%
41 - 45	0	0.00%
46 - 50	1	4.00%
51 - 55	0	0.00%
56 - 60	0	0.00%
61 - 65	0	0.00%
66 - 70	0	0.00%
71 - 75	0	0.00%
76 - 80	0	0.00%
MC	1	4.00%
WD	0	0.00%
Total	25	100.00%

Tiger Woods (1997 - 2022)		
Placement	Frequency	Percentage
1	3	15.00%
2	0	0.00%
3	2	10.00%
4	1	5.00%
5	0	0.00%
6	2	10.00%
7	1	5.00%
8	0	0.00%
9	1	5.00%
10	0	0.00%
11	0	0.00%
12	1	5.00%
13	0	0.00%
14	0	0.00%
15	0	0.00%
16	0	0.00%
17	0	0.00%
18	0	0.00%
19	0	0.00%
20	0	0.00%
21 - 25	3	15.00%
26 - 30	1	5.00%
31 - 35	0	0.00%
36 - 40	0	0.00%
41 - 45	0	0.00%
46 - 50	0	0.00%
51 - 55	0	0.00%
56 - 60	0	0.00%
61 - 65	0	0.00%
66 - 70	1	5.00%
71 - 75	0	0.00%
76 - 80	0	0.00%
MC	4	20.00%
WD	0	0.00%
Total	20	100.00%

Comparative Summary		
Player	**Wins**	**Win Percentage**
Nicklaus	3	12.00%
Woods	3	15.00%
Variance	**0**	**-3.00%**
Player	**Top-5s**	**Top-5 Percentage**
Nicklaus	16	64.00%
Woods	6	30.00%
Variance	**10**	**34.00%**
Player	**Top-10s**	**Top-10 Percentage**
Nicklaus	18	72.00%
Woods	10	50.00%
Variance	**8**	**22.00%**
Player	**Missed Cuts**	**Missed Cut Percentage**
Nicklaus	1	4.00%
Woods	4	20.00%
Variance	**(3)**	**-16.00%**
Player	**Withdrawals**	**Withdrawal Percentage**
Nicklaus	0	0.00%
Woods	0	0.00%
Variance	**0**	**0.00%**

PGA Championship Placement Comparison Rollup

Jack Nicklaus (1962 - 1986)				Tiger Woods (1997 - 2022)		
Placement	Frequency	Percentage		Placement	Frequency	Percentage
1	5	20.00%		1	4	18.18%
2	4	16.00%		2	3	13.64%
3	3	12.00%		3	0	0.00%
4	2	8.00%		4	1	4.55%
5	0	0.00%		5	0	0.00%
6	1	4.00%		6	0	0.00%
7	0	0.00%		7	0	0.00%
8	0	0.00%		8	0	0.00%
9	0	0.00%		9	0	0.00%
10	0	0.00%		10	1	4.55%
11	1	4.00%		11	1	4.55%
12	0	0.00%		12	0	0.00%
13	1	4.00%		13	0	0.00%
14	0	0.00%		14	0	0.00%
15	0	0.00%		15	0	0.00%
16	2	8.00%		16	0	0.00%
17	0	0.00%		17	0	0.00%
18	0	0.00%		18	0	0.00%
19	0	0.00%		19	0	0.00%
20	0	0.00%		20	0	0.00%
21 - 25	2	8.00%		21 - 25	1	4.55%
26 - 30	0	0.00%		26 - 30	3	13.64%
31 - 35	1	4.00%		31 - 35	0	0.00%
36 - 40	0	0.00%		36 - 40	3	13.64%
41 - 45	0	0.00%		41 - 45	0	0.00%
46 - 50	0	0.00%		46 - 50	0	0.00%
51 - 55	0	0.00%		51 - 55	0	0.00%
56 - 60	0	0.00%		56 - 60	0	0.00%
61 - 65	1	4.00%		61 - 65	0	0.00%
66 - 70	0	0.00%		66 - 70	0	0.00%
71 - 75	0	0.00%		71 - 75	0	0.00%
76 - 80	0	0.00%		76 - 80	0	0.00%
MC	2	8.00%		MC	4	18.18%
WD	0	0.00%		WD	1	4.55%
Total	25	100.00%		Total	22	100.00%

Comparative Summary		
Player	**Wins**	**Win Percentage**
Nicklaus	5	20.00%
Woods	4	18.18%
Variance	**1**	**1.82%**
Player	**Top-5s**	**Top-5 Percentage**
Nicklaus	14	56.00%
Woods	8	36.36%
Variance	**6**	**19.64%**
Player	**Top-10s**	**Top-10 Percentage**
Nicklaus	15	60.00%
Woods	9	40.91%
Variance	**6**	**19.09%**
Player	**Missed Cuts**	**Missed Cut Percentage**
Nicklaus	2	8.00%
Woods	4	18.18%
Variance	**(2)**	**-10.18%**
Player	**Withdrawals**	**Withdrawal Percentage**
Nicklaus	0	0.00%
Woods	1	4.55%
Variance	**(1)**	**-4.55%**

BIBLIOGRAPHY

Books

Barkow, Al. <u>The History of the PGA Tour</u>. New York: Doubleday, 1989.

Capps, Gil. <u>The Magnificent Masters</u>. Boston: Da Capo Press, 2014.

Connors, Jimmy. <u>The Outsider</u>. New York: HarperCollins, 2013.

Davis, Martin. <u>Jack Nicklaus: Simply the Best!</u> Greenwich: The American Golfer, Inc., 2007.

Lewis, Catherine M. <u>Bobby Jones and the Quest for the Grand Slam.</u> Chicago: Triumph Books, 2005.

McCormack, Mark H. <u>The World of Professional Golf Mark H. McCormack's Golf Annual 1976</u>. New York: Atheneum, 1976.

Nicklaus, Jack, and Herbert Warren Wind. <u>The Greatest Game of All: My Life in Golf</u>. 4th Printing. Ohio Promotions, Inc., 1969.

Nicklaus, Jack, and Ken Bowden. <u>Jack Nicklaus: My Story</u>. New York: Simon & Schuster, 1997.

Sagebiel, Neil. <u>Draw in the Dunes.</u> New York: Thomas Dunne Books St. Martin's Press, 2014.

Magazines

Golf Digest

Golf Magazine

Web Sites

www.golf.com   www.golfdigest.com   www.masters.com
www.nicklaus.com   www.owgr.com   www.pgatour.com
www.sportsillustrated.com   www.tigerwoods.com   www.usatoday.com

Lightning Source UK Ltd.
Milton Keynes UK
UKHW011954141122
412210UK00012B/172/J

Lightning Source UK Ltd.
Milton Keynes UK
UKHW011954141122
412210UK00012B/172/J

9 781665 569583